DEUTERONOMY FOR DISCIPLES

DEUTERONOMY
FOR
DISCIPLES

Alfred Nicholls

THE CHRISTADELPHIAN
404 Shaftmoor Lane
Hall Green
Birmingham
B28 8SZ

2006

First Published 2006

ISBN 085189 168 3

Printed and bound in England by:

THE CROMWELL PRESS
Trowbridge
Wiltshire
BA14 0XB

CONTENTS

FOREWORD

THIS is a book worthy to be read in day and night and never to be out of hands. For it is the most excellent of all the books of Moses. It is easy also and light and a very pure gospel that is to wete, a preaching of faith and love: deducing the love to God out of faith, and the love of a man's neighbour out of the love of God. Herein also thou mayst learn right meditation or contemplation, which is nothing else save the calling to mind and a repeating in the heart of the glorious and wonderful deeds of God, and of his terrible handling of his enemies and merciful entreating of them that come when he calleth them, which thing this book doth and almost nothing else.

THUS wrote William Tyndale in his prologue to the Book of Deuteronomy (1530), and it is probable that his comments reflect the attitude of the Lord Jesus to the fifth book of Moses. Deuteronomy records Moses' re-telling of the wilderness history for the benefit of the new generation of Israelites who were about to enter the land of promise, from where Moses was barred because of his failure to be fully obedient to God's word.

Jesus was the obedient Son, and learned his Father's ways as he meditated on all that had been revealed about God's purpose in His word, and manifested in the history of His people Israel. God brought His Son out of Egypt by the hand of Moses, and led him through the wilderness to prove and test him. No wonder the Lord Jesus saw in the message of Deuteronomy sound advice as he was proved and tested throughout his lifetime of service among his own people.

The message, and the words of Deuteronomy are therefore often found on the lips of the Lord. If they were on his lips, they should also be on the lips of his disciples.

This is the theme of this work. The author wrote about Deuteronomy because he saw in it sound counsel for today's disciples – counsel about the importance of honouring God, and about showing love for Him by loving neighbour, the fatherless and widows.

The message of Deuteronomy is shown to be the foundation of many principles that are more fully explained in the teaching of the Lord and his Apostles; a valuable reminder of the need to remember all the way we have come, and how the Lord God bears us on eagle's wings to bring us to Himself.

Birmingham, 2006   MICHAEL ASHTON

1

INTRODUCTORY

THE TITLE chosen for this book is an indication of the general method of treatment to be followed. There will be no verse-by-verse exposition, although all the main aspects of the record will be surveyed in the course of our study. The scholar may be disappointed to find that there is no detailed discussion of such facts as the date of the book, which some claim was written towards the end of the days of the Kings; or any analysis of other "problems", such as those of language, grammar or style, except where such details give a deeper insight into what the Lord was saying to His people. Those concerned with such matters will find that they have been adequately dealt with elsewhere.* Our purpose is to consider, for the people of God to whom they were first spoken, the significance of *The Words* (which is the meaning of the title given to the Book of Deuteronomy in the Hebrew Bible), and to assess their relevance for our own community today.

A focal point in Scripture

All Scripture is given by inspiration of God and it is all profitable for the man of God. So it is not right to speak of one book of the Bible as being of greater importance than any other. Nevertheless we can recognise the special quality of a book which gathers up the record of God's dealings with men from Creation to the time when Israel came to the banks of the Jordan and forms a point of reference for most of the later writers of the Old Testament.

Deuteronomy is unique in its very character. It is highly poetical, although very little of it is written in verse. It is not entirely history, nor is it prophecy, though both history and prophecy form the basis of what Moses has to say. It is not strictly narrative; it is neither a legal code nor a devotional work. Nevertheless from it we may understand God's law and be moved to worship by the tale it has to tell. Oratory it

---

* For example in a series of 17 articles on "The Antiquity of Deuteronomy" in *The Christadelphian*, beginning in September 1951.

certainly is in large measure, but oratory calculated to stir the listeners not by rhetorical devices but by phrases which impart to the book its principal characteristics. "Hearken", "hear", "observe", "keep", "do", "take heed", "remember", "forget not", "therefore thou shalt"—all these are words of "exhortation". For Deuteronomy is made up mainly of the last words of Moses, in effect of his patriarchal blessing, spoken to the people of Israel, who stood on the threshold of the Land of Promise into which he knew that in this life he would not enter.

The purpose of the book is underlined by the position which it occupies in the Old Testament. It is the last in the Pentateuch, and is evidently built around all the principles laid down in the preceding four books. In them God had been revealed as the great Creator, Sustainer, Sovereign and Judge of all mankind, who makes promises to those who fear Him and keep His commandments. Those promises were honoured in the Lord's taking of their descendants out of the house of bondage, to bring them unto Himself and make them His own people, a holy nation and a royal priesthood (Exodus 19). To that nation God had revealed Himself as a God of covenant. In fact, He had chosen to be known by the Name which expressed the covenant relationship: He was who He was, and would be for His people many wonderful things which are revealed in this book—He was the Lord. The terms of that covenant the Lord had revealed in the Decalogue, the Ten Words spoken with the living voice of God at Sinai. And that "fiery law" (33:2) He had expounded in a system of worship first established in the wilderness.

"When thou art come into the land"

Now that same law was to be expounded in terms of the people's life, both nationally and individually, "when thou art come into the land"—another constant refrain in Moses' speech. The far-reaching principles enunciated here were to extend far beyond even the nation's tenure of the Land. When on account of their disobedience to God's law, Israel were judged and cast out of the Land, as Moses foresaw they would be, they would no longer be able to carry out in practice many of the details of the commandments which the Book of Deuteronomy expresses. Yet the principles of the Law, as enshrined in the Ten Commandments, could still be kept even in Israel's dispersion, and indeed are binding upon all God's people even today. This point we shall consider in greater detail as we proceed.

A principle for us today

Another principle emerges from the book, which underlines its relevance for our community today. For the words were not spoken to the eye-witnesses of the events at the Red Sea and at Horeb but to their immediate descendants, who were nevertheless addressed as though they had been there. The responsible generation, of twenty years old and upward at that time, had all perished. As 2:14 suggests, the Brook Zered, or "Pruning", was probably so called because by the time the Israelites had crossed over it, "all the generation of the men of war were wasted out from among the host, as the LORD had said".

Any of the children of that epoch were now between forty and sixty years old; the main body of the people then in their prime had been born in the wilderness. Yet all were addressed as though they had come out of Egypt, had seen and heard all the phenomena attendant upon the giving of the Decalogue and the ratification of the covenant, were the people of the covenant, and responsible for the keeping of it. And so they were, since by their circumcision, the token of the covenant, they were constituent parts of a living body, a nation belonging to God—a privilege and a responsibility which centuries later God brought home to His people through the words of the prophets, often in the very terms used in the Book of Deuteronomy.

By the same token we today, as members of the "chosen generation, a royal priesthood, an holy nation, a peculiar people" (1 Peter 2:9), share the privileges and responsibilities of what was done at Pentecost, the anniversary of the making of the covenant at Sinai, when the "ecclesia", or the congregation of the living God, was founded upon the basis of the new covenant in Christ. See Acts 7:38 for Stephen's reference to Israel as "the ecclesia that was in the wilderness". Just as Israel, whether in the Land of which the constitution was the Law of God, or scattered abroad and therefore unable to fulfil the details of the Mosaic code, were still able to live by the unchanging principles of the "*Torah*", the Law in a wider sense (of which more later); so we, in all the different circumstances of time and place which surround our lives, can and must fulfil the Law in our hearts.*

---

* For further discussion of this point see the chapter on "Baptized with the Holy Spirit" in the author's *The Evangelical Revival* and published by *The Christadelphian*, 1983.

An analogy

Bearing in mind that an analogy is not a "strict" parallel, there are also exhortations here for us as Christadelphians of the third and fourth generation. We have entered, not into a land but a community, which other men have laboured to build, with so much of our life and worship—even our very name—easily taken for granted. We need to be exhorted, and the study of Deuteronomy will help us to that end, to "remember the days of old" (32:7)*, lest we forget how and why the Brotherhood came into being, what it stands for and how it is to be preserved. We shall also be humbled and rebuked as we remember that to be *called* the people of God is of itself no guarantee of our whole-hearted service and devotion. Careful attention must be paid to the the Law of God: it must be in our hearts as well as on our lips, if we are truly to be a people taken out of the Gentiles for His Name.

---

* For an examination of some distinctive features of Scripture teaching as they have been understood from the beginning of the history of the Christadelphians as a separate community, the reader is referred to the author's *Remember the Days of Old*, published by *The Christadelphian* in 1978.

2

THE FORM OF THE BOOK

ARCHAEOLOGICAL evidence of the period of the Exodus reveals that there was a standard form of covenant between, say, a ruler and his people, or a master and his servants, which is reflected in all the records of covenants in the Pentateuch. This is, of course, one argument for the antiquity and authenticity of these early books of the Bible, both of which are assumed without question in the pages of this book. The form of the covenant as set out by the superior party displayed the following pattern:

1. *A Preamble*, identifying the author of the covenant.
2. *A Prologue*, recounting the benefits bestowed by the author of the covenant, and forming the basis of it.
3. *General Stipulations*, defining the basis of the continuing future relationship between the parties concerned.
4. *Specific Stipulations*, giving the practical details for the keeping of the covenant.
5. *Ratification of the Covenant*, and the deposit of a copy of it before witnesses.
6. *Sanctions of the Covenant*, spelt out in the form of blessings and curses.

The covenant at Sinai closely followed this pattern: Exodus 20:1 answered to (1), 20:2 to (2), the Ten Commandments to (3), and 24:1–8 to (5). See also the renewal of the covenant under Joshua 24:2–7, where the same form of covenant document can easily be recognised.

In many respects the Book of Deuteronomy, or the "Repetition of the Law", follows this outline in even greater detail. Chapter 1:1–5 corresponds to (1), 1:6–4:49 to (2), chapters 5 to 11 to (3), chapters 12 to 26 to (4), chapters 27 to 28 to (6), and 30:19; 31:19 and 32:1–43 to (5).

To these aspects of the covenant we shall refer as we proceed. It will be more convenient in many respects, however, to set out the following more detailed analysis, to enable the reader to obtain a clearer view of the outline of the book. Acknowledgements are made to the author of the section on Deuteronomy in Ellicott's *A Bible Commentary for English Readers*, of which our analysis is an adaptation.

ANALYSIS OF THE BOOK OF DEUTERONOMY

1. 1:1–5   *The Title of the Book*

2. 1:6–4:40   *Moses' Introductory Speech*
A Review of Israel's journey from Sinai to the Jordan (Establishment of 3 cities of refuge on east bank, verses 40–43)

3. 4:44–28:69 *The Deuteronomy, or Repetition of the Law*
    (a) A Title (4:44–49)
    (b) Repetition of the Ten Commandments
    (c) Exposition of the Ten Commandments
        (i) Generally, as creating a relation between the Lord and His people (chapters 6 to 11)
        (ii) Particularly, in relation to the Land which was
            (a) The seat of the Worship of the Lord (12:1–16:17)
            (b) The seat of the Kingdom of the Lord (16:18–18:18)
            (c) The sphere of operation of particular rules of person, property, society, behaviour (chapters 19 to 27)
    (d) The Ten Commandments become the Law of the Land, written on Mount Ebal, enforced by blessings and curses (chapter 27)
    (e) Their sanction in Israel, for all time, by a denunciation of rewards and penalties still in force (chapter 28)

4. 29:1–30:20 *The Second Covenant*
To redeem Israel from the curse of the Sinaitic Covenant

5. 31:1–34:12 *Conclusion*

    (a) Moses resigns charge to Joshua. He delivers the Law to the priests and elders, and the Book to the Levites (chapter 31).

    (b) Moses' last Song (chapter 32)

    (c) Blessing of the Tribes (chapter 33)

    (d) Death of Moses (Chapter 34)

3

THE TITLE OF THE BOOK (1:1–5)

THE WORD Deuteronomy is from the Greek title in the Septuagint, meaning "Second Law". Given the proper understanding of the word "law" it is an adequate description of the book. It is not a repetition of the Mosaic law as defined in Exodus, Leviticus and Numbers, but a restatement of the covenant with special emphasis on "when thou art come into the land". In the Hebrew Bible the title is *Devarim*, "The Words", from the opening words of the book. So Genesis is known as "In the Beginning", and Exodus as "The Names", and so on.

"A whole family"

In the title passage are also identified the time and place of the delivery of the speeches, and the audience. The audience was "all Israel"—the "whole family which I brought up out of the land of Egypt" (Amos 3:1)—a form of speech to be used twelve times in the book. This implies much more than that the representatives of the two and a half tribes whose inheritance was "on this side Jordan" were assembled with their brethren to hear these final exhortations. It was a *whole people* God had redeemed, and upon a *whole people* that He would bring His blessing or curse. The later division of the kingdom, of which the seeds were sown in the lives of Jacob's sons and germinated in the dissension in the wilderness, only emphasised the impartiality of God in the matter, since He sent His prophets to warn both groups alike.

We may draw lessons for ourselves from this. The lamentable divisions in the Brotherhood, whether revealed in actual schism or in the existence of "wings" or "groups", often identified by quasi-political titles, are no part of the will and purpose of Him who is working towards the unity of all things in Christ. We are, however, like Israel, caught in a historical situation and find that it proves far more difficult to heal divisions on a sound Scriptural basis than ever it was to allow them to develop in the first place.

The immediate context of Scripture must determine for us the sense of "on this side Jordan", or literally "at the side, or passage of Jordan". Its meaning depends upon the point of view of the observer, but besides its variable meaning it became a technical expression for "east of Jordan", which is manifestly the meaning here. Not all the places named can be identified with certainty, but they are evidently on the way from Sinai to "the land of Moab" where Moses "began to declare this law" (verse 5). The best explanation of this first verse is that Moses delivered exhortations and warnings at various places on the journey (as they came to Kadesh in full expectation of entering immediately into the land, much of the content of Deuteronomy would have been relevant); and that he had gathered up the substance of all these words into his farewell address, when perhaps they were also written down for the first time (see 31:24–26).

A long lapse of time

The date in verse 3 is no doubt meant to shock the reader who has just read verse 2. If it was but eleven days' journey from Horeb by the way of Mount Seir unto Kadesh-barnea, the "Holy Door" into the land, then why were they on *this* side Jordan at almost the end of the fortieth year? The intervening record from Numbers 14 onwards supplies the answer, and forms the basis of Moses' first address. By this time Aaron had been dead six months and all those over twenty at Kadesh, with the exception of Joshua and Caleb, had perished. Within two-and-a-half months, with the reproach of Egypt finally rolled away, the people would eat their first passover in the Land of Promise (Joshua 5:2–11).

Moses began "to declare this law". *Torah* is "teaching", sometimes specific teaching, or a body of religious precepts (compare chapters 12–26), but equally moral guidance, and is a very comprehensive term. All Old Testament Scripture is *torah*, being either a revelation of God's principles or a commentary upon them. Thus, the Lord Jesus can say, "It is written in your law", when in fact the reference was to Psalm 82:6, which itself contains a quotation from Exodus 22. The relation between *torah* and judgements, statutes and precepts we consider in chapter 5.

4

MOSES' INTRODUCTORY SPEECH (1:6—4:40)

THE FINAL CONQUEST on "this side Jordan" was now complete. Under the leadership of Moses Israel had "slain Sihon the king of the Amorites ... and Og the king of Bashan" (verse 4). They both figure in greater detail in the later part of this introductory speech, where we shall consider the incidents connected with them. After his final exhortations and the declaration of "this law", Moses has now no more to do but hand over his charge to Joshua and his spiritual responsibilities to the priests and Levites.

(a) "I have set the land before you"
(1:6–8)

The speech begins with "the LORD our God spake". Even allowing for the fact that Hebrew uses personal pronouns sparingly and a name is often repeated where we should use "he", "him" and "his", the Name of the Lord appears very frequently indeed in this book. Yahweh alone occurs over 230 times, and in combination with the expressions "thy God", "your God" or "our God" about 300 times more; to which may be added another seven times in such phrases as "the LORD God of our (thy, your) fathers".

Plainly, Israel were being reminded of the covenant and of the Lord of the covenant, as He should have been remembered in all the details of their daily lives. For Deuteronomy emphasises the personal and exclusive relationship between the Lord and Israel, and the fundamental difference between Israel's God and those of the surrounding nations.

God's declaration, "Ye have dwelt *long enough* in this mount (Horeb)", reminds us that the wilderness journey was no haphazard wandering from place to place. Every removal, every period of rest, was under the Lord's control, as appears further from 2:3: "Ye have compassed this mountain (Seir) *long enough*". In the second case the record explains the significance of this expression in verses 7 and 14: the period was long enough to complete the process of purging out the generation of the men of war "as the LORD sware unto them". It was then time to turn northward and conquer.

For the explanation of 1:6, however, and for much that forms the background of this introductory address, we must consult the records of Exodus and especially Numbers. "Long enough" in the present instance was from "the third month" after the children of Israel had left Egypt (Exodus 19:1) until "the twentieth day of the second month, in the second year" (Numbers 10:11). The intervening period had been spent in the construction of the tabernacle (Exodus 36–39), the arrangement of the camp in its four-square and its marching formations (Numbers 2), the allocation of the Levites to duties connected with the moving of the tabernacle and its furniture (Numbers 4), and the construction of the two silver trumpets to serve, amongst other things, as a signalling device for the orderly execution of the marching orders by so vast a company (Numbers 10). It has been estimated that the account of this year and all its institutions fill up exactly *one third* of the Pentateuch.

The Israelites were then to "turn" and take their journey by way of Kadesh into the territory later to be assigned to Judah, conquer the hill country, the plain, the Negev and Lebanon and ultimately extend their territory to the river Euphrates—a programme sadly interrupted by their lack of faith. Not until the days of Solomon, and ironically for a brief period under Jeroboam II, on the very eve of the final disaster to the Northern Kingdom of Israel, would Israel's inheritance approach anything like the extent promised by God. The fulness is yet to come, when in the terms of the patriarchal blessing, Abraham's seed would possess the land "from the river of Egypt unto the great river, the river Euphrates" (Genesis 15:18).

The tragedy of Kadesh, which Moses takes up later in this speech (Deuteronomy 1:19–46), can only be accurately assessed when we realise that at that point the whole land was set before them, and they were about to "go in and possess it", having come only eleven days journey from Horeb (verses 8 and 1). In fact it was to take them nearly four decades to achieve only a part of what they had turned their back upon. We note also the categorical statement that the Lord had sworn the land "unto your fathers, Abraham, Isaac and Jacob, to give unto them and to their seed after them". The land was a central feature of the kingdom to come, and the concept of the resurrection of the patriarchs as an integral part of the promises, truths which form the foundation of our own hope, are not just inferences to be drawn from the record but positive features of the Lord's own words.

It is important that disciples should bear this fact in mind in days when great emphasis is being laid upon the "spiritual" blessings of the Gospel, to the exclusion, or at least the relegation to a minor place, of the reality of a future kingdom, and real inheritance and material blessings. That the Lord would be merciful and longsuffering, that He expected His people to be like Him in their dealings with their fellow men, that thus to manifest His Name would bring His people into a close communion with Him—all that is clearly contained in His declaration of Himself in His covenant Name. But so is the certainty that He would keep the oath that he had sworn by Himself, that the fathers should walk as owners through the length and breadth of the land in which they had been but strangers and sojourners. To deny their resurrection and future inheritance, and consequently to diminish the force of the promises, is to err, "not knowing the scriptures, or the power of God".

(b) "Take you wise men, and understanding" (1:9–18)

Two important exhortations, both connected with the Divine principle of leadership, for our present day community emerge from the next section of Moses' first speech. It is remarkable how often in Scripture a practical arrangement, entered into because of some development or crisis which has rendered it necessary, has been endorsed by God, thus imparting a spiritual sanction to the decision. One such crisis arose in the wilderness, as the people multiplied to become "as the stars of heaven for multitude". Directly related to the Lord's fulfilment of His promise to the fathers ("so shall thy seed be") was the need for Moses to delegate some of his responsibility.

The Shepherd of Israel

The Lord Himself was the Shepherd of Israel, who led Joseph like a flock (Psalm 80:1, a reference to the order of marching, where the tribes of Ephraim, Benjamin and Manasseh followed immediately after the ark of the cherubim); yet the visible leadership and pastoral care was vested in a chosen man. The same principle runs throughout the Divine arrangements, seen for example in David—taken by the Lord from following the sheep "to feed Jacob his people, and Israel his inheritance" (Psalm 78:70–72)—in all the kings, and in the appointment of men like Timothy and Titus at a time of crisis in the ecclesias in Ephesus and Crete. The privilege and the responsibility was also a burden, as Moses declared in Deuteronomy 1:9 and 1:12, and additional help was needed. We learn a great deal of the character of this man who could rejoice at the evidence of the Lord's blessing, praying even that it might be increased a thousand times (verse 11), even though the blessing imposed upon him the people's "cumbrance, burden, and strife" (verse 12). The word "cumbrance" is echoed in Isaiah 1:14, where even the Lord Himself had to say of Israel, in their keeping of the appointed feasts, "they are a *trouble* to me, I am weary to bear them".

Though Moses himself had voiced no complaint originally, it had early been apparent to his father-in-law, Jethro, that the ordinary pressure of judging the cases brought by the people, besides the military and spiritual charge he bore, would wear him away, "both thou, and this people that is with thee" (Exodus 18:18). This is in itself an informative remark, since it was Jethro's opinion that the people themselves would not ultimately be best served by an over-burdened leader. It was he who then suggested that there should be made a choice of "able men" out of all Israel, to judge the people at all seasons under the general oversight of Moses. This happened as they were approaching Sinai.

It was shortly after the departure from Sinai that Moses was constrained to appeal to the Lord, saying, "I am not able to bear all this people alone, because it is too heavy for me" (Numbers 11:14). It would appear that he was seeking something beyond the help in the day-to-day affairs he was already receiving. For the people, though being led on their way by the cloud of the Divine presence, had provoked the Lord to anger with their lust for flesh. Moses was instructed to bring before Him seventy men "whom thou knowest to be the elders of the people, and officers over them", who would receive of Moses' spirit to give them a more formal, heavier share of the burden carried by their leader. It was to this incident specifically that Moses was referring in Deuteronomy 1, although the earlier incident was no doubt also in mind.

At any rate, the principle involved was the same as that which had been summed up in Jethro's words: "I will give thee counsel, and God shall be with thee ... If thou shalt do this thing, *and God command thee so*" (Exodus 18:19,23). In other words, it was a human suggestion, made with the furtherance of the Lord's work in mind, submitted to Him for approval, and ultimately carried out in accordance with His command. In Numbers 11 it was the Lord Himself who took the men nominated by Moses and formally ordained them to share his burden (verse 16). Dr. Thomas clearly followed the principle in the early days of the Brotherhood:

"If (God) prescribe to us no organisation for modern times We ... must organise ourselves ...

"I believe (God) would not be displeased at any system of rule and order they (His children) might devise promotive of their own improvement of heart and understanding, and growth in faith, humbleness of mind, brotherly kindness and love; and which would enable them to support the truth and sound it out effectively in the world; all of which premises that their system embody the principles inculcated in the word ...

"No organisation, not even an apostolic one, can work well, that is scripturally, which is not composed of elements more zealous for the advancement of the truth, and the promotion of the glory of its divine Author, than of their own notions and exaltation ... Without this disposition (i.e. as 'little children'), which is 'peaceable, gentle, easy to be intreated, full of mercy and good fruits, without partiality and without hypocrisy', no organisation could work harmoniously and efficaciously, though framed and administered by the apostles themselves. Even a bad organisation with good materials would work better than a good one with a self-willed, heady, factious, and self-glorifying people."

Herald of the Kingdom and Age to Come,
1854, pages 7 and 9

Guidance for the Twenty-first Century

We need not fear, therefore, in the absence of direct Spirit guidance for our twenty-first century ecclesias, and lacking the system of a Spirit-directed eldership chosen by the apostles themselves, to come to the best practical arrangements we can for ordering our affairs. There are two important provisos: the end in view must be the best service to the Lord and the maintaining of the highest spiritual standards for the flock; and both the arrangements and the men chosen to carry them into effect must be committed to God in prayer for His blessing. Such was the principle followed in Acts 6.

The first crisis in the Jerusalem ecclesia led to the appointment of deacons, nominated by the body of the ecclesia (verse 5) and commended to the Lord in prayer (verse 6). The arrangement was abundantly blessed as the sequel showed (verse 7). Such indeed is the spirit behind our own "Ecclesial Guide", or to give it its full title, *A Guide to the Formation and Conduct of Christadelphian Ecclesias*, which should be required reading by every brother and sister who is serious about his or her part in the ecclesia, and should certainly be part of the equipment of every arranging brother.

There was another principle to be followed in the selection of the men, closely associated with the one outlined: "Take you wise men, and *understanding*, and *known* among your tribes ..." (Deuteronomy 1:13); or as Jethro had put it earlier: "Such as fear God, men of truth, hating covetousness". The same principle holds good for us, if we are to make our practical matters, our "ecclesial business", into the affairs of the spirit they ought to be, contributing to the feeding of the flock and the edifying of the people.

There may be a need of skilled administrators, sound financiers, shrewd businessmen or men of learning, to cope with all the many activities which make up the life of the ecclesias and the organisations of the Brotherhood at large, and so make the most efficient use of the resources, both financial and intellectual, available. If such can be found, so much the better. But they must all be first and foremost wise men and understanding, fearing God and grounded in the Truth, if they are to take any kind of oversight, or exercise any kind of leadership among us. They must also be "known among us" if their work is to command the confidence and the support which it is our spiritual responsibility to give them, once they have been properly chosen and prayerfully commended to God for the work they have to do. This theme has been dealt with at greater length in the author's book on *The Letters to Timothy and Titus*, published by *The Christadelphian*, 1991. See the relevant pages in chapters 9 to 11.

The charge to the elders

The opportunity was taken at Kibroth-Hattaavah to complete the organisation of the Lord's holy nation (or possibly the records of Jethro's suggestion and some other hitherto unrecorded incident are combined here), since as Moses says (Deuteronomy 1:15), the "wise men, and known" were made into leaders with the function of captains, officers and judges, thus covering the military, administrative and legal aspects of the life of the people. There is a pleasing alliteration in the Hebrew words for these elders, who were *sarim*, *shoterim* and *shophetim*.

Their functions were to be exercised for the benefit of both the native Israelite "and the stranger that is with him", and were to be without partiality between small and great. The stringent qualifications alluded to above, and the lists given in Acts 6 and in expanded form in 1 Timothy 3 and Titus 1, had been set with good reason: "for the judgment is God's."

This statement of high responsibility, which demanded that in all dealings with men, especially with the congregation of the Lord, His people must be impartial because God is no respecter of persons, merciful because He is merciful, and just because He is just, should bring home to twenty-first century ecclesial servants the greatness of their own responsibility. For the modern ecclesia is no less "the flock of God, which he hath purchased with his own blood" (Acts 20:28), than was the ecclesia at Ephesus. The work is God's: we must have only God's own standards in carrying it out.

It is interesting to see how this phrase, "the judgment is God's", is expanded by Paul in Romans 13:1–4, although in this case it is not being used as an exhortation for brethren and sisters to exercise judgement themselves, but humbly to submit to the authority of the powers of this world which He has ordained.

(c) "Fear not, neither be discouraged"
(1:19–21)

The journey from Horeb to Kadesh may have been only eleven days, and the distance about 120 miles, but the way led through the wilderness of Paran in the direction of the hill country of the Amorites ("the way of ..." is usually to be taken as meaning "the way towards ..."). The route probably lay along a waterless limestone plain. Even so, there were the manifest tokens of the Lord's presence in the cloud by day and the fire by night, and the people should have been able to recognise that "upon all the glory shall be a defence. And there shall be a tabernacle for a shadow in the daytime from the heat" (Isaiah 4:5,6).

But it was not likely that a people who had danced before a golden calf, saying "These be thy gods, O Israel, which brought thee up out of the land of Egypt", in the very sight of the mount which still burned with fire and almost immediately after hearing the commandment proclaimed,

16

"Thou shalt have no other gods before me. Thou shalt not make unto thee any graven image", would lose the opportunity for murmuring at the difficulties of the way "through all that great and terrible wilderness" (Deuteronomy 1:19).

The record in Numbers—there are only two chapters beween Sinai and Kadesh—tells of the affairs at Taberah and at Kibroth-Hattaavah and the murmuring of Miriam and Aaron. The fire on the mount must have been still visible when "the fire of the Lord burnt among them" because they had complained. It is a salutary lesson for us to remember that great experiences, ever visible reminders of the power and majesty of God, are in themselves no guarantee that the observers will be thereby made more spiritually minded. The people that murmured and provoked the Lord to anger in the wilderness were those who had passed through the Red Sea and had witnessed the mighty acts of the Lord. The earth itself may have trembled "at the presence of the Lord, at the presence of the God of Jacob" (Psalm 114:7), but the people did not always do so. The incident to be unfolded at Kadesh was a disastrous, yet classic example of human perversity.

For at that point the rigours were behind them. They had come to "The Holy Door" to the land and were about to enter into the blessings and the rest which God had promised. Therefore Moses said to them:

"Behold, the LORD thy God *hath set the land before thee*: go up and possess it, as the LORD God of thy fathers hath said unto thee; fear not, neither be discouraged."

(Deuteronomy 1:21)

The response was the request that the spies be sent, and the acceptance of their majority report marked a turning point, not only in the history of that generation but in the long history of God's people until their expulsion from the land in the days of Nebuchadnezzar. The details and the implications for that generation, indeed for our own, are to be considered in the next few chapters.

d) "It is a good land ..."
(1:22–25)

It was appropriate, with Israel actually standing at the crossing of the Jordan on the point of entering the Land of Promise to possess it, that Moses should recall the time, almost forty years earlier, when their fathers had also stood upon the threshold of the Land but had drawn back. It is true

17

that incidents such as the defeat of Sihon and Og, demonstrating the Lord's power to give His people victory over their enemies, were still fresh in their minds; whereas the previous generation had had little or no practical experience of warfare beyond the skirmish with the Amalekites at Massah (Exodus 17:8–16). Yet that generation had passed safely through the Red Sea, where the might of Pharaoh's pursuing army had been annihilated; they had seen the tokens of the Lord's presence amongst them, and they had actually heard His voice at Horeb. However, they had learned little from these experiences, and nowhere was their disposition to "come short of the glory of God" more clearly manifest than at Kadesh.

An act of unbelief

At first sight it had seemed prudent to send men to "search us out the land ... by what way we must go up, and into what cities we shall come" (verse 22). Indeed, the record in Numbers says that the Lord had so commanded them. But this in conjunction with Moses' statement—"The saying pleased me well: and I took twelve men of you, one of a tribe" (verse 23)—reveals another of those incidents (see verses 9–18) in which a human arrangement received the Divine sanction. The people put forward the request, Moses endorsed it and the Lord gave the terms on which it was to be carried out: a man for each tribe and "every one a ruler among them".

There can be little doubt that in this speech of warning and exhortation Moses was presenting the people's initiative as an act of unbelief which the next generation was at that time to be careful especially to avoid. They seem to have done so in this regard at least, and the record of Joshua's campaigns states that all of them were carried out specifically at the Lord's command and not Joshua's. He was obeying the clear instructions of "the captain of the LORD's host", whom he had met before Jericho.

The search of the Land had been thorough and extensive, and the evidence of its fruitfulness proved impressive to a people who had been over twelve months in the wilderness. "It is a good land which the LORD our God doth give" (verse 25) was the unanimous summary report.

The Book and the Land

It will give added point to what follows to consider now another characteristic of the Book of Deuteronomy, its references to the Land. The theme of Moses' exhortation is in effect "When thou art come into the land ...", and the land itself is kept before the people's minds by the constant repetition of phrases concerning it. The following list gives both the first occurrence of some of these phrases and the frequency of the same phrase or similar ones which have to do with entry into the Land. Those dealing more specifically with the blessing they will find there will be given later.

1. "The land which the LORD *sware unto your fathers*" (1:8; 27 times)
2. "... which the LORD our God *doth give unto us*" (1:20; 39 times)
3. "... *for an inheritance*" (4:21; 10 times)
4. "Go in and possess the land ..." (1:8; 33 times)
5. "A good land ..." (1:25; 10 times)
6. "... flowing with milk and honey" (6:3; 6 times)

At Kadesh-barnea, therefore, Israel had been on the very threshold of fulfilment of all that the Lord had promised. His purpose was firm—had He not sworn by Himself, since there was none greater?—the Land was theirs to inherit, and untold blessings lay at their feet. They had simply to rise up in faith and take possession.

(e) "Ye would not go up"
(1:26–33)

Ten of the twelve princes who searched the land must bear responsibility for what happened next. The people said, "*Our brethren have discouraged our hearts*" (verse 28) and the manner of giving the report rather than its content must have been the cause. After all, Joshua and Caleb had also seen the same great cities "walled up to heaven" and the "sons of the Anakim". Yet they could say, "Let us go up at once, and possess it; for we are well able to overcome it", and "If the LORD delight in us, then he will bring us into this land, and give it us" (Numbers 13:30; 14:8). The people refused to be "stilled", however, and accepted the majority report of the men that went up with the faithful two and said, "We be not able to go up against the people; for they are stronger than we".

A terrible responsibility

We may well pause a moment to consider the frightening responsibilities of all who are called upon to act as representatives or delegates in matters affecting the welfare of the Brotherhood at large, or even of a small area of its

19

operations. The community must, of course, bear its own responsibility, as the congregation of Israel did, for what it refuses or accepts when reports and proposals are made. But so much depends upon the faith, zeal and integrity of those called upon to act on its behalf when spiritual issues are at stake. The course of Israel's history was radically and inevitably altered by the revolt against the Lord at Kadesh, as is clearly shown by the record, not only of the wanderings in the wilderness but of all the events up to the exile.

For the glory had departed; the generation of the Exodus which the Lord had redeemed for Himself and which formed the nucleus of the great nation that was to be, would perish. The subsequent record, especially of the Book of Joshua, became the history of the *failure* to conquer the Land completely, not even within the area bounded by the Jordan, let alone all the land which God had sworn to give to their fathers. The events leading up to the division of the kingdom and the destruction of the national life now seemed inevitable.

It is important both in ecclesial and community matters to recognise when we come to a virtual Kadesh-barnea, a critical turn in our spiritual affairs. That there have been occasions when decisions made have set the course of our own history for a generation or more to come cannot be doubted; although there will be a variety of opinions on whether some of those decisions were entirely good or entirely bad. The vital things to remember are first, that it is easier to be aware of the errors of the past than to correct them. Every community has to live with its history and we can make no effective progress if we ignore that fact and try to make a clean sweep. To leave to join another group or a different community is simply to link oneself with a different set of unalterable facts with all their consequences. "We live our lives forwards, but only understand them backwards" is as true of spiritual history as of any other.

Second, keen spiritual insight is needed to recognise when a crisis is reached and to make decisions which will prove beneficial and not disastrous for our own time and for at least the generation to come. And third, the Lord's purpose is not finally frustrated by the failure of men: He works even amidst disaster with a faithful remnant, be they like Caleb and Joshua, only two among a multitude.

Drawing back at Kadesh

The perversity of the human nature we all bear is illustrated in the spirit that prevailed at Kadesh. Israel as a nation rarely, if ever, comprehended the true glory of the Lord who had set His Name in the midst of them. They said:

"Would God that we had died in the land of Egypt! or would God that we had died in the wilderness!"

(Numbers 14:2)

Nehemiah tells us in 9:17 that they actually carried out the proposal to appoint a leader to take them back to the land of captivity. In Deuteronomy 1:27 Moses reminds them of the words which had revealed all that was in their heart:

"*Because the* LORD *hated us*, he hath brought us forth out of the land of Egypt, to deliver us into the hand of the Amorites, to destroy us."

When one has seen "how that the LORD thy God bare thee, as a man doth bear his son, in all the way that ye went, until ye came into this place" (verse 31); when there has been abundant evidence, as described in detail in Numbers 10:33–36, that the Lord "went in the way before you, to search you out a place to pitch your tents in, in fire by night, to shew you by what way ye should go, and in a cloud by day"—in such circumstances how is it possible to think the unthinkable, and say "Because the LORD *hated* us"?

The answer is, by the same process by which we too can in effect say, "Is the Lord among us or not?"; when, knowing that our Lord shared our nature and is touched with a feeling of our infirmities, sickness, privation or doubt comes upon us and we draw back from full surrender to His will and say, "Why should this happen to *me*?" Or when, on the very eve of the coming of the Lord Jesus and the establishment of his Kingdom on earth, we say in our hearts, "Perhaps, after all, we have been wrong for over a century. Let us return unto the place from which our fathers came out".

There is more of Deuteronomy in Hebrews than we may have imagined. The Epistle gives us a valuable insight into the spiritual meaning of the Law and its significance for the twenty-first century disciple. But its clear message to us is:

"Today, if *ye* will hear his voice ..."   (Hebrews 3:7–4:9)

and

"Now the just shall live by faith: but if any man draw back, my soul shall have no pleasure in him. But we are not of them who draw back unto perdition; but of them that believe to the saving of the soul."   (10:38,39)

(f) "Take your journey into the wilderness" (1:34–40)

The account in Deuteronomy of what happened next is awe-inspiring. At Kadesh the people had been deaf to Moses' appeal to consider how the Lord had dealt with them as a father with his son, and had sworn to give them the Land. They were now to know the full meaning of the Lord's faithfulness, even as He had proclaimed it to Moses in Horeb. He had shown that He was truly for them, as He had been for their fathers and would be for all generations:

"God, merciful and gracious, longsuffering, and abundant in goodness and truth, keeping mercy for thousands, forgiving iniquity and transgression and sin."

(Exodus 34:6,7)

But when His very capacity to be all these things for them, nay, even the fact of His presence among them, was called in question, what could He do, since "he cannot deny himself", but show "the immutability of his counsel" and demonstrate that He would also be sanctified in them that come nigh Him? He could not in faithfulness forgive the rebellion and provocation which denied that He was Almighty, or that He would keep covenant with Abraham, and that proclaimed in effect that He had "brought them out", but could not "bring them in" (Deuteronomy 6:23).

So the Lord heard the words of the people "and was wroth, and *sware*", saying that none of the men of that "evil generation" should enter the Land of Promise, *save* Caleb. His judgement upon iniquity is as sure as His faithfulness to the covenant: it is confirmed by the same oath by which He had confirmed the mercy to Abraham: "By myself have I sworn", or "As truly as I live" (see Genesis 22:16–18; Numbers 14:21–24; Hebrews 6:13).

It is interesting to note that Caleb is here mentioned as the one exception among the faithless *people*, while Joshua is already being singled out for *leadership*. The promise to Abraham would have its partial fulfilment in Caleb "because he had another spirit with him." He like the patriarch was to be granted "the land that he hath trodden upon", a promise realised in Joshua 15.

But note the quality of this man, who was apparently of Edomite descent, although accepted in the tribe of Judah as head of the family of the Kenizzites: "he hath wholly followed the LORD." The Hebrew idiom is literally "he hath filled (himself) with the LORD", expressive surely of the complete

22

dedication which should be the hallmark of every disciple. And as he was wholly for the Lord, so the Lord was wholly with him. For the faith which gave him the evidence of things not seen enabled him to declare to a dejected people, "Let us go up at once, and possess it, for we are well able to overcome it" (Numbers 13:30); and when the substance of his hope was realised, it is written that he was indeed able to "drive thence the three sons of Anak" (Joshua 15:14).

There was a terrible irony in the fact that Moses' words were now being addressed to the next generation. For many of them had been numbered among the "little ones, which in that day had no knowledge between good and evil", and who their fathers said would be a prey to the inhabitants of the Land. With victories over two powerful kings behind them, they were about to go in and possess it. Would this generation be any better than their fathers? This is a question each generation disposed to be critical of the way by which their community has come ought to face with self-critical honesty.

(g) "Ye abode many days in Kadesh" (1:41–46)

The speech in Deuteronomy is deliberately selective, only the incidents which serve Moses' immediate purpose being related. We cannot, however, miss the implications of verses 41–46 where Israel is addressed in the second person plural rather than the usual "thou" and "thee" forms: "So I spake unto *you*; and ye would not hear, but rebelled ..." The responsibility of the nation as a whole could not be more clearly spelled out, nor the long-term effects of what had happened more surely emphasised. We must therefore go back to the Numbers record to fill in some of the instructive details which lay behind Moses' words.

One of the most remarkable manifestations of the glory of the Lord took place at Kadesh, from which several Divine principles emerge which we must take note of. We are confirmed in our understanding of Paul's definition of sin as "coming short of the glory of God" (Romans 3:23), for at the climax of the rebellion, "the whole congregation bade stone them with stones"—that is, Joshua and Caleb, and probably Moses and Aaron as well since it was their leadership that was being rejected (Numbers 14:4,5). At that very moment "the glory of the LORD appeared in the tabernacle of the congregation before all the people", as it did at similar crises of Israel's faithlessness or perversity in the wilderness (Exodus 16:10; 33:10; Numbers 16:19,42). The visible and

23

dramatic sign of the Lord's presence among them now revealed that He had also drawn near in judgement.

Yet, for His Name's sake, the Lord yielded to the pleading of Moses that He should not destroy the whole nation. Such a plea revealed the depth of Moses' understanding of the Name, for not even the prospect of becoming a greater nation in his name (Numbers 14:12) could lead him to contemplate for one moment the unjustified slander that could be uttered by the Egyptians if the Lord's people did not eventually enter the Land. So Moses prayed to *Adonai*, "the great and dreadful God", of sovereign majesty, to let the *power* of His Name be revealed even as He had spoken, "... saying, The LORD is longsuffering, and of great mercy ..." (verses 17,18).*

In granting pardon the Lord added, "But as truly as I live, all the earth shall be filled with the glory of the LORD" (verse 21). The promise of the Name stretched far beyond the disaster of that day, and would be fulfilled, not only in terms of the promise that Abraham's seed should enter into the land of the patriarch's sojourning, but that in him and his seed should all nations of the earth be blessed when the glory of the Lord was revealed and all flesh should see it together.

The men who brought the evil report died by the plague. The generation of the Exodus, who had so fallen short of the glory of which they should have been a part, would die in the wilderness, though they had been spared the immediate annihilation which they had deserved. Rash should we be to speculate on the future fate of those who perished in the wilderness. As a generation none of them would enter the Land at that time: there was no reversal of that condemnation. But who can tell what effect the Lord's pardon may have had upon individuals, to make them turn in faith to the promise that lay beyond, and hope that they might eventually enter in, together with Moses who was also to die on "this side Jordan"?

We learn, moreover, that there is an end to the time for repentance. The longsuffering of God will wait, but not indefinitely: and once the Lord has sworn in His wrath there is no further room for repentance, either on His part or on man's. Israel had not been convinced of this. Fearful to enter the Land whilst the Lord was with them, they recklessly

---

* See the chapter on "Lord, the Great and Dreadful God" in the author's *The Name that is Above Every Name*, published by *The Christadelphian*, 1983.

tried to do so after He had declared that He was not (14:42–45).

(h) "I have given Mount Seir unto Esau" (2:1–23)

The Children of Israel abode in Kadesh "many days". The Divine sentence was not repealed, which declared: "I the LORD have said, I will surely do it unto all this evil congregation, that are gathered together against me: in this wilderness they shall be consumed, and there they shall die" (Numbers 14:35). The men that brought up "the evil report upon the land, died by the plague *before the LORD*"—a signal act of judgement indeed. The others, with the perversity of human nature, then decided to rise up and enter the land, but the raid proved abortive because the Lord was not with them, and they were forced to retire in confusion.

Events in Kadesh-barnea

The narrative in Deuteronomy was no doubt intended to provoke a reaction in Moses' audience. They would discover soon enough that it was easier to look back and criticise the folly of an earlier generation than it would prove to face similar dangers themselves. Moses passes over the details of the "many days" in Kadesh, which we can read in Numbers 15—20. Events included the rebellion of Korah, Dathan and Abiram, the budding of Aaron's rod, the giving of sundry laws, the death of Miriam, and the smiting of the rock that was to result in the exclusion of Moses himself from the Land, a matter to which he alludes twice in this first address.

We gain the impression from Numbers 20 that the embassy to Edom with a request to pass through their borders was an attempt to take a short cut and avoid the wilderness of Mount Seir. As it was, because Edom had denied them passage (Numbers 20:21), the people were forced to turn south-eastwards, and to "compass Mount Seir many days" (Deuteronomy 2:1). Again the Divine command, showing clearly that God was overruling their affairs, proclaimed: "Ye have compassed this mountain *long enough*: turn you northward" (verse 3).

"Long enough" had been thirty-eight years, and the crossing of the brook of Pruning (Zered, verses 13,14) would fulfil the sentence upon the generation that had left Egypt:

"For indeed the hand of the LORD was against them, to destroy them from among the host, until they were consumed." (verse 15)

What followed in Moses' exhortation proves not only instructive as to God's dealings with those outside His covenant, but of vital importance for the twenty-first century disciple. The Israelites were warned to behave with the utmost circumspection as they passed by the territories of Edom, Ammon and Moab. They were to attempt no conquest, nor meddle with, nor distress the inhabitants of any of these countries (verses 4–6; 9–12; 18–23). For the Lord Himself had granted these territories to Esau and the children of Lot for their possession.

From this we learn that God does indeed bless men and give them their portion in this life, even though they are not of His covenant and therefore do not partake of the eternal blessings promised to the people He has brought unto Himself. True, the Edomites, Moabites and Ammonites were blessed because they were of the families of Isaac and Lot. But who is to say that when men acknowledge God as God, trust in Him for their material blessings and thank Him for their benefits, the Lord does not even today grant them their heart's desire, though He does not redeem or grant eternal life except upon a saving knowledge and a living faith?

A nobler portion

But secondly, and this is a harder lesson to learn, the people of God have always had to wait for their inheritance. Like the children of Israel, they know that,

> "the LORD thy God hath blessed thee in all the works of thy hand: he knoweth thy walking through this great wilderness: these forty years the LORD thy God hath been with thee; thou hast lacked nothing." (verse 7)

But they have not attained unto their rest, as the Edomites had before ever Jacob went down into Egypt. Some of the saints may at times be disposed to think wistfully of the careers they might have had, the wealth that could have been amassed, the leisure time in which others ply their hobbies, sail their yachts or tour around the world. The meek, however, do not yet inherit the earth, and the Lord has nevertheless been with us in the wilderness so that we have truly lacked nothing. He has "brought us out, that he might bring us in."

The last lesson must surely be that of the contrast between the spirit of the Edomites, whose father did not inherit the blessing, and that of the Israelites who did. For of the land of Moab God said,

26

"The Emims dwelt therein in times past, a people great, and many, and tall, as the Anakims ... but the Moabites call them Emims. The Horims also dwelt in Seir beforetime: but the children of Esau succeeded them, *when they had destroyed them before them, and dwelt in their stead.*"
(verses 10–12)

The same was said of Ammon, the descendants of Lot—"that also was accounted a land of giants ... *but the* LORD *destroyed them*; and they succeeded them and dwelt in their stead even unto this day".

What an indictment of the men of Kadesh-barnea! Generations before their distant kinsmen had dispossessed men every bit as fierce and terrible as the giants of Canaan because the Lord had given them the land. Israel, however, murmured: "Our brethren have discouraged our hearts, saying, The people is greater and taller than we"!

Is spiritual Israel of the twenty-first century any more courageous? It was forty years before Moses could add to his account of the exploits of Esau the words, "as the Israelites did unto the land of his possession, which the LORD gave unto them" (verse 12).

(i) "I have given into thine hand Sihon the Amorite" (2:24–37)

The description of the Anakim and the way in which Moab, Ammon and Edom had destroyed them, to dwell in their land, was in fact a parenthesis in Moses' speech after 2:20. The thread of his narrative is resumed in verse 24 with the Lord's command:

"Rise ye up, take your journey, and pass over the river Arnon: behold, I have given into thine hand Sihon the Amorite, king of Heshbon, and his land: begin to possess it, and contend with him in battle."

So, as we learn further from verse 31, the new initiative in conquest had come from the Lord Himself. If the crossing of the Zered had spelled the end of the generation of the Exodus, the passage of the Arnon marked the first step in the inheritance of the Land. One looks in vain for a meaning of the word *Arnon*, apparently a "rushing stream", which would parallel that of *Zered*, and give a neat balance to the symbolism of the "pruning away" of the rebels in the inheritance of their children. Scripture does not work that way, however, and indeed it is probable that the name Zered

27

was given afterwards because of its significance in Israel's history (verse 14), rather than that the name happened to fit.

What the Lord had promised long before, which the faithless generation had celebrated in song and then forgotten, would now begin to come to pass:

"This day will I begin to put the dread of thee, and the fear of thee upon the nations that are under the whole heaven, who shall hear report of thee, and shall tremble, and be in anguish because of thee."

(verse 25; Exodus 15:14,15)

Rahab confirmed this to the two spies when she told them, forty years after the Exodus, that "your terror is fallen upon us". The account of the crossing of the Red Sea had evidently left a deep impression on the inhabitants of Canaan, although it had faded from Israel's memory. But when it was reinforced by the news of the conquest of Sihon and Og, then, as Rahab added:

"As soon as we had heard these things, our hearts did melt, neither did there remain any more courage in any man, because of you: for the LORD your God, he is God in heaven above, and in earth beneath." (Joshua 2:11)

It is worth a moment's reflection on the relevance of Rahab's words for the disciple today. The deliverance from Egypt is matched, rather surpassed, by the deliverance from the bondage to sin and death. When like Israel we cry out, groaning "within ourselves, waiting for the adoption, to wit, the redemption of our body", then we rejoice in the consolation of the Truth, and marvel at what the Lord has done. But in moments of prosperity or ease the joy of salvation can fade from the memory. Israel could not be reminded often enough of whose they were and what He had done by His strong hand and outstretched arm. Let spiritual Israel eagerly accept the exhortation of this great book of Deuteronomy and "take heed", "remember", "observe" and "do".

"The iniquity of the Amorites"

The time had come which God had spoken of to Abraham. "The iniquity of the Amorites" being now full the time of their destruction was at hand. But though they were far outside the scope of the widespread blessing upon Abraham which, in temporal matters at least, extended to some of his kinsmen after the flesh, there was still an opportunity for them to co-operate with the purpose of the Lord with His people. Moses sent an embassage of peace, which makes it clear that the original intention had been to pass through Sihon's territory as the people had through Edom and Moab, "until Israel shall pass over Jordan into the land which the LORD our God giveth us" (Deuteronomy 2:29). Just as Pharaoh had had the opportunity to glorify God's Name by letting Israel go, but had been forced to glorify Him through his own destruction, so it was with Sihon. Difficult though the concept may appear to us that the hardening of Pharaoh's heart, like that of Sihon, was of the Lord (verse 30), we must not put forward a fatalistic view of God's control of events and assume that the initial refusal to obey God was an involuntary act. The Lord then, as now, was not willing that any should perish where destruction was either avoidable or unnecessary, and this aspect of His nature became enshrined in a law for Israel:

"When thou comest nigh unto a city to fight against it, *then proclaim peace* unto it. And it shall be, if it make thee answer of peace, and open unto thee, then it shall be, that all the people that is found therein shall be tributaries unto thee, and they shall serve thee. And if it will make no peace with thee, but will make war against thee, then thou shalt besiege it ..."   (20:10–12)

"Begin to possess"

The hortatory nature of Moses' first address is brought out from time to time in the comments he makes upon the events recapitulated. The disaster at Kadesh had been related as a warning to the next generation who inherited the consequences of that action. The conquest of Sihon, and later, Og, was an encouragement to them to enter in and take possession where their forefathers had failed: "From Aroer ... even unto Gilead, there was not one city too strong for us (RV has "too high", even though it had seemed that the cities were "walled up to heaven", 1:28!): the LORD our God delivered all unto us" (2:36).

(j) "Og the King of Bashan came out against us" (3:1–11)

With the experience of the campaign against Sihon behind them, Israel was encouraged by the Lord to go up against Og, king of Bashan (3:2). There is no reference this time to a separate embassage being sent to him, nor was it strictly necessary for Israel to take the Bashan road (verse 1) so far north in order to cross the Jordan, which they did later over ninety miles further south opposite Jericho. It is plain, however, that although the occupation of this territory west

29

of Jordan arises as the result of a request to Moses from the princes of the two-and-a-half tribes, the Lord was in fact leading the people towards the full conquest of the land promised to Abraham. This comprehended "this land from the river of Egypt unto the great river, the river Euphrates" (Genesis 17:18).

The victory was complete: "There was not a city which we took not from them, threescore cities", all well fortified, "beside unwalled towns a great many" (Deuteronomy 3:4,5).

The further summary statement, reinforced by another reference to Sihon, in verses 6–10, has to be viewed in the light of Moses' intention to press home the implications of these victories. To draw back now as their fathers had done would leave them entirely without excuse: the Lord had revealed Himself in their preliminary conquests and it could only be the utter faithlessness on the part of His people not to complete what had been so triumphantly begun. Moreover, the campaign was important from a strategic point of view, since at the crossing of the Jordan the right flank of the host encamped during the preparations and the actual crossing would have been exposed to attack. As it was, of Og and all his people "none was left to him remaining" (verse 3).

Although Og's kingdom was an Amorite kingdom, he himself is described as the only one that "remained of the remnant of giants", or Rephaim (verse 11). Rephaim are specifically mentioned in the Abrahamic covenant as being among the inhabitants of the land to be dispossessed by Abraham's seed, but they are unknown as the name of a race or nation outside the Bible record. In Psalm 88:10 and elsewhere, the word *rephaim* is rendered as "the dead", and it is thought that the idea derives from the fact that all the "aboriginal" inhabitants of Canaan were now dead.* Since they were evidently a formidable people, to be compared in stature with the Anakim (Deuteronomy 2:21), it is obvious that the rendering "giants" in verse 11 is appropriate.

Moreover, verse 11 tells that "his bedstead was a bedstead of iron … nine cubits was the length thereof, and four cubits the breadth of it, after the cubit of a man". This "bedstead" was in all probability a sarcophagus, prepared against the day of Og's death after the fashion of the Pharaohs of Egypt, or actually made to receive his corpse after his defeat at the hands of the Israelites. At all events, a coffin with the

---

* See "Even Giants Die", *The Christadelphian*, 1972, pages 119, 162; also "Giants", 1973, page 450).

dimensions of 4.1 x 1.8 metres (13½ x 6 feet) was certainly an exhibit worth viewing in "Rabbath of the children of Ammon"!

(k) "The LORD your God hath given you this land" (3:12–20)

In the allocation of the land east of the Jordan to the two-and- a-half tribes we have another interesting example of the Lord's willingness to co-operate with man's arrangements if they in fact further His purpose. As we have seen, the covenant with Abraham envisaged territory ultimately beyond the bounds of Canaan. The request that it be occupied then and there, however, originated from the tribes themselves, because that land was ideal for their needs. At first Moses raised a protest: for some to enter into their rest immediately would not only deprive the other tribes of their assistance in the conquest, but would positively discourage them. "Shall your brethren go to war, and shall ye sit here? And wherefore discourage ye the heart of the children of Israel from going over into the land which the LORD hath given them?" (Numbers 32:6,7). Had they come to a second Kadesh-barnea? asked Moses in effect, and his attitude was perfectly understandable.

There is no record that this matter was laid before the Lord, except by implication from Numbers 32:31. The solemn promise of the two-and-a-half tribes that the men at arms would cross with their brethren and would not return until the Land itself was settled, was both an act of generosity and of faith, since they had to leave behind families and property with none except the Lord to defend them. The record makes it clear that they discharged their promise honourably and in full (Joshua 22).

Indeed, the Lord Himself had also confirmed His word. In His mercy He had reinforced the faith of His people, granting them the benefit of a notable sign that Israel could do more than they could ask or think if only they put their trust in Him. Moses' exhortation to Joshua brings this out clearly:

"Thine eyes have seen all that the LORD your God hath done unto these two kings: *so shall the LORD do unto all the kingdoms whither thou passest.* Ye shall not fear them: for the LORD your God he shall fight for you."

(Deuteronomy 3:21,22)

Alas, the mention of Joshua and the Land brought home to Moses with full impact the Lord's pronouncement on himself: "Thou shalt not go over this Jordan." In Deuteronomy Moses reveals what a heart-rending effect these words had had upon him. This we shall next consider.

(1) "But the LORD was angry with me" (3:23–28)

Only two personal requests made by Moses are recorded in the Pentateuch. Otherwise his prayers are intercession on behalf of the people when they had sinned or appeals to the Lord that He should remember His covenant for His Name's sake. The first request followed the sin of the golden calf, when after receiving the assurance that the Lord would pardon the people, and go with them on the journey, Moses prayed, "I beseech thee, show me thy glory" (Exodus 33:18). The whole episode reveals both the compassion of the Lord and the deeply personal relationship shared with Him by Moses, to whom God said, "Thou hast found grace in my sight, and I know thee by name". We also learn much about the spiritual perception of Moses who realised that the glory of the Lord was revealed as much, if not more, in such an act of forgiveness as in the fire and smoke of Sinai. He was rewarded with an exposition of the Name by the Lord Himself (Exodus 34:5–7).

A longing for the land

The second, intensely emotional request of Moses was that he should after all be allowed to enter the promised Land. Three times he refers to the matter in his first Deuteronomy speech, in 1:37, 4:21,22, and here in chapter 3, where we can read the actual words of his prayer. There can be no doubt that Moses was profoundly affected by the Lord's sentence upon him and that his longing to see the Land was kindled by every reference to the impending entry into it.

The incident of the striking of the rock which led to Moses' exclusion from the Land (Numbers 20:12,13) has received many different explanations. The fault lay in striking the rock whereas the Lord had commanded Moses and Aaron to speak unto it. In the realm of type or allegory the rock was Christ (1 Corinthians 10:4), and was rightly smitten once that the living water might flow out of it (Exodus 17:1–7), even as "with his stripes we are healed". The Lord is not to be smitten twice, however, the simple request being all that is necessary for the soul thirsting for salvation.

There is beauty and no doubt truth in this explanation of this symbolism. In any case, God Himself gives the reason for His anger with Moses and Aaron, and Moses elaborates upon it sufficiently to make all plain. He first introduces the matter in his speech when he refers to the exclusion from the Land of the generation that came out of Egypt because of their manifest lack of faith at Kadesh. Nearly forty years lie between the events recorded in Deuteronomy 1:3 and 4:37,38, which are a parenthesis in the report of the Lord's sentence upon the faithless people. Moses too, like Joshua and Caleb, had borne the burden of the forty years' wandering which the people had incurred, but the very mention of it painfully recalls what the Lord had said to him at the second provocation of Meribah:

> "*Because ye believed me not* (believed not in me, RV) to sanctify me in the eyes of the children of Israel, therefore ye shall not bring this congregation into the land which I have given them." (Numbers 20:12)

An absolute principle

Not bring them in? For this very cause Moses had been summoned from following the flocks; for this cause the Lord had revealed His Name at the Bush; for this cause He had brought them out of Egypt; and for this cause Moses had borne the burden of the people, pleading for them, interceding for them—it had been his whole life! "Also the LORD was angry with me for your sakes" (Deuteronomy 1:37). Never did the Divine principle stand out more clearly or appear more absolute and without partiality: "I will be sanctified in them that come nigh me (*are nigh me*, RV margin), and before all the people I will be glorified" (Leviticus 10:3).

"For your sakes" means quite obviously "on your account", but the implication is deeper than the single idea that Moses suffered because of what the people had done. Moses bore the special responsibility of leadership, and the standards were higher: "My brethren, be not many masters, knowing that we shall receive the greater condemnation" (James 3:1). The Lord in fact could not show Himself a respecter of persons, even of the person of Moses, when the elders who ruled in Israel were commanded, "Ye shall not respect persons in judgment ... for the judgment is God's" (Deuteronomy 1:17). Psalm 106 is all-revealing:

> "They angered him also at the waters of strife, so that it went ill with Moses for their sakes: because they provoked his spirit, *so that he spake unadvisedly with his lips.*"
> (verses 32,33)

The exemplary character of the sentence upon Moses was recognised by him, and formed the basis of his urgent exhortation when he returned to the matter in Deuteronomy 4:21,22: "Furthermore the LORD was angry with me for your sakes ... but I must die in this land, I must not go over Jordan: but ye shall go over, and possess that good land."

A Personal Relationship

The certain knowledge that Moses was to hand over his charge and die gave a solemn quality of patriarchal blessing to his speech and reinforced his urgent words: "Take heed unto yourselves ... For the LORD thy God is a consuming fire, even a jealous God." In the light of this, however, the verses we are considering in 3:23–28 are even more instructive. They bring out clearly the personal relationship between the Lord and His servant. For in spite of his reverential awe for God, Moses can still venture to plead with Him even though the Lord is impatient of His request. The form of address is solemn—"O Lord GOD (*Adonai Yahweh*)", Almighty Sovereign Lord of heaven and earth, yet the Maker of a covenant with Thy chosen.* Twice only does Moses use this combination of Name and title in Deuteronomy.

We can gauge the sense of urgency in his pleading from 9:26, where he describes how he fell down before the Lord forty days and forty nights, and said, "O *Adonai Yahweh*, destroy not thy people ...". With the same urgency and emotion he now pleads for himself. The ground of his plea was that the Lord had begun to reveal His mighty hand in the conquest of Sihon and Og, the earnest of the conquest of the land. He no longer seeks to lead the people, only to see the land. The refusal is final: "Speak no more unto me of this matter." Yet there was justice and mercy in the response. There would be no crossing of the Jordan, yet from the top of Pisgah he could lift his eyes and behold the land from afar.

As he stood there, did he recall that Abraham had once been told to lift his eyes "and look from the place where thou art northward, and southward, and eastward, and westward" (Genesis 13:14) and realise that even to walk in the land as Abraham had done was not the fulfilment of the promise? Did he look beyond the present and the joy denied to him to the fulness of what God had promised, to that better thing which Abraham and Moses will receive with faithful disciples of all ages (Hebrews 11:40)? He had "endured as seeing him

---

* See the author's *The Name that is above Every Name*, chapter 4, published by The Christadelphian Office, 1983.

who is invisible" (verse 27) and was surely consoled as he lay down to sleep in peace.

Divine appointment

For the present one thing was ordered and sure:

"Charge Joshua, and encourage him, and strengthen him: for he shall go over before this people, and he shall cause them to inherit the land which thou shalt see."

(Deuteronomy 3:28)

The succession of human leadership, therefore, would be neither a power struggle nor a democratic process: it was a matter of Divine appointment.

(m) "For what nation is there so great?" (4:1–8)

The previous chapter concludes with the words, "So we abode in the valley over against Bethpeor". From 34:6 we learn that this was in a valley of Moab, but the exact location is unknown. Moses was to be buried in this region, so he has now come in effect to the end of his account of the long and circuitous journey from Horeb to the crossing of the Jordan. The rest of this first speech is taken up with practical exhortations for the generation who heard it:

"Now therefore hearken, O Israel, unto the statutes and unto the judgments, which I teach you, for to do them, that ye may live, and *go in and possess the land which the LORD God of your fathers giveth you.*" (verse 1)

The relationship between the Law and the statutes and judgements we shall illustrate when we come to Deuteronomy 6. It is sufficient here to say that they are practical details by which the eternal principles are translated into daily life. It was not only from the record of what had happened to the previous generation that Moses was to draw his warnings. The valley of Bethpeor had seen the death of 24,000 of the generation that was to inherit, even after the Brook of Pruning had been crossed. "Your eyes have seen what the LORD did because of Baal-peor: for all the men that followed Baal-peor, the LORD thy God hath destroyed them from among you" (verse 3).

The incident is recorded in detail in Numbers 25, and by piecing together the account of Balaam in 22–24 and the laconic note in 31:8 of the slaying of Balaam when the Lord was avenged of the Midianites, we may safely assume that the affair of the Midianitish women had been instigated by that false prophet as the only way of doing harm to the people of the Lord, who had forbidden him to curse them.

The name of the Baalim

The incident was of prime importance. Although the account of it lays emphasis upon the acts of whoredom, it also makes it evident that these were connected with idolatrous worship (Numbers 25:2,3). The very name of Baal implied a lordship other than that of the God of Israel. At times during their history Israel used the name in a kind of "ecumenical" spirit. Baal-berith, for example, means "the lord of the covenant", but the idol to which it was attached was something very different from the true Lord of the covenant with the fathers. So the prophet said that the Lord would take the name of Baali, My lord, out of the mouth of His people, even though it was being used with reference to Himself; so that the Baalim should no more be remembered by name (Hosea 2:17).

The word Baal-peor, moreover, had particularly distasteful connotations, and rightly earned the prophet's term of "that shame" (Hosea 9:10). Such facts as these lie behind the categoric Divine command that Israel were to make no league with the inhabitants of the land, but were to destroy both them and their idolatrous systems. The Lord again showed Himself impartial in His judgements: Israel were to blot out the memory of the idolatrous worship from the land. But if this people should prefer the evil to the good, they were to be destroyed with the system they espoused.

It was appropriate, therefore, since Israel had been deceived before ever they entered the Land, that Moses should draw on this experience in stern warning, pointing also the lesson that "ye that did cleave unto the LORD your God are alive, every one of you this day" (Deuteronomy 4:4).

Wisdom and understanding

There was another reason, said Moses, why Israel should keep the statutes and judgements which "I have taught you … even as the LORD my God commanded me" (verse 5). Their obedience was, as it were, a preaching witness. It was to be their wisdom and their understanding "in the sight of the nations, which shall hear all these statutes, and say, Surely this great nation is a wise and understanding people" (verse 6). The converse of this was that the Lord's Name would be blasphemed on account of their disobedience (Romans 2:24; Isaiah 52:5). So Israel were indeed the Lord's witnesses, as He said:

"Ye are my witnesses, saith the LORD, and my servant whom I have chosen: that ye may know and believe me, and understand that I am he: before me there was no God formed, neither shall there be after me. I, even I, am the LORD; and beside me there is no saviour. I have declared, and have saved, and I have shewed, when there was no strange God among you: therefore ye are my witnesses, saith the LORD, that I am God."   (Isaiah 43:10–12)

So Israel were witnesses to the Lord's omnipotence, to His covenant love and mercy, to His justice in punishing for their iniquities a people whom He had known above all the nations of the earth (Amos 3:2), and to the fact that He had a purpose with the earth and had in Israel revealed things to come—the very sign that He is God alone.

All the true servants of God have recognised the greatness of Israel (Deuteronomy 4:7,8). They have also recognised that the nation did not achieve greatness in its own right, but by virtue of the fact that they had "God so nigh unto them, as the LORD our God is in all things that we call upon him for". The gods of the nations were idols, able neither to hear, nor see, nor speak, and needing to be borne upon men's shoulders (Psalm 135:1–18; Isaiah 46:1,2). Israel's God, however, had borne *them* upon eagle's wings and brought them unto Himself. The wonder of this was brought home to David when God promised to perpetuate His Kingdom and His purpose in David's line:

"Who am I, O Lord GOD? and what is my house, that thou hast brought me hitherto? And this was yet a small thing in thy sight, O Lord GOD; but thou hast spoken of thy servant's house for a great while to come ... Wherefore thou art great, O LORD God: for there is none like thee, neither is there any God beside thee, according to all that we have heard with our ears. And what one nation in the earth is like thy people, even like Israel, whom God went to redeem for a people to himself, and to make him a name, and to do for you great things and terrible ...?"

(2 Samuel 7:18–23)

It is worthy of note that in this prayer David uses the same solemn address of reverential pleading, "O Lord GOD"— *Adonai Yahweh*—upon which we have already remarked (page 34).

The greatness of Israel was reflected not in their military achievements, though these were a necessary preliminary to their entry into the Land of promise, but in the *constitution* of the nation. As Moses put it:

"And what nation is there so great, that hath *statutes and judgments so righteous* as all this law, which I set before you this day?" (Deuteronomy 4:8)

(n) "Only take heed to thyself"
(4:9–13)

The changes from the second person singular ("thou") to the plural ("you"), obscured by most modern translations, are worthy of careful study for the understanding they offer us.

We do not claim to have grasped all the points of emphasis made by these variations, but the following may be stated as a general principle for the book of Deuteronomy. "Ye" and "you" are addressed to the people as a multitude of persons, whilst "thou" and "thee" refer to the nation as a corporate whole—the "Son" whom God called out of Egypt (32:6; Hosea 11:1), or to single individuals. So in verse 8, Moses sets the law before "you", all who were assembled to hear; but Israel as God's "whole family", "all Israel", were to take heed to "thyself", the nation as a single entity. The message went deeper, however, since only by the righteous conduct of *each individual*, especially of *each leader* of the nation, could the nation as a whole keep the LORD's covenant.

This exhortation Paul uses with great force in his charge to Timothy, which in many respects follows closely the pattern of Deuteronomy. The problems at Ephesus, "the house of God, the congregation of the living God", needed careful handling if the ecclesia was not to be eaten up with the canker of the "other-teaching" of men like Hymenaeus and Philetus. The careful choice of elders as men of character and integrity would be of prime importance. But above all Timothy's own conduct would offer both example and cure:

"*Take heed unto thyself,* and to thy teaching. Continue in these things: for in doing this thou shalt save both thyself and them that hear thee." (1 Timothy 4:16, RV)

The same is true of the twenty-first century disciple in the ecclesia. It is vain for us to talk of "the state of the Brotherhood", or "the future of the ecclesias" as though either were something from which we ourselves were detached. The real need is for each one to bring to our ecclesia and our Brotherhood a love for the Lord and a concern for our brethren and sisters, founded upon a clear understanding of Divine truth and principle, and a resolve to practise both—to "truth it in love" (Ephesians 4:15). In short, *to take heed unto ourselves*. If however we ourselves forget the things which our eyes have seen of the Lord's redemptive work and they depart from our hearts, we shall neglect to "teach them thy sons, and thy sons' sons" (Deuteronomy 4:9).

The nature of God

The details of the experience at Sinai are recalled very vividly indeed (verses 10,11), since they were of importance for the people's understanding of the nature of their God and His attributes. When they entered the Land they were to be left in no doubt of the terms of their inheritance—"I will *make* them hear my words". All the phenomena at Sinai had been impressive, both visually and audibly. To "the things which thine eyes have seen" in the Exodus were added further tokens of God's power and presence, as "the mountain burned with fire *unto the heart* (RV) *of heaven*, with darkness, clouds and thick darkness".

The record in Exodus adds the details of the thunder and the trumpet which sounded with a great crescendo to herald the Lord's descent upon the mountain in fire, to the accompaniment of an earthquake (Exodus 19:16–19). This was the *first* trumpet in Scripture, and it is worth comparing it with the *last* trumpet, described in similar terms in 1 Thessalonians 4:15–18, but this time sounded to herald the consummation of a purpose and the judgement of the Lord's people.

And then—the Voice!

"And the LORD spake unto you out of the midst of the fire: ye heard the voice, but saw no similitude; only ye heard a voice." (Deuteronomy 4:12)

The importance of seeing "no similitude" is discussed below. But surely we cannot escape the conclusion Moses himself is drawing from this experience of God at Sinai: God communicates with His people by means of His word, and they keep His covenant by doing it. Time and again, especially in the Psalms, God's prophets return to this theme:

"I am the LORD thy God, which brought thee out of the land of Egypt ... But *my people would not hearken to my voice*; and Israel would none of me." (Psalm 81:10,11)

The existence of God and His presence amongst His people are testified by the same means today: His word has come to all, whether they received it direct, as at Sinai, or through the medium of the prophets in their writings or utterances. And ever since, the exhortation has gone forth, through Moses, through the Psalmist and through the Apostle:

"Today, if ye will hear his voice, harden not your heart,
as in the provocation, and as in the day of temptation in
the wilderness: when your fathers tempted me, proved me,
and saw my work."   (Psalm 95:7–9; Hebrews 3:7,15; 4:7)

The finger of God

The "covenant, which he commanded you to perform"
(Deuteronomy 4:13) was the Ten Commandments—the
Decalogue, or Ten Words—which were written on two tables
of stone. There was deep significance in this writing. The
cloud dispersed, the fire died down and the voice of the
trumpet was stilled. Indeed, for reasons Moses will tell us
later, even the living voice of God was to be heard no more
directly by the people. The very memory of the experience
was to fade, and generation after generation would arise
without any repetition of it. Yet over three thousand years
later we know what was said. The writing, "written with the
finger of God" was like all Scripture, *God-breathed* as much
as the audible words had been.*

Another important reason lay behind the fact that the
Decalogue was committed to writing. At the commencement
of our study there was offered a comparison with the
standard form of covenant known to the contemporary world
(page 5), included in which was the provision for the deposit
of a copy of it in the presence of witnesses. The two tables of
the testimony were that copy, and we have the interesting
reflection that there were two of them, not because there was
insufficient room for the Ten Words on one, as the popular
illustrations suggest, but because the *two parties* to the
covenant each had their own copy. And where more
appropriate for the copies to be deposited as a lasting witness
to what the Lord had done than in the ark of the covenant, or
the ark of the testimony, where the Lord had promised to
meet with His people?

(o) "The LORD thy God is a consuming fire" (4:14–24)

According to verse 14 Moses was commanded "at that time"
to begin the exposition of the Ten Commandments in the
form of statutes and judgements to be observed "in the land
whither ye go over to possess it". Indeed, Exodus 20:22–23:33
saw the beginning of that exposition which followed the
detailed instructions for the building of the tabernacle. The

---

* See the Essay on "By Inspiration of God" in the author's *Letters to
Timothy and Titus)*.

complete exposition, however, was overtaken by events, notably the making of the golden calf and the shattering of the stone tablets, which indicated Israel's breaking of the covenant; and then the affair at Kadesh-barnea which deferred the entry into the Land for forty years. The Deuteronomy, or Repetition of the Law, is therefore the proper occasion for this exposition, which occupies chapters 5–26 inclusive.

"Ye saw no similitude"

The entry into the Land would expose the generation born in the wilderness to a fresh danger—that of the Canaanite culture and worship. Accordingly Moses here anticipates the repetition of the Second Commandment (5:8–10) and its detailed setting forth in "statutes and judgments" by warning against any attempt to represent the Lord in a physical manner. Though the reality of God's presence at Sinai could not be doubted, the experience was essentially spiritual and awesome. No form was visible, and in their first subsequent attempt to represent the *Elohim* who had brought them out of Egypt the people had corrupted themselves (verse 16; Exodus 32:4,7,8), dishonouring the Lord with an inadequate image of Him as one His own creatures.

Moses' first warning, in verse 16, is against making any statue in human form whether male or female. Since Israel's God was a *personal* God, the temptation to represent Him thus must have been very great indeed. But man was created in God's image and after His likeness: to reverse the rôles was to do despite to the Lord since "the heaven, even the heaven of heavens" cannot contain Him, much less a temple made with hands. How woefully inadequate then the graven image of a man!

> "They have mouths, but they speak not; eyes have they, but they see not; they have ears, but they hear not; neither is there any breath in their mouths."　(Psalm 135:16,17)

The disciple should also remember that *any* attempt to limit God, by our own definitions or unscriptural concepts of Him, since our thoughts and our ways are so much lower than His, is virtually to fashion Him into an image of ourselves. We need a statement of our faith about God, but God is not confined in it any more than He was in Solomon's temple. He dwells with him that is of a contrite and humble spirit, and His best representatives are they who tremble at His word.

Symbol and reality

Verses 17,18 forbid resort to other aspects of Creation in an attempt to make God "real". The sojourn in Egypt had only too deeply influenced the generation of the Exodus, as the incident of the golden calf showed. It is important to note that the Israelites would no doubt have felt themselves at one with those today who need a statue or a relic or a symbol to stimulate or orientate their devotions. It is claimed that it is not the symbol which is revered, *but what it represents*. Israel said in effect the same thing: the golden calf represented their God and their feast to it was a feast to the Lord: "These be thy gods (*elohim*), O Israel, which have brought thee up out of the land of Egypt" (Exodus 32:8). So did Jeroboam claim later for the images he set up at Bethel and at Dan (1 Kings 12:28).

The deities of Ancient Egypt included a wide range of the animal creation. Even the most important ones were depicted as a cow, an ibis, a falcon, or even in human form with animal characteristics, such as the jackal-headed Anubis. Winged or fiery serpents together with other creeping things were common symbols in antiquity: the people should have remembered with good cause that in the eyes of the Lord they were the symbols of sin or judgement (Numbers 21:6,7). Forty years is not a sufficiently long time for racial memory to die out, and Canaan, with a new set of grotesque forms and shapes to its idolatry lay ahead. Moses' appeal, therefore, is urgent, and we are being prepared for the stern command that the people should destroy all the sights that beguiled and corrupted as well as the people of the land who practised them.

For not only had the Lord created man in His own image, but He had set him over the works of His hands. The fulfilment of the Divine purpose in creation would come when the Son of man entered into his dominion over:

"all sheep and oxen, yea, and all the beasts of the field;
the fowl of the air, and the fish of the sea, and whatsoever
passeth through the paths of the seas."   (Psalm 8:7,8)

How vain, then, to *worship* created things instead of the Creator! It was not simply a question of a pardonable lapse in understanding: there were moral results of this folly, which are expounded in some detail in Romans 1, which violate every one of the Ten Commandments.

Sun, Moon and stars

Perhaps there was something of prophetic vision in the prohibition against worshipping the hosts of heaven, which were also the work of God's fingers. Such worship was more characteristic of Persia than of Egypt or Canaan, but Israel's contact with it as a fully developed religious system was as yet a long way off. Nevertheless the temptation to such idolatry was always there and could prove more subtle in many ways than the actual making of an image. Careful thought might lead a man to see the wisdom of such reasoning as we find in Isaiah, where God pours scorn on the man who selects a good piece of wood, kindles a fire to warm himself, cooks himself a meal and with the remainder makes himself an idol before which he bows in worship (Isaiah 44:14–20).

To walk abroad beneath the vastness of heaven, however, and see the glory and the beauty of the great lights, and the stars set for signs and seasons, kindles a response which should be one of awe and reverence for the Maker of heaven and earth. Nevertheless, Moses acknowledges that Israel could be "*driven* to worship them" or "*drawn away*" as the Revised Version has it (Deuteronomy 4:19), even as that perfect man Job explains:

"If I beheld the sun when it shined, or the moon walking in brightness; and my heart hath been secretly enticed, or my mouth hath kissed my hand: this also were an iniquity to be punished by the judge: *for I should have denied the God that is above.*" (Job 31:26–28)

It is important for our consideration of the Second Commandment, when we come to chapter 5, to note that the above remarks of Job were prefaced by reference to another form of idolatry: "If I have made gold my hope ... If I rejoiced because my wealth was great ..."

Symbols of the Covenant

The stars of heaven were the symbols of the covenant made with Abraham: they were not to be worshipped as if they were the Lord of the covenant Himself, for it is He "who maketh the seven stars and Orion", Who can "bind the sweet influences of the Pleiades, or loose the bands of Orion ... bring forth Mazzaroth in his season ... or guide Arcturus with his sons" (Job 38:31,32).

There was yet another reason given why the host of heaven should not be worshipped as divine:

"The LORD *thy* God hath divided (the host of heaven) unto all nations under the whole heaven. But the LORD hath taken you ... to be unto him *a people of inheritance*, as ye are this day" (Deuteronomy 4:19,20).

It is ironical that Israel should either have forgotten or at least treated very lightly their special status in the eyes of God, or at times arrogantly presumed upon it as though they were in themselves superior people, entitled to God's protection while flouting His commandments. Either attitude was disloyalty. On the one hand, if Israel could worship the gifts which He had imparted to all men, they lost the concept that the Lord was their God, with an exclusive claim upon their love and worship because He had redeemed them.

On the other hand, they could not be truly His people, and therefore like Him in their ways, if they did not recognise that God had created all nations under the sun and sent His rain upon them all without partiality. For disciples the Lord Jesus uses the same argument: if their Heavenly Father made His sun to rise upon the just and the unjust, how much greater should be His children's desire to be perfect as He is by displaying the same generous spirit.

"A people for his name"

There is another consideration for the twenty-first century disciple and it needs stressing urgently. The spirit of ecumenism, which is abroad and which is affecting even some members of the Christadelphian community, loses sight of one important aspect of Christianity: its object is to "take out of the Gentiles a people for his name". True disciples are called upon to be a separate people, sanctified unto God. It is as important for them as it was for Israel of old to remember that the terms of the covenant in Christ's blood, by which they are constituted a holy nation, were laid down by God and not by themselves. Through God's grace, and not through any wisdom or merit of their own, they have a distinctive understanding of the way of salvation, and share a distinctive faith and hope. This exclusiveness is of God and not of man.

The vivid description of Egypt in verse 20 as "the iron furnace" became an established Scriptural metaphor, conveying the sense of the hardness and travail endured by the people in bondage. We know how they cried out to be delivered, just as we in our turn have groaned being burdened, as we wait for our ultimate deliverance from sin and the redemption of the body. From the earliest times iron was associated with captivity in Egypt, as the Psalmist wrote of Joseph:

> "He sent a man before them, even Joseph, who was sold for a servant: whose feet they hurt with fetters: his soul entered into the iron."   (Psalm 105:17,18, RV margin)

In his prayer of dedication of the Temple Solomon pleaded with the Lord for forgiveness for the people, should they depart from Him, with the special plea echoing Moses' words:

> "For they be thy people, and thine inheritance, which thou broughtest forth out of Egypt, from the midst of the furnace of iron ... For thou didst separate them from among all the people of the earth."   (1 Kings 8:51–53)

Jeremiah, on the other hand, recalls the same words to emphasise the penalty for breaking that same covenant:

> "Cursed be the man that obeyeth not the words of this covenant, which I commanded your fathers in the day that I brought them forth out of the land of Egypt, from the iron furnace, saying, Obey my voice, and do them ..."
>
> (Jeremiah 11:3,4)

A theme to remember

Once more Moses refers to his approaching death and the Lord's sentence upon him. He was moved no doubt by the further mention of the inheritance of the Land he was not to enter. There is surely a pang in his heart as he contrasts "*this* land", where he will die with "*that good* land" which his contemporaries were to possess (Deuteronomy 4:21,22). The recollection, however, only serves to emphasise the character of his speech as true exhortation, a patriarchal blessing in which he leaves them what will prove to be most precious if only they will keep it: *Take heed unto yourselves, lest ye forget the covenant of the Lord your God*. It is scarcely possible to avoid repetition in our study: but then, why should we, since Moses himself did not, and we ourselves need reminding no less frequently than did Israel of whose we are and whom we serve. In contemplating the love of God we must never lose sight of the fact, reiterated in that great Letter to the Hebrews which sets forth the new covenant against the background of the symbolism of the old:

> "For the LORD thy God is a consuming fire, even a jealous God."   (verse 24; Hebrews 12:29)

(p) "I call heaven and earth to witness"
(4:25–31)

In many respects this introductory speech can be viewed as a synopsis of the rest of the Book. It recalls the memory of Sinai which is further expounded in 5:1–33; indicates that the Ten Commandments are to become the law of the Land in terms of "statutes and judgments" (6:1–8:20); reminds the children of Israel of their former rebellions as the basis of warning and exhortation (9:1–11:32); stresses the faithfulness of the Lord to His part in the covenant and prophesies Israel's departure from Him (28:1–68); calls heaven and earth to witness against them (32:1–43); and names Joshua as Moses' successor who will lead the people into their inheritance (31:1–23).

The Lord, jealous and merciful

Verses 25–31 contain in effect another of those wonderful expositions in practical terms of the Name of the Lord. The last section concluded with "For the LORD thy God is a consuming fire, even a jealous God", an attribute which would be demonstrated in His punishment of the people if they corrupted themselves by making any likeness of things in heaven, in earth or under the earth. The theme is continued in a strongly prophetic vein, for Moses takes his hearers into the future, their own future and beyond, when they "shall have remained long in the land, and shall corrupt" themselves (verse 25). The fact that they will break the Second Commandment is spoken of as a foregone conclusion, for Moses goes on to leave them in no doubt as to what will follow.

"I call heaven and earth to witness against you this day." If they will not accept that their God, the Creator, changes not, then His unchanging covenant of day and night, summer and winter and all the ordinances of heaven will attest to that fact: their casting off is as fixed and determined as the movement of the stars in their courses. On the other hand, just as Abraham had been taken forth abroad to hear the Lord set the assurance of the blessing in the glory and the beauty of the stars, so later, through Jeremiah, He declared His promise of fulfilment through the New Covenant based on forgiveness to be equally immutable:

"Behold, the days come, saith the LORD, that I will make a new covenant with the house of Israel, and with the house of Judah ... for I will forgive their iniquity, and I will remember their sin no more. Thus saith the LORD, which giveth the sun for a light by day, and the ordinances of the moon and of the stars for a light by night, which divideth the sea when the waves thereof roar; the LORD of hosts is his name: If those ordinances depart from before me, saith the LORD, then the seed of Israel also shall cease from being a nation before me for ever." (Jeremiah 31:31–37)

All this is anticipated in these few verses in Deuteronomy now under consideration. For the covenant Name speaks of the mercy of the Lord as well as of His judgement. If He is jealous, it is not the jealousy of man but that of a heavenly Father who sees His children seduced from a love and obedience in which their chief, their only blessings can be found. And if He is a consuming fire, it purifies what can abide it as well as destroys the worthless, as Isaiah found in his own experience (Isaiah 6:7). So Moses declares:

"… even in the latter days, if thou turn to the LORD thy God, and shalt be obedient unto his voice; (For the LORD thy God is a merciful God;) he will not forsake thee, neither destroy thee, *nor forget the covenant of thy fathers which he sware unto them.*" (Deuteronomy 4:30,31)

The New Covenant

No clearer understanding of the covenant name can be imagined: the Creator and Sovereign Lord of heaven and earth is to be remembered and adored for His covenant with Abraham of justification and inheritance. His Creation is both the guarantee and the witness to His faithfulness. But if His mercy endureth for ever His judgements must be likewise unchanging. When He poured them out on Israel it was because *they* had changed and had forsaken their covenant loyalty to Him. They would, however, find that in His constancy the Lord would restore to them His mercy, His covenant love, if they would only repent or *change back*, to serve Him once more. In terms strongly reminiscent of Deuteronomy did Solomon dedicate the house prepared for Him whom the heaven of heavens cannot contain (1 Kings 8), to be both a focal point of the people's worship when they had become settled in the Land, and a stimulus for the yearnings and devotion of a people scattered from it for their iniquity, yet seeking to return unto the Lord in spirit and in truth. The Lord on His side would have His eyes open towards that house night and day, "even toward the place of which thou hast said, My name shall be there" (1 Kings 8:29, 46–52).

These same principles are to be seen in the manifestation of the Lord's Name in His Son. He "gave His only begotten Son, that whosoever believeth in him should not perish … but he that believeth not …" Having manifested such love and waited with longsuffering, not willing that any should perish, God will eventually send again His Son unto whom He hath committed all judgement, to take vengeance upon those who have despised His love.

It is worth noting here that the New Covenant in Christ's blood is essentially the covenant with Abraham, as Paul tells us in Galatians 3. The Old Covenant was concerned with dwelling in the Land on the basis of the Law of Moses; the New with *eternal inheritance* of the earth on the basis of righteousness through justification by faith.

Moses' warnings and exhortations had both a positive and a negative basis. If the children of Israel would persist in violating the Second Commandment, then they would be scattered among all nations and "be left *few in number* among the heathen" (Deuteronomy 4:27)—surely a tragic condition for those who were heirs of a covenant which would have made them as the sand of the seashore for multitude! But they would also find that amongst the heathen they had no option but to serve other gods, since their own God was far from them (verse 28). God would in effect "choose their delusions, and will bring their fears upon them; because when I called, none did answer; when I spake, they did not hear: but they did evil before mine eyes, and chose that in which I delighted not" (Isaiah 66:4). The disciple also should beware (2 Thessalonians 2:11).

(q) "For ask now of the days that are past" (4:32–40)

There was another basis for the people's faith besides that of the unchangeableness of the ordinances of heaven: it was the evidence of their experience in their own history. They could search the full extent of human history from the days that were before them "since the day that God created man upon the earth". There need be no geographical limit to their enquiry, "from the one side of heaven unto the other". Never had there been "any such thing as this great thing is, or hath been heard like it". The actual words of Moses are more powerful than any paraphrase can be in expressing the wonder of the two unique events, the Exodus and at Sinai:

"Did ever people hear the voice of God speaking out of the midst of the fire, as thou hast heard, *and live*? Or hath God assayed to go and take him a nation from the midst of another nation, by temptations, by signs, and by wonders, and by war, and by a mighty hand, and by a stretched out arm, and by great terrors, according to all that the LORD your God did for you in Egypt before your eyes?"

(verses 33,34)

The significance of this goes deeper yet. For the redemption of His people was as much a witness to the glory of the Lord as was creation itself; for He had set His glory above the heavens, as David puts it (Psalm 8). Or, to quote Moses once more:

"Unto thee was it shewed, *that thou mightest know that the LORD he is God; and there is none else beside him.*"

(verse 35)

The *Torah*, the "law" or "teaching", therefore had its foundation in the fact of Israel's redemption. It was true "doctrine" in the Scriptural sense of that word, for the New Testament use of it has the same sense. It is not a theological code but a code of behaviour based upon a knowledge of the historical facts of God's salvation and an understanding of their implication in the life of God's people. In the case of Israel their instruction depended upon the fact that "*out of heaven* he made thee to hear his voice" and "*upon earth* he shewed thee his great fire" (verse 36).

Nowhere in the whole of the Book of Deuteronomy, or indeed in any of the historians or prophets, are the historical facts of the Red Sea and Sinai ever out of mind. Moreover the classification of books in the Hebrew Bible calls the history writers "the former prophets", because God spoke to His people in the events through which they passed, and the prophets as such are "the latter prophets", who interpret the meaning of the events for their hearers.

Knowledge and experience

It is important for the twenty-first century disciple to remember, especially when so much emphasis is laid upon "experience" as the basis of the knowledge of God, that Israel learned very little from their experience. It was not the fire upon earth which explained their God to them. Had He not spoken to them then the significance of all the phenomena of Sinai would have been lost upon them. As the apostles were to emphasise in their preaching, they had "received the law by the disposition of angels, and have not kept it" (Acts 7:53). The evidence of the presence of God and of "the finger of God" at work, even the great deliverance at the Red Sea, were forgotten by a people who did not have *the Law of God* in their hearts.

For those who did, however, then the sights and sounds brought the conviction that "the LORD he is God in heaven above, and upon the earth beneath: there is none else" (Deuteronomy 4:39). That uniqueness of their God was to be emphasised again and again, until they understood that the first and greatest of all the commandments was:

> "Hear, O Israel: the LORD our God is one LORD: and thou shalt love the LORD thy God with all thine heart, and with all thy soul, and with all thy might." (6:4,5)

The Deuteronomy proper—the second telling of the Law—takes up that theme and expounds it in great detail. With a final exhortation to keep the statutes and commandments "that it may go well with thee, and with thy children after thee", Moses brought his introductory speech to a conclusion (4:40). If he felt it necessary to repeat and underline his theme so frequently, then we too should be prepared to listen often, and hearing, to obey.

(r) "Three cities on this side Jordan" (4:41–43)

Since the territory on the east of Jordan had already been allocated to the two-and-a-half tribes, it was logical to set aside three cities of refuge before the main body, including those who would be responsible for the administration of the Land, crossed over the river into Canaan. The regulations for the separating of six cities of the Levites are recorded in Numbers 35 and the more detailed ordinances described in Deuteronomy 19, where we shall consider them in due course.

One or two reflections, however, are worth recording here. The institution has some spiritual lessons to teach us beside the symbolism of the refuge from the avenger of blood which we all need in our salvation from death. We are brought face to face with some of the realities of our human existence. It was a Divine principle that "whoso sheddeth man's blood, by man shall his blood be shed" (Genesis 9:6). In the days when the family was the unit of society the duty of avenging the blood of the slain devolved upon his next of kin. There was a corresponding duty to help in other ways, to play the part of a *goel*, or redeemer, a title which Job gives in prospect to the Lord Jesus, our kinsman "according to the flesh". Both these responsibilities were legislated for when Israel came into the Land.

"A law unto themselves"

It is interesting to note in passing that other nations had wrestled with the problem of the responsibility of individual vengeance, and in due course brought it under the control of law. Perhaps this is an illustration of what Paul says in Romans 2:14,15 about the Gentiles who have not the law doing by nature the things contained in the law, and so "are a law unto themselves". Be that as it may, the Divine Law enabled the justice and rigour of the law about killing to be mitigated in the provision of a way of escape. There was no disguising the fact, however, that life would never be the same again after the incident involving the loss of a life. The one who had committed the act was forced to flee to the city, leaving his home and occupation, not to return until the death of the high priest freed him from the obligation to reside therein. Refusal to flee or to accept the discipline of the law left him exposed to death. But by complying with the Divine requirements the slayer was freed from all *guilt* and from the forfeiture of his life.

Thus once more we are taught that we cannot escape the consequences of our actions and the hard facts of life do not enable us to distinguish between the accidental or the premeditated as far as the results are concerned. We can take comfort, however, from the fact that God is merciful and delivers us from the burden of our guilt, not only in the case of the common occurrences of daily life but in the greater responsibility of our human nature and the inevitability of our sinning before Him. If we try to worship in sincerity and truth, "he is faithful and just to forgive us our sins, and to cleanse us from all unrighteousness".

As for the Israelite in the land, so for the disciple there is a "strong consolation" for those who "have fled for refuge to lay hold upon the hope set before us". But we must abide in the refuge for ever, since our High Priest dies no more, being "for ever after the order of Melchizedek" (Hebrews 6:18–20).

5

THE REPETITION OF THE LAW

(a) Introduction to Moses' second speech
(4:44–49)

THE SECTION opens with the words: "And this is the law which Moses set before the children of Israel". Some have taken the words as marking the conclusion to the previous speech, but the alternative explanation is preferable, from a comparison with the opening words of the Book. "The testimonies, and the statutes, and the judgments" are here said to have been spoken "on this side Jordan, in the valley over against Beth-peor, in the land of Sihon ..." (verses 45,46), whereas in 1:1 other places along the way from Sinai are named as well. So we adhere to the original suggestion that Moses warned and encouraged the people at various places on the journey through the wilderness, then gathered up his words in a farewell address, when perhaps they were written down for the first time to form what we have considered as his introductory speech.

The Law to be presented in chapters 5—26 is nevertheless identified as the same law that had already been proclaimed at Sinai (verse 45), but expressed in more detailed terms. Perhaps a simple example will help us to see the relationship between the *law* and the *statutes* and *ordinances* connected with it.

It was a part of God's Law that His people should ever keep in memory their deliverance from the house of bondage. So He instituted a *statute*, or decree, that this law should be honoured in the keeping of the Passover. The *ordinances* and *judgements* were those detailed regulations governing the manner of observance of the Passover. As we go through the remaining chapters we shall see that all the Divine principles receive a similar exposition in terms of statutes and ordinances, to give us what we have several times referred to as the translation of the Ten Commandments into practical living. And as we have also remarked before, the principles have not changed. It is as much a law for us that we should remember how the Lord has become our salvation even though observance of the Passover is no longer necessary or even possible for us.

So we come to the *Deuteronomy* proper, not the "Second Law" as one translation of the Greek word could suggest, but a restatement of the old covenant in a form especially applicable to a people on the threshold of the Land. The verses immediately under consideration do in fact offer a brief recapitulation of chapters 1—3 since 2:26–37 and 3:29 are gathered up in verse 46, 3:1–11 in verse 47 and 3:8–22 in verses 48,49.

In the chapters which follow we shall see the Land viewed as the place where the Lord is to be worshipped, as the place of His throne and therefore the focal point of His Kingdom, and as the place in which His law is the constitution of a nation, until the "law goes forth from Zion, and the word of the LORD from Jerusalem" throughout the world. We shall be continually impressed with the value of the book as a foundation study and a book of wisdom and devotion for us today.

(b) "Hear , O Israel, the statutes and the judgments" (5:1–5)

The concluding verses of chapter 4 were introductory to this second major section of Moses' final address. In it the Law and the exposition of it now to be presented were identified as that which had been proclaimed at Horeb already, although as we shall see it will be expressed slightly differently in its new context. The reasons for this we have just set out when considering the question of the eternal, unchanging law of God in its application to the changing circumstances in which the people of His covenant find themselves.

"The whole family"

In chapter 5 verses 1–5 the people are summoned to hear the restatement and exposition of the Law: the call was to "all Israel", the *whole* people. Some of the implications of this form of address, both for Israel and the modern disciple have already been discussed (page 8), including the reminder that God Himself is not party to the schisms and dissensions which His people create among themselves. In addition to the appeal in these verses Israel are constantly reminded of their national identity and family unity in other phrases and titles characteristic of the book of Deuteronomy. The following list gives the first reference to each of them and the frequency of its occurrence in the 34 chapters of the book:

1:1	"All Israel"	(12 times)
4:1	"(Hear) O Israel"	(5 times)
7:6	"A holy people"	(5 times)
7:6	"A peculiar people"	(3 times)
1:16	"Brethren", "brother"	(28 times)
10:18	"The stranger, the fatherless, and the widow"	(10 times)

The children of Israel were thus left in no doubt that in recalling to their attention the scene at Horeb, when the Lord talked with them "out of the midst of the fire", Moses' object was to spell out the obligations of the new generation to the terms of the covenant. "The LORD our God made a covenant *with us* in Horeb." Many people have stumbled over these words, especially when they are viewed in conjunction with the following verse:

"The LORD *made not this covenant with our fathers,* but with us, even us, who are all of us here alive this day."

The majority of those present, all about sixty years of age or under, except for Moses, Joshua and Caleb, had not been eyewitnesses of the events described. Those between forty and sixty would have memories, vague or vivid according to their age at the time, of being present at the scene with their now deceased parents. How then could the words of Moses be accurate?

Heirs of privilege and responsibility

A moment's reflection provides us with the answer, upon which we have already touched briefly when discussing the theme of corporate responsibility and the lessons from Deuteronomy to be learned by the Brotherhood today (page 3). The covenant was made with *all* Israel, with generations then unborn who in their turn became heirs of both the privileges and the responsibilities of being God's own people. Moses is reminding the people that the covenant was not a dead letter because it was made with their fathers, as if God would deal with them on a different basis. He is emphasising that as members of the holy nation, the Lord's own people, they had been there, on the same principle that Levi paid tithes to Melchizedek through Abraham (Hebrews 7:9,10). Hence arises their great privilege as well as their duty to speak of it in the fullest detail to their children, who would themselves have to bear the same responsibility in due course.

The interesting expression "face to face" deserves notice here, since it recurs in other books, especially in the Pentateuch, and seems to contradict another principle clearly emphasised to Moses himself:

"Thou canst not see my face: for there shall no man see me, and live ... my face shall not be seen."

(Exodus 33:20–23; also John 1:18; 1 Timothy 6:16)

The meaning becomes plain when we remember that the Hebrew word for "face", or more literally "faces", refers more specifically to the *presence* than the *aspect* of a person. Thus the tabernacle shewbread is strictly "the bread of the faces", "the bread of the presence" which, if the reader will ponder this for a little, will call forth a profitable meditation on the manifestation of the glory of the Lord in the faces of the cherubim and in the living bread sent down from heaven.

So when God declared that He talked with Moses face to face ("mouth to mouth" in Numbers 12:8), He meant that their communication was direct and not through a mediator or in a vision. Exodus 33 is instructive as to how this took place, since it is clear that Moses was enveloped in the cloud of the Lord's presence as they talked "face to face" at the tabernacle door (verses 8–11). The children of Israel, therefore, had been in the very presence of the living God at Sinai, hearing His voice directly and witnessing or hearing every aspect of His power and glory revealed except the Divine countenance itself.

"I stood between the LORD and you"

That the people did not continue in that direct relationship with the Sovereign Lord of heaven and earth who was nevertheless their God, was a matter of their own choice. True, they had been kept at a distance as far as their physical contact with the mount was concerned; only Moses, disciplined and purged by his own experiences, was invited up into the midst of the devouring fire, although chosen representatives were invited closer than the people as a whole (Exodus 24:1,2; 9–11). The fear aroused in the hearts of those who heard the Voice and their request that Moses should mediate for them received sympathetic consideration on the part of the Lord, and thus began the ministry of the prophets to which we shall give further consideration in its appropriate place.

We remind our readers of what has been said about the correspondence between the form of the Lord's covenant and that of covenants familiar to dwellers in the Ancient World (page 5). We list below further characteristic phrases of the book of Deuteronomy, to show the aspects of covenant-relationship which are fundamental to Moses' final exhortation to the people about to enter into their inheritance:

4:37	"Love" (with God as subject)	(5 times)
5:10	"Love" (with man as object)	(12 times)
4:4	"Cleave unto him"	(5 times)
4:49	"With all thy heart and soul"	(9 times)
4:10	"Fear him"	(13 times)
6:12	"Beware lest thou forget"	(4 times)
7:24	"Blot out the name" (referring to what God would do to Israel for their neglect, or what they should do to the false gods for His sake)	(6 times)
5:7	"Other gods" (to be warned against, destroyed etc.)	(13 times)
11:28	(Gods) "which ye (thou, they) have not known"	(7 times)

(c) "I am the LORD thy God" (5:6–21)

We repeat some of the information previously given about the form of ancient covenants as set out by the monarch or superior party, since it will be helpful to bear the following general pattern in mind when considering the Ten Commandments.

1. A *Preamble*, identifying the author of the covenant.

2. A *Prologue*, recounting the benefits bestowed by the author of the covenant, and forming the basis of the covenant.

3. *General Stipulations*, defining the basis of the continuing future relationship between the parties concerned.

4. *Specific Stipulations*, giving the practical details for the keeping of the covenant.

5. *Ratification of the Covenant*, and the deposit of a copy of it before witnesses.

6. *Sanctions of the Covenant*, spelt out in the form of blessings and curses.

Both *Preamble* and *Prologue* are set out in verse 6 of this chapter: "I am the LORD thy God, which brought thee out of the land of Egypt, from the house of bondage". That Israel's God was the Lord was more than a declaration of relationship, important though that was. A sovereign had the right to dictate the terms of the covenant, but Israel's God was Sovereign Lord of heaven and earth—a far wider concept of sovereignty or lordship than could ever be claimed for the gods of the nations which were "no-gods". He was also *Yahweh*, to be remembered as a God of covenant love as He had already revealed Himself in bringing them out of the house of bondage. Israel were to keep this continually before their minds: "Hear, O Israel: the LORD our God is one LORD" (6:4). This says more than that Israel's God is one, as distinct from the gods many and lords many of the nations: there was only One like Him, unique in mercy as in might.

The basis of the Covenant

There was no question therefore that the Lord would keep covenant with His people. The basis of the covenant was simply "I am the LORD thy God". All that follows depends upon the recognition of that fact. The content of the Ten Words needed no further explanation or justification. There had been established a relationship between the Lord and His people. The basis of the *continuing relationship* was the observance of the general stipulations now proclaimed by the God of Israel.

Viewed in this light the Decalogue is evidently not an abitrary set of rules but a declaration of love and condescension. Of His very nature God is to be sanctified by them that come nigh Him. So He is to be loved with all the heart, all the soul, and all the strength:

"Thou shalt have none other gods before me."

There is much to be written about the Ten Commandments particularly in terms of their importance for the disciple, and this we intend to do when we come to the exposition of them in terms of the *Specific Stipulations* of chapters 12–27. Several points of importance and interest can be made here, however, as we discuss them in terms of the relationship created by them between the Lord and His people. For example, "before me" is literally *before my face*. Anything considered of greater worth than the Lord not only *comes between* Him and His servant: it obscures the manifestation

57

of His glory. Coming short of the glory of God is one definition of sin (Romans 3:23). To give time and energy to any pursuit which cannot be "sanctified by the word of God, and prayer", or to anything which cannot be received with thanksgiving can only lead us away from God.

The second commandment carries the thought a stage further:

"Thou shalt not make thee any graven image, or any likeness of any thing ..."

The worship of other gods is prohibited; therefore the representation of them as objects of worship is equally prohibited. There is always the danger that what has been used as a symbol is taken for the reality, and the pagan world was obsessed by the worship of the creature more than the Creator.

The making of the brazen serpent in the wilderness provides a classic example of this. By God's command Moses made a serpent of brass and set it upon a pole for the healing of the nation after they had been bitten by the fiery serpents (Numbers 21). The serpents were the symbol of their sin in limiting the power of God to provide for His people in the desert. There was a powerful concentration of symbolism which it is tempting to expand upon here. We content ourselves with remarking that the word *nachash*, a serpent, is related to the words for "hiss", "beguile", "bright or shining" and "brass". A wealth of meaning lies here, easily to be found by the student who reads 2 Corinthians 11, John 3 and 12 and other passages, and who realises the significance of brass as a symbol of fleshly reasoning which is the counterfeit of the fine gold of faith.

"A thing of brass"

It is plain, however, that what had healing virtue when viewed with the eye of faith and in understanding of the Divine principles displayed in it, became a destructive influence when revered for its own sake. Although we hear nothing further of it until the days of Hezekiah, we can guess at the malign influence it exercised upon the minds of the people when we read that as part of his reforms Hezekiah "brake in pieces the brasen serpent that Moses had made: for unto those days the children of Israel did burn incense to it"(!) Hezekiah, however, recognised it for what it really was: "and he called it Nehushtan", that is, a piece of brass (2 Kings 18:4).

58

The evil of image worship lies in the fact that even though it be the likeness of a man, or of anything else that God has made, it is at best *an inadequate* and at worst *a completely false representation* of the Creator. Our own mental images or our theological definitions of God can be equally false or inadequate, coming between us and the glory and the grace of the King, immortal and invisible, whose ways are not as our ways, nor His thoughts as our thoughts. We can no more confine God within our own limitations than could the children of Israel within the four walls of the Temple. So our concept of Him must be that which He gives us in the revelation of Himself in Christ. Otherwise there can be no true covenant-relationship.

The Third Commandment

The third of the general conditions of the covenant bears a close relationship to the first two:

"Thou shalt not take the name of the LORD thy God in vain."

This was primarily concerned with the false or trivial oath. It is in a sense an attempt to manipulate God, and to involve Him in one's own deceit or dishonour Him by bringing Him down to man's own level. A moment's thought makes us realise the full meaning of what follows: "for the LORD will not hold him guiltless that taketh his name in vain".

The matter ranges far beyond the use of the oath in the process of law or in the sealing of a compact between two parties. In that sphere the Lord demanded that all commercial dealings be on the basis of "a false balance is abomination to the LORD", and all justice must be administered on His principles and as in His sight: "I am the LORD". The practice of emphasising one's words or seeking to give credence to a simple statement by invoking the Lord as witness was itself productive of evil. It was a casual use of the Name, inconsistent with the behaviour of a people whose prayer was "Hallowed be thy name", and the Lord Jesus condemns it in his teaching (Matthew 5:33–37).

The modern disciple should consider this carefully. We live in an age of slovenly speech when additional expletives of one kind and another are commonplace. Some of them are entirely blasphemous and to avoid such expressions surely needs no second thought on the part of God's children. There are a large number of other words, however, which are substitute expressions for the blasphemous but are considered "mild" or "innocent" in their use—of which strangely enough "good lord" is an example, or "good heavens", "gracious me", or "by Jove" (a doubly doubtful one this, if one thinks about it!). While it is not contended that the users of these and similar expressions do so with any concept of an oath or vain use, it is worthwhile considering the importance of guarding the tongue, in the light of the Lord's warnings against swearing by heaven or earth, the throne or footstool of God, and the apostolic exhortation to "let your speech be always with grace, seasoned with salt" (Colossians 4:6).

The Sabbath Law

The instruction to "Keep the sabbath day to sanctify it" in the Deuteronomy version reveals some significant differences from the account in Exodus. It will be seen that they are consistent with a restatement of the principle for a people about to enter into the Land. It is plain from Scripture that the sabbath day rest was amongst other things prophetic of the consummation of God's purpose. God Himself sanctified the seventh day since it marked the completion of the work of creation. The day was set apart from all that preceded it by this very fact: it was a *cessation* that marked a coming to perfection.

Into this perfect state man was eventually to come, and throughout all their history "there *remaineth* therefore a rest to the people of God" (Hebrews 4:9). In remembrance of the Lord's own sabbath the children of the Exodus were instructed to set the day apart, in faith that the Lord would bless them and they would lose nothing material thereby. They thus could honour the principle and contemplate the ultimate glory to which they were being led. On the threshold of the Land, however, they were about to enter into a rest, and were to keep the sabbath in memory of their great deliverance from Egypt.

The sabbath law linked creation with the creation of a people, and looked forward to the New Creation in the fulfilment of the promise to Abraham and his seed. This is what one writer has called "the Gospel of the Pentateuch". The Deuteronomic version of the Fourth Commandment had yet another variation appropriate to a people about to settle in a land. Besides the general term "cattle" the labouring ox and ass are specifically mentioned and there is an additional reason given for the commandment: "That thy manservant and thy maidservant may rest as well as thou".

The Law and the life

Thus was the *Torah*, or teaching, revealed in its true form: it set forth the historical basis of the commandment proclaimed and taught the people how to live as the people of the Lord. They were to treat those dependent upon them with the same consideration they had received from God. He had brought His people out of bondage and they were glad. They would honour Him and keep His law by showing that same spirit of compassion: "And remember that thou wast a servant in the land of Egypt, and that the LORD thy God brought thee out thence ... *therefore* the LORD thy God commanded thee to keep the sabbath day".

The whole law, said the Lord Jesus, can be summed up in the commands to love the Lord with all the heart and one's neighbour as oneself (Matthew 22:35–40). "First" and "second" in this context is an order of importance and not a numerical sequence, and the reason for the order is plain to see. Genuine love of God always brings love of man in its train; love of man does not necessarily lead to love of God. In fact, it does so rarely, as the wide range of humanitarian movements of today, all of them sincerely seeking to benefit mankind, plainly indicates. They are for the most part humanist rather than Christian in their motivation. If we ponder this we see the sense of the Lord's saying that the second commandment is "like unto" the first, since love of one's neighbour is an integral part of wholehearted love of God. We can deduce this from the inspired arrangement of the Decalogue.

The commandment to honour father and mother marks the natural transition from the concept of the love of God illustrated in the preceding four to that of the social behaviour which that love should engender. The family is the fundamental unit of society, and it is from God the Father that the whole idea of family derives: or as Paul expressed it:

> "From (him) every family in heaven and on earth is named." (Ephesians 3:15, RV)

The Divine arrangement

From our parents, who under God have given us life, we gain our first experience of others beside ourselves. It begins with a totally dependent relationship, in which the parents exercise the sacred responsibility of sustaining in being the child they have brought into the world. Experience of the wider society and, above all, the knowledge of God are learned (we are speaking of the Divine arrangement, indeed,

61

of God's commandment to His people) at first from parents and then from others, until the age when the child becomes the man, bearing his own responsibility and able to enter into a personal relationship with the great Creator and Father of all. It can rightly be said, therefore, that in the true order of things our parents are, by His own appointment, as God to us in our infancy. There is thus laid upon them a great privilege and duty and upon the child the obligation of honour and obedience.

We shall see that the duty to honour parents is extended in the Law to cover a more general field of the relationship between the generations. Leviticus 19:32 may be cited by way of example: "Thou shalt rise up before the hoary head, and honour the face of the old man". The reason given for this command is worthy of our closest attention: "... *and fear thy God: I am the* LORD". Paul has called the Fifth Commandment "the first commandment with promise" (Ephesians 6:2) and leaves us in no doubt that it is as binding on the twenty-first century disciple as on the second generation Israelite.

For neglect of the mutual obligations of one generation to anothe,r the knowledge and understanding of God and of the privileges and responsibilities of being a covenant people were gradually diminished, and it is surely significant that the Lord Jesus, challenging the Pharisees in the matter of their tradition and particularly that of compounding their duty to parents into a Temple offering, said:

> "Well hath Esaias prophesied of you hypocrites, as it is written, This people honoureth me with their lips, but their heart is far from me ... Full well ye reject the commandment of God, that ye may keep your own tradition. For Moses said, Honour thy father and thy mother; and, Whoso curseth father or mother, let him die the death." (Mark 7:6–13)

A stable family unit is the very foundation of society, and how much more so when that unit is based upon "the nurture and admonition of the Lord". All the commandments would be honoured, the Lord's covenant kept, and so their days would "be long upon the land which the LORD thy God giveth thee". Implicit in that "commandment with promise" is the fact that the Lord would keep covenant also.

"Thy neighbour as thyself"

It is important to remember that the Sixth Commandment is a prohibition on *murder*, that is the premeditated killing of one member of the Lord's people by another for personal and unlawful reasons. It cannot therefore be cited as an argument against military service or the death penalty, since the Law of Moses recognised both and legislated for it. (Our objection to military service, be it noted, is based upon different principles, though having their own connection with the concept of a holy nation belonging exclusively to God). Emotive phrases like "mass murder" and "judicial murder" are used by the pacifist or those opposed to the death penalty in the modern state, and this commandment is often cited in support. As we have already seen, manslaughter was the subject of legislation also, the cities of refuge being provided for the accidental killer.

It is easy to see the connection between this commandment and those preceding. It is a usurpation of Divine prerogative, and therefore a dishonouring of God who alone can give life and has the right to take it away. The Seventh Commandment has an even more special relation to the covenant, if that were possible. Adultery, as distinct from other sexual offences, which are the subject of some fairly detailed legislation in Deuteronomy 22–25 which will be considered in its place, has to do with sexual relations between two people of whom one, at least, is someone else's marriage partner, or betrothed. It is pre-eminently therefore an act of unfaithfulness to a covenant, which is in itself an act unworthy of the people of the Lord, whose very Name is a covenant-name.

"A great mystery"

Adultery would be a sin if for no other reason than that the Lord forbade it. When we remember that marriage is the closest of human relationships and is intended to be the very symbol in human life of the covenant-relationship between God and His people—a relationship of love, of sustaining on the one part and of reliance on the other, of mutual trust and commitment—then we can the better realise the terrible nature of this act.

The twenty-first century disciple, living as he does in a society which tolerates loose sexual behaviour and makes light of the marriage tie, assuming that divorce is the solution to all marital problems, would do well to keep to the fore this idea of covenant-relationship, remembering that he has made a covenant with God as well as with his partner. It will not only teach him discipline but that attitude of mind which the Lord's apostle enjoins upon him, when he speaks of the great mystery of Christ and the church, and exhorts him to follow the mind of Christ in care, self-sacrifice and abiding love. Human compassion should teach him not to do violence to his partner's emotions and affections or wantonly take that which is supremely and uniquely someone else's. The reminder that his covenant was with God as well as with his wife should even further strengthen his resolve never to leave her or forsake her for another. The exhortations and warnings for the wife are parallel and equally strong.

In a world which is only too familiar with kidnapping and the hijacking of aircraft for personal advantage, it is interesting to note that several commentators make special application of the Eighth Commandment to man-stealing, rather than to the stealing of property. There seems no adequate linguistic reason for this opinion, since the word for "steal" is in no way specialised, but there is no doubt that the principle of hijacking or kidnapping does violence to Divine law as well as to the laws of the land. In any case both forms of stealing are condemned in the Book of Exodus, the stealing of goods in 22:1–4 and the other in 21:16:

> "And he that stealeth a man, and selleth him, or if he be found in his hand, he shall surely be put to death."

The penalty for depriving a man of liberty was the same as that for depriving him of life, and there was no appeal against that sentence!

"For three transgressions, and for four"

We digress for a moment to comment further upon another aspect of this particular crime, especially as it features in Amos' denunciation of the Philistines. The description of the "three transgressions" and the "four" for which the Lord visited judgement upon the nations surrounding Israel served to throw into relief the nature of the transgressions of Judah and Israel.

The deed for which each of these nations was condemned was an example of a breach of a commonly held code of behaviour amongst ancient peoples, who "having not the law, did by nature the things contained in the law ... and are a law unto themselves ... their conscience also bearing witness" (see Romans 2:13–15). And Amos' point is essentially Paul's point also: if the Lord will judge a world for the violation of "natural law" (for want of a better expression, although this law has its origin in God's own basic code governing the relation of man with man), what will be the judgement of a people to whom God has committed His oracles and revealed His attributes? For Judah to despise the law of the Lord (Amos 2:4) and Israel to sell the needy for a pair of shoes, turn aside the way of the meek, and for a man and his father to go in unto the same maid (verses 6,7), was on a par with the sin of Gaza, who "delivered up the whole captivity to Edom" (1:9).

Slavery as an institution was accepted among the nations, and certain aspects of the Mosaic law were devoted to its regulation. It is *slave-trading* which is in question here, however, and the selection of Gaza as the representative of the Philistines in this is appropriate, since it was essentially a commercial transaction for which they were notorious. The fact that the "whole captivity" was delivered up to Edom is further evidence that it was not simply a matter of war and conquest. The Babylonians carried captives to Babylon as a political measure; the Philistines delivered a defenceless population into other ruthless hands. They were "men-stealers", against whom there were laws in Athens and elsewhere besides in this eighth commandment of the Decalogue. (See also 1 Timothy 1:10, where Paul lists men-stealers as among those lawless and disobedient ones for whom the law was "made").

Whichever way one interprets "Thou shalt not steal", it concerned an offence against a man, either in his person or in the wealth which God had given him. There was another kind of damage that men can do to each other: "Neither shalt thou bear false witness against thy neighbour". Again we see the close connection between all the commands of the second part of the Decalogue. If "false witness" be confined to legal procedures, then a man's life or liberty are put in jeopardy. The case of the Lord Jesus and of Stephen are classic examples of the danger into which the innocent could be brought by a false or "vain" testimony (the word is the same as that used in the Third Commandment for taking the Lord's name "in vain"; He was not to be called upon as a witness for the wrong reason).

The prohibition goes even further, however, to cover baseless rumour, idle gossip, about a person, not necessarily in connection with a legal process. Such an extension of meaning is consistent with Christ's own teaching to his disciples in the Sermon on the Mount, and from which the modern disciple draws his own understanding of the true Torah. For Jesus takes us to the motive behind the act, as in the case of murder and adultery. So idle gossip would in his eyes be as evil as false witness in the court of law, since both are equally destructive of that good name which is better than precious ointment (Ecclesiastes 7:1); it is a manipulation of another for one's own advantage—an act of unfaithfulness to one's brother, and therefore to the Lord of the covenant Himself:

> "LORD, who shall dwell in thy tabernacle: or who shall rest upon thy holy hill? ... He that hath used no deceit in his tongue, nor done evil to his neighbour: and hath not slandered his neighbour."
>
> (Psalm 15:1,3, Coverdale Version)

"All these have I kept ..."

The Deuteronomy version of the Tenth Commandment shows three principal variations from that in Exodus. Deuteronomy places the wife before the house, and uses a different word in respect of her from that applied to the neighbour's property. The woman is not to be *desired*, the goods not to be *coveted*. Also the "field" is added to the list of forbidden objects.

The express mention of the field is to be explained quite naturally by the fact that the people were about to enter the Land, which was to be allotted to them by God's own appointment. To be content with what had been granted in this, as with other Divine gifts, is an expression of trust and confidence in Him as well as of love to one's neighbour. So in a sense this commandment sums up all the rest: "Love worketh no ill to his neighbour". Indeed, as we have seen above, it is with the desire and the motive that the Lord Jesus was principally concerned in the fulfilling of the Law. To belittle one's brother and esteem him a vain fellow, to be angry with him without a cause, to cast covetous eyes on his goods—herein lies the root of murder, theft and false witness.

The coveting of another man's wife is something different, as is explained by the emphasis given by the word "desire". The lustful thoughts engendered, which the Lord calls "adultery already in one's heart", arouse stronger passions even than the lust for gold. It is appropriate, therefore, that even in the commandment which restrains all kinds of selfishness this particularly base form of it should be set apart, even though like all the others it is the subject of a separate commandment. Unlike the seizing of another's property, in which the covetous desire grows in the mind of one person, adultery involves the kindling of desire in another, the stealing of a heart, and an act of theft for which there can be no restoration. How well the Psalmist, sensing the evil in himself, caught up the spirit of the Divine Law:

> "Against thee, thee only, have I sinned, and done this evil in thy sight ... Behold, thou desirest truth *in the*

inward parts; and *in the hidden part* thou shalt make me to know wisdom ... For thou desirest not sacrifice; else would I give it: thou delightest not in burnt offering. The sacrifices of God are a broken spirit: a broken and a contrite heart, O God, thou wilt not despise." (Psalm 51)

The Tenth Commandment, therefore, being the only one that can be broken in secret, the transgression of the others being open to at least one other person, deals essentially with a man's personal relationship with the Lord. The young man with great possessions found this out when, having been reminded of the early commandments by the Lord's rebuke for ascribing goodness to any other than God Himself, and having professed his lifelong obedience to the others, was unable to part with what had really stolen his heart and give his goods to the poor:

"Mortify therefore your members which are upon the earth; fornication, uncleanness, inordinate affection, evil concupiscence, and covetousness, *which is idolatry*."

(Colossians 3:5)

The Voice of God fell silent as dramatically as it had begun to speak: "And he added no more". Indeed, there was no more to add. All that followed could only be the practical application of the great Torah, that which may be known of the Lord Himself and of His covenant with His people. In fear and trembling they declared, "All that the LORD hath spoken will we do, and be obedient".*

(d) "O that there were such an heart in them" (5:22–33)

With a great voice the Lord had spoken out of the midst of the fire, of the cloud, and of the thick darkness. The people were terrified at the awesome sight, and from the Letter to the Hebrews we learn that even Moses said, "I exceedingly fear and quake" (Hebrews 12:21). In this at least "all Israel" were united, and immediately there came a deputation of the heads of all the tribes and elders to plead that in future Moses would act as mediator between God and the people. We note that although they had seen that day "that God doth talk with man, and he liveth" (verse 24), they were still afraid that any further repetition of the experience would be

---

*See further comment in *Ten Commandments in the 20th Century*, A D Norris [published by Tamarisk].

disastrous: "If we hear the voice of the LORD our God *any more*, then we shall die."

"This great fire"

There is no doubt that of all the phenomena it was the fire that had filled them with so much dread and alarm, since it is mentioned by the elders three times in their speech, in addition to Moses' comment upon it twice in the preceding verses. Even the fire, however, was but the visible sign of the sanctity of the Mount as the place where the Lord had "come down". Again we have the Apostle's inspired commentary from Hebrews:

> "For they could not endure that which was commanded,
> And if so much as a beast touch the mountain, it shall be
> stoned, or thrust through with a dart." (12:20)

In rejoicing that we "are not come unto the mount that might be touched, and that burned with fire, nor unto blackness, and darkness, and tempest", we must not forget the lessons of God's holiness which the phenomena were designed to impress. We might think that had we witnessed the events at the Red Sea and at Sinai they would have been burned into our heart as well as our senses. Not so, as the Deuteronomy record goes on to emphasise, and as is implicit in Apostolic commentary. "See that ye refuse not him that speaketh ... For our God is a consuming fire" (Hebrews 12:25–29). The possibility of receiving the "better thing" based upon "better promises" makes it all the more important that no man should "fail of the grace of God". But it is contrary to all that the Scriptures teach about human nature to believe that "the things which are seen" (by apostolic definition, the things which also are temporal) are of themselves a help towards obedience to the Divine commandments. The fire continued to burn on the mountain long after the words spoken by God had ceased (see Exodus 24:17), and the children of Israel danced around the golden calf in full view of it!

"Who is there of all flesh ...?"

For a brief moment "all Israel" recognised their unique relationship with the Lord their God: "Who is there of all flesh that hath heard the voice of the living God ...?" Their instinctive dread is in itself a testimony to the fact that man was intended to bear the Divine likeness and be holy like God. Otherwise they would have had no conscience or sense of coming short of His glory by reason of their being part of "all flesh". They also recognised the even closer relationship which Moses bore to God, since they added to their request that they should no more hear the living voice the plea that Moses should be their mediator. He should go near to hear all that God said, return to tell them, and "we will hear it, and do it".

The Lord's comment upon the people's words provides the key to the remainder of the Old Testament and, indeed, to the rôle of the Lord Jesus Christ himself. We have another example of a principle set out at the beginning of our study (page 12), where a practical arrangement put forward by the leaders of the people because of some crisis or development which had rendered it necessary, had been endorsed by God, and thus given a spiritual sanction. "They have well said all that they have spoken" was such an endorsement of the mediatorial work of Moses which was now proposed (Deuteronomy 5:28).

Perhaps it is not always fully realised that this was the foundation of *the ministry of the prophets*, in which the Lord would reveal Himself in some form to a spiritually qualified man, who would then speak forth the words of God with all the authority of God Himself. The prophet would become the living voice and his written words the "God-breathed" words which were able fully to equip the man of God who took heed to them in all wisdom and knowledge.

As far as we can discern, the voice of God spake no more from heaven until that day when, in fulfilment of all that God's servant Moses and His servants the prophets had declared should come, the heavens opened, the Spirit descended upon the Lord Jesus, "And lo a voice from heaven, saying, This is my beloved Son, in whom I am well pleased" (Matthew 3:16,17). It is not recorded who besides the Lord heard the voice. The probability is that none except himself heard it, or that if they did they were unable to distinguish the words, any more than those who heard what they thought was the sound of thunder when, immediately before the crucifixion, the Father declared His intention of glorifying His Name in His Son (John 12:28).

On the other hand, the three disciples who were with the Lord on the holy mount of transfiguration heard and understood the voice, when to the declaration of God at the baptism was added the commandment, "Hear him" (Luke 9:35). All this was in the fitness of things, since the hearing of the audible voice from heaven evidently marked men out for special service in the word of God (see also Acts 9:6,7 with

22:9: the *sound* of the voice was audible, but its words were not discernible to the bystanders).

"In the hands of a mediator"

We need exercise little imagination to realise the immense responsibility that was now laid upon Moses. Nor do we have far to seek in the record to understand how fully qualified he was for the task—through the grace of God. He was careful for the honour of God, seeking with all his heart the fulfilment of the promise of the Name and the manifestation of the glory of God in His people. Hence came his anger at their lack of faith and his uncompromising action in dealing with their sin in the making of the golden calf. But he was also a shepherd of his people, bearing the burden of their strife and pleading for them before the Lord in the most desperate moments of their wilderness journey. And "the secret of the LORD was his".

That secret was, in this case, an understanding of the true nature of atonement. It could not be brought about by the sacrifices and offerings, even the solemn ceremony of the Day of Atonement itself, which were all based upon the covenant of which he was the mediator. At every point that covenant spoke of a perfection yet to be revealed, an offering for sin once and for all which could not be effected in the oft repeated sacrifices of the Law. Such forgiveness could be brought only by one who, jealous of the Name yet touched with the infirmity of his people, would offer himself, that mercy and truth might meet together, and righteousness and peace might kiss each other (Psalm 85:10):

> "Oh, this people have sinned a great sin, and have made them gods of gold. Yet now, if thou wilt forgive their sin—; and if not, *blot me*, I pray thee, *out of thy book* which thou hast written." (Exodus 32:31,32)

"O that there were such an heart in them!"

It is likely that the promise of the "prophet like unto Moses" was first given at Sinai, and it was the nature of his ministry that was more fully defined in the further exposition of the law unfolded in the Book of Deuteronomy. We shall consider this therefore in its place (page 176). In acknowledging the people's awe before His presence and granting them a mediator in answer to their request, the Lord added:

> "O that there *were* such an heart in them, that they would fear me, and keep all my commandments always, that it might be well with them, and with their children for ever!" (Deuteronomy 5:29)

The Lord their God was a jealous God, but the nature of His jealousy is revealed in these words. He sought the love and obedience of His people for their own sakes as well as for the honour and glory of His Name—"That it might be well with them, and with their children for ever". The original plea is in the form of a question: "Who will give that there shall be such an heart in them …?" God Himself provided the answer through the prophet Jeremiah:

"Behold, the days come, saith the LORD, that I will make a new covenant with the house of Israel, and with the house of Judah … *I will put my law in their inward parts, and write it in their hearts*; and will be their God, and they shall be my people … for I will forgive their iniquity, and I will remember their sin no more."   (Jeremiah 31:31–34)

That time had not yet come. The fire still burned upon the mountain-top, but Israel had to get them unto their tents again. They had to teach every man his neighbour, and above all his children, saying, "Know the LORD"; and prominent in that work would be the prophets raised up from among their brethren. One of the greatest of them all until the coming of John the Baptist and the Lord Jesus, Moses remained before the Lord to hear all the commandments, the statutes and the judgements which he was to teach them.

6

THE EXPOSITION OF THE TEN COMMANDMENTS

(a) "Thou shalt love the LORD thy God" (6:1-9)

THE FIRST COMMANDMENT is now expounded at some length, since it is the greatest of them all, and upon it hang all the law and the prophets. There was no excuse for Israel if they misunderstood the nature of the covenant or their part in it. The Lord emphasised it time and time again, and so must we as we come to each verse. Accordingly 6:1–3 spells out the fear of the Lord and the benefits of obedience, "that thy days may be prolonged ... that it may be well with thee ... in the land that floweth with milk and honey".

"Hear, O Israel"

The verb in the commandment "Hear, O Israel", often repeated in Deuteronomy, has given its name to the whole commandment in the Hebrew liturgy: it is the "*Shema*", "*Hear*, O Israel: The LORD our God is one LORD", which is proclaimed daily in the synagogues. In Islam there is also the daily proclamation that *Allah* is one, an expression of a rigid monotheism which many have compared with the *Shema*. The meaning of the *Shema* goes far deeper, however, than a declaration that the worship of Israel was monotheistic, true though that should have been. Moreover, its implications for the twenty-first century disciple go far beyond a simple declaration that our God is a Unity and not a Trinity, which is also true. For the second part of the *Shema*, "And thou shalt love the LORD thy God with all thy heart, and with all thy soul, and with all thy might" is an intrinsic part of the same statement of faith.

For Moses does not say that the Lord is one *God*, but that He is one Lord, which is altogether a different matter. The expression has its parallel, or shall we say, fulfilment, in 1 Corinthians 8:5,6:

"For though there be that are called gods, whether in heaven or in earth, (as there be gods many, and lords many,) but to us there is but *one God, the Father*, of whom are all things, and we in him; and one Lord Jesus Christ, by whom are all things, and we by him."

Yahweh was Israel's God, and there was none like Him. He alone was the Creator of heaven and earth, He alone their Sovereign Lord. He alone was the Sustainer of all that He had made and to Him alone did all creatures owe obedience. He alone was the Maker of the covenant with Abraham, Isaac and Jacob, and He alone had become the Saviour of His people. Without Him they were no people and apart from Him there was no land flowing with milk and honey, no inheritance.

But as the Lord was one, so should His people have been in His service. It was *one people*, a "whole family", "all Israel", who were called upon to serve the Lord. His worship should have been the delight of the whole man, who loved the Lord his God with *all* his heart, with *all* his soul, and with *all* his might—not a man of many parts, each of them devoted to a special interest which led him to divide his loyalty between God and affections centred upon self. This was the practical implication of the First Commandment; for if the tabernacle worship was designed to show the people how they could be gathered up, as it were, in the sacred service of the representative Levites, draw nigh in the sacrificial ministry of the priests, and even enter into the presence of the living God in the person of their High Priest and mediator, it was also designed to exhort them to complete dedication and commitment to the Lord who was so completely committed to them.

The disciple is taught so too. In the Letter to the Ephesians Paul describes how God is working towards the unity of all things in Christ—"that in the dispensation of the fulness of times he might gather together in one all things in Christ, both which are in heaven, and which are on earth; even in him" (Ephesians 1:10). Those who are privileged to receive the "adoption of children by Jesus Christ to himself" are exhorted to "walk worthy of the vocation wherewith ye are called", and by their conduct (which manifests the lowliness, meekness, longsuffering and forbearance of the Lord, just as the people of the Lord were to manifest His attributes) to "keep the unity of the Spirit in the bond of peace". The Letter is almost an apostolic commentary on the *Shema*:

> "There is one body, and one Spirit, even as ye are called in one hope of your calling; one Lord, one faith, one baptism, one God and Father of all, who is above all, and through all, and in you all." (4:4–6)

The implications of that are tremendous: we must "truth it in love", that we "may grow up into him in all things, which is the head, even Christ".

"Thou shalt teach them diligently"

Such was the import of the words which Moses said "shall be in thine heart". The memory of Sinai had been recalled for those who had witnessed the drama and were now aged between forty and sixty. The words of Moses in the Book of Deuteronomy brought it to life for the others who, as we have seen, were equally the people of the covenant, privileged and responsible, though they were not yet born at the time of the Exodus. But how were succeeding generations to know? The answer is clear and unmistakable:

"And thou shalt teach them diligently unto thy children, and shalt talk of them when thou sittest in thine house, and when thou walkest by the way, and when thou liest down, and when thou risest up. And thou shalt bind them for a sign upon thine hand, and they shall be as frontlets between thine eyes. And thou shalt write them upon the posts of thy house, and on thy gates." (Deuteronomy 6:7,8)

The fact that later generations concentrated upon the formal compliance with the above commandment, making broad their phylacteries and touching perfunctorily the *mezuzah*, or small case containing parchment inscribed with the Shema and fastened to the doorpost, must not make us miss the beauty of the description of a home and family dedicated completely to the worship of their God. Devout Jews accepted the responsibility of ensuring that, in so far as age and understanding allowed, their children shared with them all the experiences of Divine service, and that they fully comprehended why things were done as they were.

At the institution of the Passover Moses told the elders of Israel that the ordinance was to be observed by them and their sons for ever: "and it shall come to pass, when your children shall say unto you, What mean ye by this service? that ye shall say, It is the sacrifice of the LORD's passover, who passed over the houses of the children of Israel in Egypt, when he smote the Egyptians, and delivered our people." Again, at the crossing of the Jordan, it was assumed that children would ask their fathers in time to come, "What mean ye by these stones?" "Then shall ye let your children know, saying, Israel came over this Jordan on dry land", and the story of the Lord's mighty acts, including "as the LORD your God did to the Red Sea", would again unfold before the wondering child.

"His Father's business"

There were undoubtedly many occasions when such teaching was neglected in Israel; but the principle was clear. In addition to sharing the background of the home, the child witnessed and took part in some corporate religious acts and after the age of twelve began to take a fuller personal part in the life of the community. The Lord Jesus grew up in such a home (and we may be sure the choice of Mary and Joseph rested on other spiritual conditions beside their lineage) where God was worshipped and His law revered and, at the age when a child's imagination is captured and a pattern of life set, he longed to be about his Father's business.

There are plainly many lessons for our times to be drawn from this commandment of the Lord.

The love of the Lord their God was to be displayed in the manner in which the children of Israel diligently passed on the account of His great work of salvation and the things pertaining to His worship unto the generation to come. The lessons for our time are plain to see. There were to be specific occasions when the children would be encouraged to ask, "What mean ye by this service?" Also the historic crossing of the Jordan was marked by a monument which invited the question, "What mean ye by these stones?" It is surely significant that at the age of twelve, when a child's imagination can be stirred and his allegiance won, a more active personal participation in the spiritual life of the nation was called for. It was no mere coincidence that at this age the Lord Jesus asked: "Wist ye not that I must be about my Father's business?"—as though Joseph and his mother, having taken him to Jerusalem, ought to have understood the effect it would have upon him.

The ecclesial family

In an age like ours, when the world tends to separate the young from the old, treating them as almost distinct communities and taking more and more responsibility for the young away from their parents, we may well ponder the implications for ecclesial life where this outside influence is allowed to affect us.

As a community we have always exercised a care for the young. Sunday Schools were part of ecclesial life from early times, and in them devoted brethren and sisters have always played a significant part. Larger ecclesias organised Young Men's Bible Classes and many smaller groups have been fortunate enough to have a mature brother who took the young under his wing, to ensure that they combined serious study with the opportunity to discuss other issues with one who had a sympathetic ear. The original Youth Circles, born out of a wartime necessity, were *ecclesial activities*, and membership was restricted to those prepared to attend the Sunday School or Sunday evening meetings.

Family or group?

Have we ourselves, however, sometimes fallen too easily into the common assumption that children are too young to understand the Bible or that young people need to be catered for in a special manner which encourages them to attend youth weekends week after week, mingling with their own generation but rarely participating in activities involving the whole ecclesial family? We confess that it is all too easy to generalise and if we speak of observable trends it is not to criticise—having taken part in many such activities ourselves!—but to evaluate and exhort. Instances are on record where a fraternal gathering has attracted none of the younger generation, not even of the host ecclesia, while three weeks later the same hall was packed at a "special meeting for young people", at which the audience listened with rapt attention to *the same speaker with the same subject as before*!

Tragedy would it be indeed if the widespread breakdown in family life which poses such serious problems for society should occur in the ecclesial family too. We appeal, therefore, to all leaders and organisers of activities for young people to keep the concept of the ecclesial family well to the fore. Many ecclesias follow the excellent practice of integrating their Youth Weekends with the ordinary Sunday worship and witness of the ecclesia. In this way the ecclesia meets as a family with guests, and happy are those leaders who can encourage their own people returning to share their satisfaction with the older brethren and sisters who kept the ecclesial lamp burning for them at home.

There is a good case to be made out for involving children and young people more closely as observers in ecclesial activities, and certainly for giving them more detailed information and explanation. Provided it can be done with decorum it is often good to invite them forward that they may have a closer view of a baptism, for example. This is an event in which they can be encouraged to take a keen personal interest. Then the question, "What mean ye by this service?", can be answered with a practical illustration, as were the questions of the young Israelite at the Passover (significantly the *youngest* member of the family), who was then informed not only about the crossing of the Red Sea and the Jordan, but also all the promises and responsibilities of which he also would become an heir.

The individual young man and the young woman, perhaps a brother or sister not yet mature enough to carry the responsibility alone, could occasionally be invited to accompany an older brother or sister on a visit to comfort or assist, always provided that such an extra visitor would be welcomed.

Growing in wisdom and understanding

With full realisation of the practical problems posed for parents with younger children, it is suggested that where they are brought to the meetings, particularly the breaking of bread, they come with some idea, however elementary, of why the parents have come and why, at least at certain points, they should pay close attention to what is going on. If the limit of their participation is to sit quietly pursuing their own concerns throughout the entire meeting, then there may be a great disciplinary benefit to be derived, but not much advance in understanding of the fear of God. After all, in Israel there were occasions when they stood "all of you this day before the LORD your God; your captains of your tribes, your elders, and your officers, with all the men of Israel, *your little ones*, your wives, and thy stranger that is in thy camp, from the hewer of thy wood unto the drawer of thy water", to renew the covenant (Deuteronomy 29:10,11) or to hear the law read, *"that their children, which have not known anything, may hear, and learn to fear the LORD your God"* (31:13).

There is a further point worth considering. Our children and young people at school or college face tremendous pressures in the modern age, greater sometimes than even their parents and certainly the average ecclesial member over middle age not involved in modern education, can ever possibly realise. Christadelphian children have always been treated with mild amusement or a kindly shrug of the shoulders because they have gone to "meeting" instead of to "church" or "chapel". Where interest has gone any deeper, then some of the details of our faith which put us outside the mainstream of orthodox Christianity may have aroused hostility or sympathy for our naivety. Nowadays, however, the issues are deeper and concern morality, and often any who maintain standards, profess belief in the Bible, or go to Sunday School are "marked men".

It can be particularly difficult for the late teenager who may be among a very small minority in the school class who have had no sexual experience. There is a case on record where a special prize was awarded to an unmarried schoolgirl mother "for academic progress in the face of special difficulties", and there is no reason to suppose that this was an isolated occurrence. Certainly not "virtue rewarded"!

The vital rôle of home and ecclesia

Now when society has no concept of sin and little of disgrace, and the schools are generally no longer on the side of the parents on questions of morality or religion, or of what shall or shall not be freely discussed in the matter of sex or perversion, the importance of the home influence and the backing of the ecclesial community, local and worldwide, is seen to be of the very greatest for the spiritual welfare of our young people. Add to this the consideration that those who have some understanding and sense of commitment often find themselves naturally drawn towards others of their generation in similar conditions whose faith and zeal find expression in the enthusiasms of the charismatic movement, which sadly has no solid Biblical foundation or saving truth, and the vital rôle of home and ecclesia in their spiritual education is even more manifest.

For neglect of the mutual obligations of one generation to another, the knowledge and understanding of God and of the privileges and responsibilities of being a covenant people were lost to view in Israel and the nation degenerated. Quite literally there was no living long upon the land which the Lord their God gave them, let alone any possibility of entering into the everlasting inheritance promised to Abraham, Isaac and Jacob. How urgent then the command for the twenty-first century disciple: "And these words which I command thee this day, shall be in thine heart: and thou shalt teach them diligently unto thy children." And how significant the Lord's choice of Abraham as the "father of the faithful":

"For I know him, *that he will command his children, and his household after him*, and they shall keep the way of the LORD, to do justice and judgment; that the LORD may bring upon Abraham that which he hath spoken of him."

(Genesis 18:19)

(b) "Then beware lest thou forget the LORD" (6:10–15)

The urgent command to teach the children to love the Lord by keeping His commandments was immediately followed by the call to discharge another responsibility. For the Lord was about to lead His people into their inheritance, in Deuteronomy 6:10 explicitly identified with the land covenanted to Abraham, Isaac and Jacob. The joy with which they would enter in is reflected in the glowing description of the land's prosperity and of the ordered and settled life upon which the wilderness generation would then begin. That there was a solemn responsibility commensurate with its delights could easily be overlooked, and it was imperative that Moses should now draw attention to it in his speech which has as its theme "When thou art come into the land ..."

"It is written ..."

There is obviously much for the disciple in a passage which the Lord Jesus used as a basis for his own overcoming of one of the temptations in the wilderness. For the occupation of the Land was to be no "pioneering" expedition. All was prepared for them — "cities, which thou buildest not, houses ... which thou filledst not, wells ... vineyards ... olive trees ...", upon none of which had they bestowed any labour. Their part was the faithful conquest of the Land and the cleansing of it from idolatry.

There are dangers in opulence equal to, and perhaps even greater than those of privation in a wilderness:

"Feed me with food convenient for me: lest I be full and deny thee, and say, Who is the LORD? Or lest I be poor, and steal [or, as Israel, murmur], and take the name of my God in vain." (Proverbs 30:8,9)

Reason as well as faith should have kept continually before the mind that the Lord was the Giver of all their prosperity, and that all should be rendered unto Him in the spirit of David:

"But who am I, and what is my people, that we should be able to offer so willingly after this sort? for all things come of thee, and of thine own have we given thee. For we are strangers before thee, and sojourners, as were all our fathers: our days on the earth are as a shadow, and there is none abiding." (1 Chronicles 29:14,15)

"This is my beloved Son"

The record tells us that "Jeshurun waxed fat, and kicked ... then he forsook God which made him, and lightly esteemed

79

the Rock of his salvation" (Deuteronomy 32:15). Not so God's other Son which He called "out of Egypt" (Matthew 2:15). The careful choice of his mother and of the home environment in which he was brought up ensured that he had been taught diligently in the law of the Lord. His determination to be about his Father's business meant that he continued to meditate therein all the day, and from it he drew his own lessons and strength. Faced with the vision of "all the kingdoms of the world, and all the glory (fulness) of them", with the suggestion that he could enter immediately upon the promised inheritance without fulfilling his Father's will unto the death of the cross, the Lord answered the challenging "*If* thou be the Son of God ..." with a true Son of God's reply: "It is written, Thou shalt worship the Lord thy God, and him only shalt thou serve". That command had been spoken from Sinai, by the same Voice that had spoken from heaven to him forty days before. It was written on the tables of stone with the finger of God Himself. And Moses had repeated it in his exposition of the Decalogue in terms of the wholehearted love of the Lord their God.

More can be said later of the Lord's victory over temptation in the context of the two further quotations from Deuteronomy which sprang to his lips, both from this same section of the book. The personal danger to the disciple of opulence for which he has put forth little effort is obvious, especially when one considers the moral degradation which seems to accompany a high "standard of living" (by no means the same thing as "quality of life").

Assuming for the present that we accept the apostolic warnings and exhortation for ourselves individually, let us now consider some of the implications for our own community. For the personal form of address used by Moses, the second person singular, pointed the exhortation to individual Israelites, some of whom managed to keep their own integrity amidst the national disasters of disobedience and apostasy. The "Thou", however, was also the nation as a whole, "the whole family" redeemed from Egypt.

Foundation principles

Provided we do not press comparisons too far, there are lessons for the Christadelphian Brotherhood in our own generation. In so far as we can claim affinity with the Israel of God, we have our roots in what God did in the founding of the church in the first century. After the principle laid down in the Book of Deuteronomy, we endeavour to carry out in the twenty-first century the spirit of all the arrangements made for worship and fellowship in the first, just as the brethren then were applying the eternal principles of God's law from the beginning in the circumstances of their newly founded ecclesias. Our life and thought must therefore be based upon the word of God.

There is another beginning to which we do well to pay heed—the origin of the Christadelphian brotherhood. Today we are an organised community—loosely organised, it is true, inasmuch as each ecclesia is "the church which is in the Father, and in the Lord Jesus Christ" wherever it may be. There is a limit to its autonomy, however, since it is linked with "all those that in every place call upon the name of Jesus Christ our Lord, both theirs and ours". Such organisation as does exist outside the ecclesias is for the support and encouragement of the ecclesias and the promotion of cooperation in work and fellowship, and can prosper only as long as it in turn receives the approval and support of those it seeks to serve.

But how often do we think back to the days when there was *no* organisation, and when that which we take so much for granted had to be carefully pondered and the practice worked out in the light of Scriptural principles? When the light of truth began to dawn upon our early brethren, and they found themselves isolated, sometimes ostracised, from the communities or churches around them, there was no Christadelphian body to join, no ecclesia to receive them. And so the *Royal Association of Believers*, basing its title upon 1 Peter 2, was formed in New York (1853), and its constitution painstakingly set out, that brethren baptized upon their belief of "the things concerning the Kingdom of God and the name of Jesus Christ" and sharing a common hope could break bread together.

Brethren in Christ

From such a beginning were developed our characteristic ecclesias later called Christadelphian. Our Constitution, introduced with its Scriptural basis in the *Guide to the Formation and Conduct of Christadelphian Ecclesias*, was drawn up by one man with foresight and Scriptural understanding. So were the first four Christadelphian Hymn Books* from which later books were derived. It still contains those compositions of early brethren, profound verses unsurpassed as expressions of our distinctive fundamental beliefs, such as the work of God in Christ (Hymn 83—"Glory

---

* *Golden Harp* (1865); 1869, 1874, 1932, 1964 and 2002 editions

and blessing be") and the hope of the Kingdom (Hymn 138—"Father Supreme'). Then there were years of worship and witness in the hired room before the acquisition of ecclesial halls.

Our settled pattern of ecclesial life; our volume of literature for study, exhortation and preaching; our *Brotherhood Near and Far* and the ease with which we can communicate with each other; the very possibility of world-wide witness such as the Day of the Watchman Project in every continent (1976)—such is the inheritance upon which the present generation has entered. Are *we*, the children of the third and fourth generation, in danger of esteeming too lightly that for which others have laboured in faith?

(c) "Ye shall not tempt the LORD your God" (6:16–19)

It is significant that the commandment not to go after other gods to serve them should be so urgently repeated (verse 14) now that Israel were on the threshold of the Land. It was because the temptation to do so would be renewed upon entry into Canaan when they would come into direct contact with the idolatrous worship of its peoples.

Why it should prove to be so seductive we intend to discuss when we come to the detailed instructions as to the behaviour of God's people in these circumstances as set out in Deuteronomy 12 and 13. It is sufficient here to recall that although there had been the incident of Baal-peor (Numbers 25), as part of a deliberate plan to destroy Israel instigated by Balaam, Israel's sins in the wilderness had not included idolatry in the strictest sense, worshipping graven images. True, at Sinai even the experience of the Lord's presence had not prevented the making and the worshipping of the golden calf, which meant that the influence of Egypt's animal cults was still powerful. Israel had been for the most part free of such influence for forty years in the wilderness, but would now be exposed to it even more sharply.

At Massah

In the warning of verse 16 we see the true meaning of "tempt" in Scripture. It means "to try out, to test" rather than "to seek to lead astray". Only in the former sense can it be applied to God, and this is the meaning underlying every statement that God tempted any of His servants or allowed His Son to be tempted of Satan. The incident at Massah preceded the experience at Sinai and concerned the provision of water in the desert. Coming as it did immediately after the Lord's giving of manna, the suggestion that He had brought them out of Egypt especially to kill the people with thirst was a singular expression of faithlessness, a challenge to the very power of the God of the Exodus finally to redeem. So the place was known as *Massah*, or Testing, and *Meribah*, Chiding, or Strife.

Although the actual name of Massah appears nowhere outside the books of Exodus and Deuteronomy, the events there ranked with those at Taberah and Kibroth-hataavah where "ye provoked the LORD to wrath". It was a place of significance in the long day of temptation in the wilderness, "when your fathers tempted me, proved me, and saw my work" (Psalm 95:7–11).

Two further points of interest emerge here. First, it was the fathers of the generation Moses was addressing who had committed the act of provocation at Massah. Yet, on the principle of corporate responsibility discussed on page 3 the next generation had also been there. Their own future had been moulded by the history of their nation. If the provocation at Massah could be repeated by their fathers as they moved on from Sinai, but still within sight of the mount whence God had spoken, then the miracle of the crossing of Jordan would not soften the hearts of the children, unless they diligently kept the commandments of the Lord their God, and did that which was right and good in His sight (Deuteronomy 6:17–19).

The firstborn of Israel

Secondly, there is a wonderful interplay of ideas here which it will be easier for the sensitive reader to appreciate than for a writer to explain in few words. According to Deuteronomy 33:8 (the details of which must be considered in due course), the work of Moses and Aaron at Massah is attributed representatively to the tribe of Levi. In subsequent incidents the Levites were "on the LORD's side" to maintain His holiness in the midst of a perverse generation (Exodus 32:26–29), or to stand in the breach when the wrath of the Lord was kindled against them (Numbers 25:10–13). So the tribe of Levi was to become the Lord's portion in Israel in place of the firstborn sons: they were the firstborn among the firstborn of the nations.

How fitting then that the Father's only begotten Son, zealous for the righteousness of God yet fitted for the work of great High Priest because "he himself hath suffered being tempted", should resist temptation in the wilderness with: "It is written, Thou shalt not tempt the Lord thy God."

(d) "And when thy son asketh thee in time to come" (6:20–25)

The reader will long ago have become aware of the repetitive character of the Book of Deuteronomy. Not only is it in itself a recapitulation of the Exodus and the wilderness journey as a basis for the exhortation and warning it contains for those about to enter the Land: the appeals themselves are repeated with different emphasis as the meaning of the covenant is unfolded in its practical application.

So we may relate 6:17,18, which promise inheritance and prosperity in the Land for the obedient, to 1:35,36; 4:1,5; 5:29 and the first verse of chapter 6. The theme will be recalled several times more as we proceed. The blessings of the Old Covenant are thus made perfectly clear: "It shall be our righteousness, if we observe to do all these commandments before the LORD our God, as he hath commanded us" (verse 25), and by that righteousness they would obtain blessings and long life upon the Land. The issues of *eternal life* belong of course to the New Covenant, which in fact antedated the Old, inasmuch as it was implicit in the covenant with Abraham. For his faith was accounted for righteousness and his inheritance of the land and the blessing belongs not to the Mosaic era but to the age to come.

A family relationship

The vital importance of relationships with the rising generation is also emphasised. We invite the reader to look once more at the passages considered in pages 74–79. There we drew attention to the occasions when the ordinances of the Passover and the raising of the memorial stones beside the Jordan prompted the enquiry, "What mean ye ... ?" from the younger generation. Here it is the testimonies, the statutes, the judgements themselves about which further information is sought.

In *The New International Commentary*, on the Book of Deuteronomy, P C Craigie makes this helpful observation (pages 174,175):

"The nature of the question implies a good family relationship, the kind envisaged by the positive implications of the fifth commandment ... The positive nature of the question is shown by the identification of the questioner with the God of the covenant, even though he was not present at the actual making of the covenant; thus he is asking questions about the commandments *which the* LORD **our** *God commanded* **you**. It is a question from a youth growing to maturity in the covenant community, already instructed in obedience, but wishing to know and understand the meaning and significance of the commandments that shaped the course of his daily life."

This beautiful picture of the ideal relationship between parents and children underlines the importance of family life for the spiritual health of the community or nation.

"That thy profiting may appear unto all"

It is interesting to see the progression in the education of the children, and we should mark it well. Family life was ordered in practical terms by the Lord's commandments. Every word of Moses and the prophets, however, was designed to bring out the *meaning* of the Law as well as the details of its observance. Indeed, Israel were roundly condemned for keeping the ordinance (often in a punctilious manner) without having the Law in their hearts. By his participation in the Passover the youngest member of the family was moved to ask about the actions performed; the older child was expected to enquire into what could be termed their theological content.

There are guidelines for us here, and it is becoming more important that we should observe them. In the junior Sunday School it is appropriate to introduce the playlet, the mime or the action song into the teaching of Scripture. They are often performed with the bright-eyed innocence and enthusiasm which in its developed form should characterise the children of the Kingdom and the fact that "The rain came tumbling down", repeated as a chorus in a song about the Flood, for example, becomes part of the children's unforgettable knowledge. Their own simple drawings, unsophisticated poems and other contributions all serve the same end—to form the basis of *realisation* of the Bible message.

The ecclesial family can find joy in the activities of its youngest members in their simplicity. But to continue what is appropriate for the young as part of the spiritual fare provided for the older ones, in method if not in content, or to introduce the same methods into the ecclesia, is to ignore the needs (as distinct from some of the wishes) of those coming to maturity by implying that the knowledge of God is all too difficult in the terms in which He has chosen to reveal Himself in Scripture. Some of the more off-beat modern versions of the Bible, to say nothing of the strip cartoon ones, have in the main served to mislead rather than inform. "Righteousness" may be a difficult concept, but *The Living Bible*'s "the way to heaven" confuses the issue completely.

The father's reply to the earnest enquiry of his son is in fact "theology" of the simplest yet most profound kind. "God revealed Himself both by act and by word. Both the acts and the words of God revealed His concern and His purpose for His people. Both the acts and the words imposed a responsibility on God's people, to revere and obey God in order that they might continue to experience His presence in history and continue to hear His words. The result of this reverence and obedience is stated in 6:25: 'It shall be our righteousness …' Righteousness in this context describes a true and personal relationship with the covenant God (see also Genesis 15:6), which not only would be a spiritual reality, but would be seen in the lives of the people of God. Thus the answer to the son's question finally focuses on the proper relationship of a man to God, and the fruit of that relationship in daily life" (Craigie, op. cit., page 175).

For ease of committing to memory (a worthwhile exercise), the above may be set out in summary form as follows:

INTRODUCTION

1. *The historical background*: Israel in bondage to the Egyptians (verse 21)

THE REVELATION OF GOD IN HISTORY

2. *Israel's experience of God*: the deliverance of the Exodus (verse 21)

3. *The judgements of God*: His dealings with the Egyptians (verse 22)

4. *The purpose of God*: To bring His people into the Land (verse 23)

THE REVELATION OF THE WORD OF GOD

5. *The Word of God*: The giving of the Law (verse 24)

6. *The conditions laid down*: Obedience and reverence for God (verse 24)

(e) "Thou shalt smite them and utterly destroy them" (7:1–26)

The contents of chapter 7 are unpalatable to modern taste since they come into that category which causes many earnest people to distinguish between a "God of the Old Testament" and the Father of our Lord Jesus Christ. It is not the place here to go over all these arguments in detail, for the reasons for the commandment to Israel utterly to destroy the Canaanitish inhabitants of the Land have been already clearly spelt out.

The substance of chapter 6 was the exposition of the First Commandment, coupled with the reassurance that God "brought us out from thence, that he might bring us in", as the introduction to that commandment in effect declared (Exodus 20:2). Chapter 7 is part of the exposition of the Second Commandment, since the treatment of the "seven nations greater and mightier than thou" was connected with the prohibition against making graven images and with the fact that "I the LORD thy God am a jealous God".

The reader is referred to a good Bible atlas or one of the newer illustrated Bible Dictionaries if he is anxious to follow up details concerning the identity of the seven peoples listed, which is not important for our immediate purpose. Some of them were migrant tribes who had settled in Canaan. The Jebusites play a part in Israel's subsequent history, being the last tribe to be brought under control when David took their stronghold and made it his capital, "the city of David". All but the Hivites are specifically mentioned by God to Abraham as those whose land was promised to his seed as part of the covenant to Abraham's seed (Genesis 15:18–21).

We surely do not miss the significance of one phrase in the covenant confirmed to Abraham, as he slept, by the passing of a lamp between the pieces of his sacrifice:

"Know of a surety that thy seed shall be a stranger in a land that is not theirs ... But in the fourth generation they shall come hither again: *for the iniquity of the Amorites is not yet full.*" (verses 13–15)

The Israelites, then, were entering into the Land in the fulness of time. The inhabitants had filled up the measure of their iniquity and were therefore ripe for destruction. The Second Commandment had proclaimed that the Lord would visit "the iniquity of the fathers upon the children unto the third and fourth generation *of them that hate me*". There was abundant evidence of that hate to be found in the Land.

It is in this context that the significance of Rahab's faith can be realised more fully. From her testimony to the two spies sent by Joshua we understand that the destruction was not to descend upon the inhabitants all unawares. She was able to say:

"I know that the LORD hath given you the land ... *For we have heard* how the LORD dried up the water of the Red sea for you, when ye came out of Egypt ... And as soon as we had heard these things, our hearts did melt, neither did there remain any more courage in any man, because of you: *for the LORD your God, he is God in heaven above, and in earth beneath.*"   (Joshua 2:9–11)

Men without excuse

The fact that Rahab was a Canaanite did not preclude her from obtaining mercy of the Lord on the basis of faith in Him and a resolve to keep His commandments. We may compare her statement with the words of Paul in Romans 1:18,19:

"For the wrath of God is revealed from heaven against all ungodliness and unrighteousness of men, who hold (hold down, RV) the truth in unrighteousness; because that which may be known of God is manifest in them; for God hath shewed it unto them ... even his eternal power and Godhead; so that they are without excuse."

If it be objected that when the Gibeonites, or Hivites, came with a similar profession to that of Rahab—"Thy servants are come because of the name of the LORD thy God: for we have heard the fame of him, and all that he did in Egypt"—then Joshua was criticised for accepting them, we can find our answer in this chapter 7 of Deuteronomy.

In the first place Joshua had not enquired of the Lord, and therefore was not capable of assessing the sincerity of the Gibeonites' profession of faith. The record says that "they did work wilily". Without Divine permission he had made a league with them, entirely contrary to the Lord's command through Moses. "League" and "covenant" (verse 2) are the same word and this knowledge throws into relief for us the reason for God's edict. The only covenant for the people of God was that which the Lord, the God of covenant, had made with them. For them to ally themselves with any other was a denial of the Lord who had brought them out of Egypt. The later history of the people in the Land, especially in the light of the prophets' commentary on it, shows clearly that the political alliances entered into from the time of Solomon had their spiritual and logical outcome in the decline and fall of the kingdom.

Mercy and covenant love

Furthermore, God's mercy even towards Israel was not on the basis of their own acts. Their "righteousness" did not lie in their own deserving, but in their keeping of their obligations under the covenant as the Lord kept His. His mercy, or *chesed*, was His *covenant love* which led Him to forgive all but the hardened, rebellious sinner for His mercy's sake. But where there was no Divine covenant, there could be no mercy, as it is written:

"Thou shalt make no covenant with them, nor shew mercy *(chesed)* unto them." (Deuteronomy 7:2)

It is in the light of this that we must also interpret verse 3. The marriages in question would be primarily political, as was the case with Solomon, designed to bind peoples together in the closest of ties. The disciple, however, can readily discern the deeper spiritual implications, for marriage is the closest and most binding of all covenants, by God's decree, because from the beginning it has always been He who "hath joined together". So just as the formation of a political alliance was for Israel a denial of the Lord's covenant, so was marriage outside of His nation:

"For they will turn away thy son from following me, that they may serve other gods." (verse 4)

(f) "Know therefore that the LORD thy God, he is God" (7:9,10)

In the quotation from the Second Commandment in 7:9,10 we have a further explanation of the instruction to root out all memory of the Canaanites from the Land:

"Know therefore that the LORD thy God, he is God, *the faithful God, which keepeth covenant and mercy with them that love him and keep his commandments* to a thousand generations; *and repayeth them that hate him to their face,* to destroy them: he will not be slack to him that hateth him, he will repay him to his face."

Mercy and judgement

As we understand from the interpretation put upon the commandment here (see also Exodus 20:6, RV margin), the loving-kindness and the judgement of the Lord are to each other in the ratio of a thousand to three or four. But judgement there must be if He is to be true to His own Name (Exodus 34:6,7). He is God, the faithful God, and "he cannot deny himself". If there is no judgement upon the unrepentant guilty, then mercy towards those who fear Him has no meaning at all.

The jealousy of God, therefore, is not that human quality which quite unreasonably resents another's sharing in his benefits. It is the yearning of parents over children who resist a loving discipline or yield to influences which are plainly to prove destructive. It is the righteous anger mixed with anxious longing of a husband or wife when another seeks to come between or loosen the loyalty of the one who is bound to the other in an exclusive relationship of covenant with each other and with God. As Paul said of the ecclesia at Corinth, who were being exposed to the deceitful words of "false apostles ... transforming themselves into the apostles of Christ":

> "For I am jealous over you *with a godly jealousy* (that is, a jealousy like that of God himself): for I have espoused you to one husband, that I may present you as a chaste virgin to Christ." (2 Corinthians 11:2)

We now link this passage in Corinthians, with its comparison between the subtlety of the serpent and the seductive words of the other-teachers in the ecclesia, and the passage in Romans 1, to enlighten us further on the Deuteronomy passage and to provide a basis for exhortation for disciples today. For the Lord's words are explicit: Israel's neglect to carry out His command would expose their children to the danger of becoming idolaters (Deuteronomy 7:4) while they ran the risk of being *snared therein* themselves (verse 25). Why was the danger so insidious? And what was so abominable in the Canaanitish practices which were, after all, part of the culture as well as the religion of the land? Indeed, although the peoples were easily identifiable separately by their origins, they shared a common culture and were often distinguished in religion only by the variation in the names of their principal deities.

We learn much from verses 12–16. The blessings of the covenant would be the inheritance of a land flowing with milk and honey. The fruitfulness of the people's life is spelled out in great detail, with emphasis upon the fertility of their own bodies, of their crops and their animals:

> "He will also bless the fruit of thy womb, and the fruit of thy land, thy corn, and thy wine, and thine oil, the increase of thy kine, and the flocks of thy sheep ... there shall not be male or female barren among you, or among your cattle." (verses 13,14)

True worship

The worship of the living God, of *Ail Shaddai*, Creator and Sustainer, acknowledged Him as the unique source of all these blessings. In Eden the practical effect of that acknowledgement would have been the thankful enjoyment of all that God had given—"every tree that is pleasant to the sight, and good for food" and the companionship of man and wife—while man recognised God's right to obedience and sought his development in wisdom and spiritual understanding by honouring the commandment. As it was, the desire for self-fulfilment led Adam and Eve to fall for the delusion that one can find satisfaction in material things alone, and wrest one's knowledge and understanding from the physical world rather than learn of Him who created it. Thence came fear, guilt, shame, pain, sorrow and death.

Thence came also paganism and idolatrous practices both ancient and modern, which consist of worshipping and serving the creature more than the Creator. There is a word employed in a unique sense in the Book of Deuteronomy which enables us to see the process most clearly. From its use there the critic has assumed he has evidence that the book was written late, long after rather than on the eve of the entry into the Land. For us, however, it is evidence to the contrary, showing that the Divine warning through Moses was exactly right, suited to the circumstances the hearers were about to encounter. For this generation the idolatry of Egypt was an historic memory: the idolatry of the land, however, would obtrude upon their daily life if they did not resist.

"From Me is thy fruit found"

The word is *ashteroth*, and it occurs here in Deuteronomy 7:13 and in 28:4, 18 and 51. It means "the flock" or "the young of the flock" and is associated with the breeding of sheep or cattle. In accordance with His covenant with the patriarchs the Lord had blessed them with increase in their flocks and they in turn recognised that all their wealth came from God. This same "covenant and mercy" the Lord would keep with Israel in the Land, if they heeded the exhortation to "hearken to these judgements, and keep, and do them". Yet they would be cursed in their flocks and all their fruitfulness in body, herd and field would waste away if they refused to hear and do all that the Lord had commanded.

In the land of Canaan they would learn a different sense altogether to the word *ashteroth*. Throughout the Semitic and Mesopotamian world, from which the wilderness generation had been largely secluded, Ishtar, Astarte, or in its plural form Ashtaroth or Ashteroth, was a "mother goddess" closely associated with love, war and fertility cults. In her depraved worship we have the perfect illustration of Paul's argument in Romans 1. The blessings which came from the Creator alone and brought no shame or sorrow with them when received with prayer and thanksgiving, were attributed to

91

some divinity, later personified, within nature itself. It could be worshipped only with superstitious fear and dread by those whose minds were given over to those things which Paul describes, with remarkable restraint, as "not convenient".

We can easily see the subtle nature of the danger to which Israel was to be exposed. The serpent in the garden had offered a plausible explanation, more satisfying to the flesh, of what God had said. Most of Eve's words in her reply to his question had been God's—*but not all*. Some commentators have drawn attention to the fact that the word for "naked" (Genesis 2:25) and for "subtil" (3:1) are the same, and suggest that we are therefore justified in concluding that the reasoning of this beast of the field which the Lord God had made answered to "the lust of the flesh, the lust of the eyes, and the pride of life". Certain it is that the immediate result of following that reasoning was an increased awareness of physical nakedness, coupled with shame and embarrassment which they had not felt before.

"The deceitfulness of sin"

The subsequent history of departure from God offers many examples of pagan names and titles which *could* be associated verbally with the true worship but had acquired a sinister connotation. The worship of Baal-berith is one example, after which the children of Israel "went a whoring" upon the death of Gideon (Judges 8:33; 9:4). It was part, says the record, of their going after Baalim, the nature deities whose cult challenged the worship of the Lord throughout their history (Ashtaroth, incidentally, was one of the consorts of Baal). Now "Baal-berith" means "lord of the covenant", and it is easy to imagine the apostate Israelite saying, "Where's the harm? Our God has always been the lord of the covenant." So abhorrent was Baal worship to God Himself, however, that through the prophet Hosea He declared (2:16,17):

> "And it shall be in that day, saith the LORD, that thou shalt call me Ishi (My husband); and shalt call me no more Baali (My lord). For I will *take away the names of Baalim out of her mouth*, and they shall be no more remembered by their name."

The dire results of Israel's neglect of the Lord's instruction implicit in the Second Commandment are plain to see. Soon after arriving in the Land they began to worship Baal and Ashtaroth, and then "the gods of Syria, and the gods of Zidon, and the gods of Moab, and the gods of the children of Ammon, and the gods of the Philistines, and (they) forsook the LORD, and served not him" (Judges 2:13; 10:6).

The cult of Ashtaroth was widespread in the days of Samuel (1 Samuel 7:3,4), who made specific reference to it in a speech to the people (12:10). It was to a temple of Ashtaroth in Bethshan that the Philistines carried Saul's armour. The ensnaring process envisaged in Deuteronomy 7:3,4 came to full fruition when the worship of Ashtaroth was given royal sanction by Solomon himself:

> "For it came to pass, when Solomon was old, *that his wives turned away his heart after other gods*: and his heart was not perfect with the LORD his God, as was the heart of David his father. For Solomon went after Ashtoreth the goddess of the Zidonians, and after Milcom the abomination of the Ammonites." (1 Kings 11:4,5)

An abomination unto the Lord

"Abomination" is by no means too strong a word. It sums up the words of Paul describing the vice, obscenity and degradation into which pagan cults lead their worshippers. Recently discovered cult objects, including a gold Astarte pendant from Tell el-Ajjul (see *The Illustrated Bible Dictionary*, page 133), emphasise the nature of the fertility rites. The theory is that the earth and the beasts of the field, even man himself can be stimulated to fruitfulness by the worship of these symbols and by engaging in the acts which they represent. In their most violent form they could include a human sacrifice; at their most humiliating they involved the sacrifice of virginity.

One of the most frightening aspects of all this is the fact that the language of the cult and the images and artefacts of worship were *the art and culture* of the peoples involved. The Astarte pendant was both a symbol and an ornament. Small wonder, then, that Moses returns to the theme in Deuteronomy 12:29–31 with:

> "Take heed to thyself that thou be not snared by following them ... and that thou enquire not after their gods, saying, How did these nations serve their gods? *even so will I do likewise*. Thou shalt not do so unto the LORD thy God: for every abomination to the LORD, which he hateth, have they done unto their gods; for even their sons and their daughters they have burnt in the fire to their gods."

And in this chapter 7 Israel are warned even against treating some of the objects as "collector's pieces" or ornaments for the home:

"The graven images of their gods shall ye burn with fire: *thou shalt not desire the silver or gold that is on them*, nor take it unto thee, lest thou be snared therein: for it is an abomination to the LORD thy God. *Neither shalt thou bring an abomination into thine house*, lest thou be a cursed thing like it: but thou shalt utterly detest it, and thou shalt utterly abhor it; for it is a cursed thing." (verses 25,26)

A heavy charge

The very repetitive nature of the warnings, which are all in character with the Book of Deuteronomy itself, can only mean that the dangers were great. This is sufficient justification for the heavy charge laid upon the people in the chapter we are considering. The Lord Himself would fight for them, and "send the hornet among" the people of the land until they were destroyed—no doubt a similar metaphor to that used in 1:44, when the Amorites "chased you, *as bees do*, and destroyed you in Seir". The Canaanites would flee before Israel until there was no hiding place for them; and though the campaign would be lengthy "lest the beasts of the field increase upon thee" and the empty land return to a wild state before the settled people could bring it under cultivation, the destruction of the inhabitants and their culture was to be complete.

It is no doubt difficult for the twenty-first century disciple to enter into the spirit of the foregoing severe commands. It was evidently equally difficult for the Israelites at the time, judging by the ease with which they were ensnared both by their new-found opulence (6:10–14, pages 79,80) and by the gods of the nations. The possibility that we too could be deceived as they were is no remote possibility, as the New Testament writers emphasise. For incredible as it may seem, when we consider the darkness of the idolatrous Canaanite, the superstitious dread which lay behind many of his acts of worship and the sheer cruelty of many of his observances, it was the way of his world. All his life, all the pattern of the Canaanite's thoughts was set against the background of his concept of divinity—the hostile power of nature which brought barrenness, famine, pestilence and death unless placated by the appropriate sacrifice. But since the practices were also indulgences of the flesh they were superficially attractive and satisfying: their destructive quality was learned too late.

A dark world

In reality nothing has changed. In the world of the first century, even in the midst of the highly developed culture of the Graeco-Roman civilisation, there was the same terror in life. Indeed, it was of this very world that Paul wrote in Romans 1, with a vivid description of its immorality, dedication to unnatural practices, hardness and implacability of heart. To be a slave in such a world was darkness and misery indeed: to be a rich man or a philosopher was to be enslaved to equally destructive forces.

For three centuries the human spirit had striven to express itself with beauty and with dignity, to fathom the nature of the universe, to bring order into human thought, to capture in unyielding marble the grace of the human form clad in garments flowing in the wind, or pour out the depths of the human soul in drama about the tragedy of man imprisoned by circumstance—or as some have described it, "the mathematical destruction of a mortal by the gods". In the shadow of one of the greatest of these human achievements in Athens, Paul had felt his spirit stirred within him because "the city was wholly given to idolatry". The artist had glorified the creature more than the Creator: the philosopher had deified the human mind—"the god within"—and between them they banished God from His own world. A man of Paul's breadth of understanding and deep spirituality could only sigh for the groaning and travailing of a world astray.

Even before they entered into Canaan Israel had become *"hardened by the deceitfulness of sin"*. This hardening process rendered them incapable of distinguishing right from wrong, the true from the false and made them fall easy prey to the opulence and idolatry of their new environment. It is this incapacity to exercise spiritual discernment which Paul calls "a reprobate mind", to which the world, whose wickedness was thrown into sharp relief by the Gospel, had been "given up".

The same spirit now works in the children of disobedience, the course of this world still flows in the same direction. We can be thankful that 2,000 years of the Lord's teaching have in some places modified the brutality of men and lifted the standards to some extent. To how limited is that extent in fact becomes even more evident as society manifests its ungodliness more openly, and terror and vice pass beyond the power of the law to control.

Our former way of life

Paul declared emphatically that where the Gospel has not been received, where there is no rising from the death in trespasses and sins, the way of life is in the same lusts of the flesh which were deified from the beginning. Surely then, we cannot claim to be free of the dangers against which Moses warned Israel, and that repeatedly. For the life and thought of our own world is reflected in its art and culture, in its patterns of speech and the variety of its entertainments. The serpent's beguiling of Eve Paul compares to the possibility that the ecclesia at Corinth would fall away from the Truth, by accepting a gospel which was no gospel at all, although all the language and vocabulary—"another Jesus", "another gospel", "false apostles", "deceitful workers", (2 Corinthians 11 throughout)—were images of the true Gospel itself.

We may well feel that such deviation is mild compared with Israel's apostasy, but in the light of their history we should be unwise to reckon that a right walk before God can be based on something which both Christ and his apostles describe as a snare. And how much graver the possibility of being deceived by the material things this world has to offer, the pleasures of second-hand participation in what God has condemned as evil and worthy of His judgements, all of which are presented to us in brilliant colour with technical expertise. There is, of course, as yet no call upon us to go forth to pull down and destroy: the idols must be cast down in our hearts.

(g) "As a man chasteneth his son"
(8:1–20)

The eighth chapter of Deuteronomy is one of outstanding interest and importance, for it expounds a principle first enunciated forty years earlier in the land of Egypt. It is a fundamental principle of the relationship between God and His people, carried over and fulfilled in our relationship with Him through the Lord Jesus. The Lord had commanded that the first words of Moses to Pharaoh were to be:

"Israel is my son, even my firstborn: and I say unto thee, Let my son go, that he may serve me." (Exodus 4:22,23)

The full meaning of the wilderness journey with its privations, its joys in the making of the tabernacle out of the willing offerings of the people, and its triumphs over their enemies—all becomes clear in the light of the exhortations of this chapter.

A double emphasis

Other commentators have already remarked that the special emphasis on the need for obedience is produced in this chapter by the use of two closely interwoven themes: *remember / forget* and *wilderness / promised land*. P C Craigie, in *The New International Commentary* already referred to, sets out the structure of the chapter conveniently as follows:

2–6: *remember the wilderness*, and God's presence there;

7–10: God will bring His people into the *promised land*;

11–16: beware of *forgetting* God in the *promised land*; beware of *forgetting* God who was present in the *wilderness*;

17–20: beware of presumption: *remember* God, the source of strength: *do not forget* God and follow other gods;

forgetfulness leads to disaster.

The wilderness had indeed been "great and terrible"; yet the Lord had been with them there. It was He who had gone before them to search out each fresh place of encampment; and the glory of the Lord had been their rearward (Isaiah 58:8). "In all their affliction he was afflicted, and the angel of his presence saved them" (Isaiah 63:9). The evidence of His presence had been seen not only in the dramatic miracles—if we can speak in such quantitative terms of miracles at all!— such as the water bursting forth "out of the rock of flint" and the manna from heaven. It was seen in the *providence* of God in a way observable only upon reflection over a long period:

"Thy raiment waxed not old upon thee, neither did thy foot swell, *these forty years*."

Discipline and testing

The question must therefore be raised as to why the people had to suffer the rigours of the wilderness at all. If the power of the Lord was such that they in fact lacked nothing and many of the usual consequences of such a long journey were miraculously averted, why did they not escape *all* the privations or be delivered from all the hardships? It is the classic question with which the unbeliever seeks to undermine faith in God. Even the believer sometimes asks the question in his heart, saying, Why should this happen to *me*? Israel's faithlessness expressed itself in "Is the LORD among us, or not?" (Exodus 17:7); and even, "Because the LORD hated us, he hath brought us forth out of the land of Egypt ..." (Deuteronomy 1:27).

There can be no more explicit, even comforting statement of the Lord's care and compassion for Israel which lay behind the experiences to which they were subjected than the declaration through Moses in this chapter 8. The renewed exhortation to keep the commandments that they might enter into the Land and "live, and multiply" was followed by the command to remember the way by which they had come. It was *"the way which the LORD thy God led thee".* Nor was it purposeless; it was—

"to humble thee, and to prove thee, to know what was in thine heart, *whether thou wouldest keep his commandments, or no."*

So there was a testing period, in which the quality of Israel's devotion to the Lord and His covenant would be put to the proof. It is important to remember that God's testing has no negative implications. It has an educative purpose whereby character is strengthened and knowledge of Him increased, and it has been an essential part of the life of the men and women of God from the beginning. The commandment in Eden was given for this purpose, as was the command to Abraham to offer up Isaac: "God did *tempt* (or, prove) Abraham" (Genesis 22:1).

The manner of the testing in the wilderness was such that the people were never left without evidence of God's presence—in the cloud and the fire, for example, or in the unfailing, daily provision of manna. They were proved but never forsaken. They had enough to eat but no surfeit, and that for good reason:

"that *he might make thee know* that man doth not live by bread only, but by every word that proceedeth out of the mouth of the LORD doth man live." (Deuteronomy 8:3)

God's true Son

This knowledge of God was to go deeper still into their heart, for they were to consider—

"that, *as a man chasteneth his son,* so the LORD thy God chasteneth thee." (verse 5)

There could be no more tender words indicative of the highly privileged status the children of Israel enjoyed for the fathers' sakes. The apostolic commentary of Hebrews 12 on the sufferings of Christ is designed to give comfort to disciples who endure affliction but it is plainly based upon Deuteronomy, as we read:

"For whom the Lord loveth he chasteneth, and scourgeth every son whom he receiveth. If ye endure chastening, God dealeth with you as with sons; for what son is he whom the father chasteneth not? ... shall we not much rather be in subjection to the father of spirits and live?" (Hebrews 12:6–9)

Passing from the wilderness into the promised Land they would then be able to "eat bread without scarceness". Human nature being what it is they would find it an equal challenge to faith when they had eaten and were full, and had built goodly houses, and dwelt therein (Deuteronomy 8:9,12). There was a danger that they would then forget God, and the evidence of their forgetfulness would be that they omitted to keep His commandments, and His judgements and His statutes "which I command you this day".

The "pride of life" is listed by John as one of the three things which characterise "the world" and are therefore "not of the Father" (1 John 2:16). Israel would manifest this sin when their heart was lifted up. They would say in their heart, "My power and the might of mine hand hath gotten me this wealth" (Deuteronomy 8:17). This trust in one's own might is characteristic of men, and many a time in Scripture it is cited as the reason for the downfall even of those who had once walked in their integrity before God. The prophet Isaiah emphasises the importance of meekness and humility when he declares:

"To *this* man will I look, even to him that is poor and of a contrite spirit, and trembleth at my word." (66:2)

"For thus saith the high and lofty One that inhabiteth eternity, whose name is Holy; I dwell in the high and holy place, with him also that is of a contrite and humble spirit ..." (57:15)

The result of disobedience

The warning against the lifting up of the heart appears several times in the Book of Deuteronomy. There was no cause for pride in Israel even though their experiences had been unique, and there had never been another nation "which had God so nigh unto them". It was because of the covenant with the fathers who had served Him in faith and humility, and so had been counted righteous before Him. So Israel were to remember that—

"the LORD did not set his love upon you, nor choose you, because ye were more in number than any people; for ye were the fewest of all people: but because the LORD loved you, and because he would keep the oath which he had sworn unto your fathers." (Deuteronomy 7:7,8)

If the privileges were great, so were the responsibilities. The testing of *the wilderness* would give way to that in *the Land*, when a desert people used to privation would be confronted with untold wealth and the allurements of the Canaanite "civilisation" which was entirely "of the world". The Lord had indeed "brought them out ... that he might bring them in", and if they *remembered* the Lord they would find that His chastening had been "to do thee good at thy latter end". But if they forgot His commandments then "I testify against you this day *that ye shall surely perish*" (8:16,19).

(h) "If thou be the Son of God ..."

To study all the implications of the foregoing for disciples of the twenty-first century it will be profitable at this point to consider further the temptations of the Lord Jesus in the context of these chapters from Deuteronomy. The importance for disciples of the experiences of the Lord surely cannot be over-emphasised.

The significance of his thrice-repeated "It is written" as a basis for his triumph in temptation should not be minimised. It touches upon the question of "sharing God's guidance" which has been discussed in the series on "The Evangelical Revival" (*The Christadelphian*, 1981, pages 83–86), since all can agree upon two things: first, according to both Matthew and Luke (4:1 in each Gospel), the Lord Jesus Christ was specifically "led of the Spirit" on this occasion; and second, that whatever measure of the Spirit gifts was granted to the disciples—and they were only "by parts" (1 Corinthians 12:4–6; 28–30; Ephesians 4:7, 11–16)—no-one has ever received such fulness of the Spirit as that bestowed upon the only begotten Son of God. "For God giveth not the Spirit by measure unto him" (John 3:24).

In the wilderness

Now the Lord was led of the Spirit for a special purpose—"to be tempted of the devil". To interpret this as a confrontation between two spirits, one of good and one of evil, with the Lord as the ground of battle between them is to miss the point completely. Moreover, the Lord's references to Deuteronomy and Israel's sojourn in the wilderness would have no meaning. The conquest of sin which has its origin in human nature could only be by man's choice of good and refusing of evil. The victory of Christ had to be won in himself before, by God's grace, his disciples could themselves become "more than conquerors" through their association with him in his death. So after the proclamation of his Divine Sonship at his baptism, the Lord's ministry began with what was both an historical event and a dramatisation of the testing he was to undergo throughout his ministry until the final agony of Gethsemane. The issue in the wilderness was the same as that in the Garden: "Not my will, but thine be done."

So although Christ was *led* of the Spirit to the place of testing, it was not by the power of the Spirit that he overcame. It was by choosing to do the will of God *as it had been revealed in the Word.* The principles of God's dealing with a Son were timeless, and were the same for the only begotten Son, unique in status as firstborn among many brethren, yet suffering being tempted like unto them, as they were for the son called out of Egypt (Hosea 11:1) to be the firstborn among the nations.

"For us temptations sharp he knew"

The forty days of fasting for the Lord corresponded with the forty years during which God suffered Israel to hunger. The absence of the daily supply of manna, however, meant that his condition was described with masterly understatement by Luke when he wrote "he afterward hungered"! All through our consideration of the temptation of Christ we must remain keenly aware of the fact that his experiences, being personal, were sharper and deeper than those suffered collectively by God's people in their wilderness. For one thing his status was higher than theirs, since he was God's *only begotten* Son. For another, the anointing without measure meant that the power to grasp at the proffered blessings was more effective than that of the nation in the Land.

So the temptation to make stones into bread would have been nothing, had he not as Son of God been able to do it. Commentators have waxed eloquent upon a presumed ecstatic state induced by hunger which made the round stones appear as loaves in the burning sunlight. The facts are, however, that not only was hunger of itself sufficient to concentrate his mind upon the need for bread and the possibility of using his power as Son of God to do so: one of the signs of his Messiahship would be that ability to *feed his people* (in Hebrew the words for "rule as king" and "feed" are the same; see Psalm 78:70–72). How great would be the desire for a man to use the power within his grasp not simply for his own ends but apparently to further the work of God at the same time—to take the short cut that avoided the suffering! So might any of us have reasoned, or "rationalised" the problem as the modern idiom has it.

The Lord Jesus, however, was "of quick understanding in the fear of the LORD". If he was the Son of God he was also the Servant in whom His soul delighteth, as the Voice from heaven had proclaimed (Luke 3:22). As Servant he would be obedient, even unto death; as Son he would know that it was written that God's Son was suffered to hunger that the supreme quality of his Sonship would be revealed and what was in his heart be made manifest. He would know also that there was no question of the Son of God perishing in the wilderness, desperately hungry though he might be and "straitened till it be accomplished".

Feeding the sheep

Luke said that at the conclusion of the temptation the devil "departed from him *for a season* (or, till an opportune time)", by which we understand that the Lord had undergone a severe test in principle, and was to face similar tests until the final victory. In the light of the wilderness experience we can understand the aftermath of the feeding of the five thousand. His compassion had been stirred, not merely because the multitude were hungry after three days, but "because they were as sheep not having a shepherd" (Mark 6:34). So "he began *to teach them many things*" as well as to feed them with bread. No wonder that when they had seen such obvious and satisfactory signs that he was Messiah, they tried to "come and take him by force, to make him a king" (John 6:14,15).

Again, how easy it would have been to ride upon the wave of popular favour, to claim that the people would be benefited by his taking the Kingdom and bringing in the blessings of bread to the hungry and riches to the poor. It was only the true Son of God who knew that the blessings of the Kingdom could come only upon a redeemed earth, and that the greatest sign of his Messiahship would be to go to Jerusalem and there be crucified for their sins—"If thou be the Son of God, *come down from the cross*"!—and be raised again the third day.

So Jesus spoke to the people about "the bread of God", the true bread by which alone man could live for ever. Like their fathers in the wilderness, the multitude all uncomprehending turned away from him, their hearts set not upon understanding of the ways of God but upon the bread of which they had eaten and been filled. The twelve, however, began dimly to perceive the truth and said, "Lord, to whom shall we go? thou hast the words of eternal life", though even they had had to learn through a rebuke in words first uttered in the wilderness—"Get thee behind me, Satan!"—that there was no short cut to the Kingdom and the glory.

The kingdoms of the world

The different order in which Matthew and Luke present the temptation in which were displayed the kingdoms of the world in a moment of time is important for the development of their own record. The Kingdom is a primary theme of Matthew's, so it is fitting that he ends the account of the Lord's temptations with Satan's offer of the kingdoms of the world, to lead directly into his treatise on the Kingdom of heaven (Matthew 4:8–11). Luke, on the other hand, makes Christ come, with the challenge to leap from the pinnacle of the temple in mind, to the brow of the hill where the people attempt to throw him down headlong (Luke 4:9–13, 28–30).

With the glory of the kingdoms apparently within his grasp, the Lord was like the children of Israel who entered upon the opulence of the Land. The Kingdom and the glory were his by right, but the suggestion that they were for the immediate taking was the error into which the people fell when they said in their heart, "My power and the might of mine hand hath gotten me this wealth" (Deuteronomy 8:17). It was a time to beware, lest they forgot the Lord, They should fear the Lord their God alone (6:10–13). The Lord Jesus, however, knew what was written not only in Deuteronomy, but also in the second Psalm: "Thou art my Son ... *Ask of me*, and I will give thee ... the uttermost parts of the earth for thy possession."

The second temptation in Luke's record, then, was the counterpart of that presented to Israel when they entered into the Land. The heart motivated merely by "the things of this world", in this case "the pride of life", would count that all things were there for the taking. Israel went further and reckoned that in some way they had acquired their wealth by their own effort. It is the classic sin of men who, being no longer thankful, become vain in their imaginations (see Romans 1:21).

No short cut for him

The true Son of God, however, recognised an even subtler temptation. The benevolent despot of this age would claim that by his rule the people prospered (it is the main plank of the political platform in the democracies also!). There is no doubt that Messiah's reign will fill the earth with untold blessings. With the kingdoms of the world now before him "in a moment of time", surely it would be right for him to take them immediately and cut short the groaning and travailing together in pain of creation which was to last until he took to himself his great power and reigned? The Lord went straight to the heart of the matter: "It is written, Thou shalt worship the Lord thy God, and him only shalt thou serve" (see Deuteronomy 6:13). He would ask of his Father and He would give him the nations for his inheritance, the uttermost parts of the earth for his possession. And that would be at a time which the Father had put in His own power.

The basis of all future blessings could only be the forgiveness of sins, and the accomplishment of *that* purpose would take the predetermined course. The temptation of the Kingdom was linked to that of the bread, as we have seen, since both had to do with the "ruling" of the people and the "feeding" of the flock. But the bread he would give was his own life and the power to heal the sick would be the sign of something even more important, the power on earth to forgive sins by "himself taking our infirmities and bearing our sicknesses" (Matthew 8:17, with Isaiah 53). This was the path of him who, taking the status of a servant, would be obedient unto death.

There was, however, a present path to tread; there were signs to give to the people that they might know that the Father had sent him. Surely here was a sphere in which the power of the Spirit that was upon him ought to be put to the fullest use.

This time also there was a relevant Scripture:

"For he shall give his angels charge over thee ... They shall bear thee up in their hands, lest thou dash thy foot against a stone." (Psalm 91:11,12)

From the pinnacle of the temple to the courtyard below was a long drop. Yet with implicit faith in the Scripture a man of God would come to no harm if he launched himself into the air. So might we have reasoned after the flesh. There is the additional thought, that if the courtyard was crowded there could have been no more forceful demonstration of Spirit power and therefore of Divine authority with which to commence a public ministry. Why should not belief in the Son of God be made as easy as possible for people! On the other hand, if the courtyard were empty, then there was an excellent opportunity to test out the power before the need for the demonstration arose.

"Ye do greatly err ..."

We notice how the three temptations were closely linked with the fact that Jesus, Son of the living God, was Messiah. There were certain signs by which the people would recognise him when he came and the power to do all of these now lay in his hands. But his anointing made him also "of quick understanding in the fear of the LORD": the Hebrew says "his scent was of the fear of the LORD"—a beautiful metaphor which carries all the overtones of having a flair for divine things, and having a presence sanctified by the incense of the sanctuary.

We too are taught the right use of Scripture by the Lord's answers on this occasion. The Lord had "brought Israel out" that He "might bring them in". He had promised to keep them in all their way through the wilderness, and had indeed given abundant evidence that He was with them (Deuteronomy 8:3,4). Moreover, He would keep them in their way forward through the land, "to cast out all thine enemies before thee, as the LORD hath spoken." To chafe under His discipline, to challenge Him to prove His presence among them by *demanding* bread in the wilderness, were acts of faithlessness. "It is written, Ye shall not put the Lord thy God to the proof, as ye proved him at Massah" (6:16; Luke 4:12).

Texts and contexts

Above all we are instructed by the realisation that for the Lord Jesus a quotation was not an isolated verse, used to prove a point by the words alone. It was *a reference to a whole situation* which could be summed up in that verse. We have seen this in the three quotations from Deuteronomy. It is borne out in the reference to the angels in Psalm 91. For the words omitted from our quotation of verses 11,12 (page 104) which do not actually occur in the records of the temptation, could be easily glossed over by the thinking after the flesh. The Lord, however, *knew* that the emphasis of the promise was in those words *"to keep thee in all thy ways"*. He would walk surely "today and tomorrow" without stumbling, bearing our sins in his own body even up to the tree of Calvary. And on the third day, when the angel who had charge over him rolled away the stone of the tomb and sat on it, he would be perfected. *This* was the greatest sign of his Messiahship, and without it no sign that caught the popular imagination could be effective.

How much more wisely should we walk as disciples if we would follow this example! How much smoother would be our ecclesial life if the wholeness and the richness of the Lord's experiences and those of the children of God of olden days were our pattern and our guide!

The principles expressed by the Lord Jesus under the private stresses of the wilderness temptations can be traced throughout his ministry. It is a fascinating study in itself to find the occasions which marked the "season" when the Lord was exposed to temptation (Luke 4:13), though we can do no more than point the reader to it here. Luke follows the record of the temptation to cast himself off from the pinnacle of the temple with the account of the turmoil in Nazareth, after Jesus had read of his mission from the book of the prophet Isaiah:

"And all they in the synagogue, when they heard these things, were filled with wrath, and rose up, and thrust him out of the city, and led him unto the brow of the hill whereon their city was built, *that they might cast him headlong.*"　　　　　　　　　　　　　　　(Luke 4:28,29)

Forcing the issue

Like the occasion already referred to when, after the multiplication of the loaves and fishes, the people wanted to take him by force to make him king, here was an opportunity to allow others to force the issue. As he fell headlong the angels would no doubt have borne him up, lest he should be dashed to pieces on the rocks below. But how then should the Scriptures have been fulfilled? So Jesus "passing through the midst of them went his way". Similarly there were occasions, notably that recorded in Matthew 16, when others tried to persuade Jesus to ride upon a tide of popular favour and avoid the cross. Luke tells us that the Lord thereupon "straitly charged them", informing his disciples with a touch of severity that "the Son of man *must* suffer many things, and be rejected of the elders and chief priests and scribes, and be slain, and be raised the third day".

The lessons of the wilderness temptation, which were the lessons of Deuteronomy, strengthened the Lord Jesus for a three years' ministry which took him through Gethsemane, where all the issues were resolved into quite simply "Not my will but thine be done". The same powerful lessons are there for us, the disciples of the twenty-first century, to take unto ourselves.

(i) "At Horeb ye provoked the LORD to wrath" (9:1–29)

The exhortation to "remember and forget not" continues with a recitation of the occasions on which Israel had manifested their stubbornness in acts of rebellion against the Lord. Chapter 9 opens with "Hear, O Israel". There follows the warning that the Lord would drive out before them "nations greater and mightier" than themselves, including the Anakim before whom the spies had trembled and persuaded the people to draw back at Kadesh, but they were not to boast in their own might in consequence. They were instead to remember the occasions when the Lord, who would be a consuming fire to their enemies (verse 3), had shown His great power in His mercy towards them when they had deserved to be utterly consumed (Numbers 14:17–21).

We notice the threefold parallelisms in the text: their God was (a) He who would cross the Jordan ahead of them as a devouring fire; (b) He who would thus destroy their enemies; and (c) He who would humble them before Israel. Israel on their part were warned that they would inherit (a) not on account of their own righteousness, but (b) on account of the wickedness of the inhabitants; and (c) Israel were a stubborn people.

From Egypt to Horeb

If the inheritance of the Land had been dependent upon Israel's righteousness instead of upon the covenant with their fathers, then they would never have entered in. For, says Moses:

> "Remember, and forget not, how thou provokedst the LORD thy God to wrath in the wilderness: *from the day thou didst depart out of the land of Egypt, until ye came unto this place*, ye have been rebellious against the LORD."
> (Deuteronomy 9:7)

It is remarkable how the foundations of true understanding and worship are laid down in the early books of the Bible which Deuteronomy recapitulates. Just as the adjective "holy" first appears in Scripture in connection with the manifestation of God as a covenant God, when the Lord revealed His Name and purpose at the Bush (Exodus 3), so the phrase "the glory of the LORD" helps to explain the apostolic description of sin as coming "short of the glory of God" (Romans 3:23). This first occurs in connection with the stubbornness of Israel.

One month was not too short a time for Israel to forget the mighty hand and outstretched arm by which the Lord had brought them out. They had seen the Red Sea cover the Egyptians and had lifted up their voices in a song of triumph to the Lord, yet in the wilderness of Sin the whole congregation murmured for lack of bread. The Lord's response was to promise both bread and meat but, significantly, the children of Israel "looked toward the wilderness, and, behold, the glory of the Lord appeared in the cloud" (Exodus 16:10). It was to remind them that, although they were about to set off into that wilderness, the Lord was ahead of them as He would always be, to provide and to protect (see Numbers 10:33–36; Deuteronomy 1:32,33) and all their faithless murmurs should have been stilled by that knowledge.

Even this signal provision of the Lord was soon forgotten. When water was abundant at Elim they had cried out for bread; at Rephidim, amidst the ample, constant supply of manna they thirsted, carrying their murmuring so far as to wish they had died by the fleshpots of Egypt!

One would have thought, however, that after they had heard the voice of the living God speaking directly to them from the mount in Horeb they would never have proved faithless again. That they were awestruck and fearful appears from the record in Exodus, and their reluctance to repeat the experience was understandable. But were it not for our understanding of human nature from the Scriptural standpoint we should find it incredible that Israel should have made the golden calf at the very foot of the mountain *while the fire still blazed above* (Deuteronomy 9:15; Exodus 24:17). And then, in spite of the Second Commandment, to call their idol their God that brought them out of Egypt and proclaim a feast unto the Lord!

Moses' intercession

In our present chapter Moses does not spare to underline the wickedness of the people. Their rebellion at Horeb took place while he was in the very presence of God to receive "the tables of stone, even the tables of the covenant which the LORD made with you" (Deuteronomy 9:9). Moreover, while he was fasting forty days and forty nights in preparation to receive the *Torah*, the Divine instruction for the people, they were sitting down to eat and drink and rising up to play. The apostolic comment in 1 Corinthians 10:6,7 suggests that something more evil than mere recreation is implied in those words. The casting down of the tables was more than a gesture of anger on the part of Moses; it was a symbolic act indicating that there was in effect no more a covenant between the Lord and His people. They had "*quickly* turned aside out of the way" which He had commanded them, and had broken the covenant on the very day that Moses was bringing them the ratified evidence of it, "written with the finger of God". There seemed no escape from the Lord's sentence:

"Let me alone, that I may destroy them, and blot out their name from under heaven: and I will make of thee a nation mightier and greater than they."

(Deuteronomy 9:14)

We have commented before upon the extraordinary insight developed by Moses into the meaning of the Name, and therefore of the attributes of the great God of Abraham. It is seen in the fact that he was prepared to plead with Him even in the face of so categorical a pronouncement of judgement. Since sacrifice and offering would be of no avail, could such wickedness be forgiven, however, by the resignation of his own part in the glory to be revealed? Exodus 32:32 shows us how close Moses had come to the fulness of the principles of the Atonement:

"Yet now, if thou wilt forgive their sin—; and if not, blot me, I pray thee, out of thy book which thou hast written."

The principle of atonement

By the following verses we are taught that atonement is not by substitution, as Moses was taught that he was not the redeemer whom God would ultimately raise up to set His people free. What the record in Exodus does not tell us is found in Deuteronomy 9:18. Moses—

"... fell down before the LORD, as at the first, *forty days and forty nights*: I did neither eat bread, nor drink water, because of all your sins which ye sinned ..."

It was after this period, in yet another visit to the top of the mount, that the eternal glory of that which was as yet unseen was revealed to Moses as he remained hidden in the rock—an experience upon which Moses drew later at Kadesh (see Numbers 14:11–21 again). The links with the Lord Jesus and his forty days fasting in the wilderness are too plain to be ignored. Noteworthy also is the Lord's displeasure with Aaron—"to have destroyed him". He who was to become High Priest needed the intercession of Moses! How privileged we are to have the Great High Priest who stands in Moses' place for our intercessor!

Some other details added by the record in Deuteronomy concern the destruction of the golden calf. The people's sin was, of course, their action in making the idol. Moses, however, calls the calf itself "your sin" and by his symbolic action showed that their sin had been taken away. First he ground the idol to powder, "even until it was small as dust" — a thorough destruction indeed. Then he cast the dust into the stream and made the children of Israel drink of it.

We do not always realise that there was a "brook that descended out of the mount", and so miss the wonderful chain of symbolism which links the smitten rock of Horeb, the cleft in the rock where Moses was hidden as it were "in the bosom of the Father" and the living water that flowed where the living Voice had proclaimed a covenant of salvation, mercy and peace. The link extends even to the prophet Elijah who, strengthened by the meat supplied by the angel, went forty days to come to a cleft in the same mountain and learn of the power of God in a still, small voice (1 Kings 19:8–12).

"Where streams of living water flow ..."

Can we see also a dual significance in the fact that Moses compelled the people to drink of the water into which the dust had been cast? It seems at first to have been a penalty they had to pay, designed to make them realise, by taking their sin unto themselves, as it were, that their act had defiled the very quality of life. But might it not also have been that the flowing stream (usually described in Hebrew as *living water*) was carrying their sin away and their partaking of it looked forward to the final cleansing by him who was "the Lord ... of the fountain" (Psalm 68:26, RV)?

Even after so signal an act of forgiveness the people showed themselves to be but flesh, striving ever with the spirit of the Lord. The tale of the further acts of rebellion, at Taberah and at Kibroth-hattaavah, we shall also consider in the present context. In them we shall find yet more to delight and warn the disciple.

(j) "The LORD had said he would destroy you" (9:22–29)

We return once more to the incident of the golden calf for it provides us with an interesting example of metonymy, a figure of speech which consists of substituting the name of one thing for the name of an attribute of it or of something closely related. Thus Israel's sin had been *the making of the calf*, yet Moses had called *the calf itself* as "your sin" and had destroyed it. This principle, like that of "personification" (for example when Wisdom in the Proverbs is treated as though it were a woman) is of great importance for our understanding of such things as the law of the sin offering and the sacrifice of Christ to which we shall draw attention later.

"Our God is a consuming fire"

The remainder of Deuteronomy 9 continues the tale of Israel's disobedience. The mention of Taberah, Massah, Kibroth-hattaavah (verse 22) and Kadesh-Barnea (verse 23) altogether makes it evident that each separate act of disobedience was but a further illustration of their basic sin—a lack of faith in the Lord which resulted in a lack of commitment to His covenant with them.

The strife at Massah had been on the way to Sinai, before the Lord's manifestation of Himself in the burning fire, although the people had already seen His mighty hand and His outstretched arm. The making of the golden calf, the complaining at Taberah, and possibly the lusting for meat at Kibroth, had been either within sight of the burning mountain or of the smoke from it and the glow which lit up the sky behind them. Taberah was three slow days' journey from Sinai, and Kibroth, if it was not another name given to the same place, could not have been more than one day further on. In any event, the former name was given because "the fire of the LORD burnt among them, and consumed them that were in the uttermost parts of the camp" (Numbers 11:1), and the name of "The graves of them that lusted" was given because the same judgement had been manifested in different form.

All these incidents were evidence of Moses' claim that "Ye have been rebellious against the LORD from the day that I knew you" (Deuteronomy 9:24). The recital of them reinforced his exhortation that as they crossed into the Land they should remember that the basis of their inheritance was the Lord's mercy and not their deserving. Moses describes his own reaction in verse 19: "For I was afraid of the anger and hot displeasure, wherewith the LORD was wroth against you to destroy you".

The full manifestation of the Name to Moses was to follow the destruction of the golden calf. However, he was evidently already so sensitive to Divine things that, while fully understanding that their God was a consuming fire, he knew that a man of a humble and a contrite heart could approach to Him in intercession. There were those who could dwell with the devouring fire (Isaiah 33:14). So he prostrated himself, with that most solemn of invocations upon his lips: "O *Lord* GOD, destroy not ..."

Adonai Yahweh

We have drawn attention before to the powerful and evocative use together in special circumstances of the Name and title of Adonai Yahweh, Lord God, as a form of address. It is almost always on occasions when the sovereign majesty of God in power and judgement are linked with His mercy and compassion for the sake of His covenant with Abraham and his seed.* There were occasions when the appeal did not turn away the Lord's wrath, as in the case of the striking of the rock and in the days of Amos. Here, however, "the LORD hearkened unto me at that time also".

Moses had already rebuked the faithlessness of the people by declaring that in redeeming them from Egypt, the Lord "*brought us out* from thence, that *he might bring us in*, to give us the land which he sware unto our fathers" (Deuteronomy 6:23). Now in his concern for the honour and glory of God he was anxious lest the Egyptians should blaspheme the Name by saying, "Because the LORD was not able *to bring them* into the land which he promised them, and because he hated them, *he hath brought them out* to slay them in the wilderness" (9:28).

This, however, could not be: "Yet they are thy people and thine inheritance, which *thou broughtest out* by thy mighty power and by thy stretched out arm" (verse 29).

We round off our consideration of chapter 9 by recalling once more the verses from Numbers which sum up all that is contained in the prayers of intercession of the great mediator which he repeated in summary form in his final exhortation. The power of *Adonai* and the compassion of the Lord of the covenant are beautifully comprehended in Numbers 14:17–19:

> "And now, I beseech thee, let the power of *my Lord* be great, according as thou hast spoken, saying, *The LORD* is longsuffering, and of great mercy, forgiving iniquity and transgression, and by no means clearing the guilty, visiting the iniquity of the fathers upon the children unto the third and fourth generation. Pardon, I beseech thee, the iniquity of this people according to the greatness of thy

---

* See pages 31–34 and the author's *The Name that is above Every Name,* published by *The Christadelphian,* 1983

mercy, and as thou hast forgiven this people, from Egypt even until now."

(k) "Destroy it not; for a blessing is in it"

Before drawing the lessons for the disciple from the foregoing, let us pursue a short meditation arising from the prayer in Deuteronomy 9:26: "Destroy not." In his book *The Titles of the Psalms*, James Thirtle puts forward the theory that the names of tunes to which certain Psalms were set, and which are a part of the Hebrew text and appear as headings in the AV, should in fact be attached to the *preceding* Psalm. We have hitherto held an open mind on the question. His idea has now been placed beyond reasonable doubt for us, however, when we looked once more at the Psalms which were set to the tune *Al-Taschith*, or "Destroy not". The matter seems to go deeper even than Thirtle suggests and raises the whole question of the relationship between words and music in Ancient Israel.

With reluctance we must defer full treatment of this fascinating theme until opportunity presents itself. We are convinced, however, that the original melodies were linked closely with the emotions aroused by the words, and had the power to evoke the sentiments if not the actual words whenever they were heard. We shall look more closely at this in connection with the Song in Deuteronomy 32.

The song was a witness for the Lord against the children of Israel and Moses taught the words, and presumably the music, to the people "until they were ended"—a phrase which suggests repetition and rehearsal. Possibly the melody was taught by a system of hand signs, rather as some of our older generation were taught tunes with hand signs representing the letters of the tonic sol-fa notation. We know that two prophets, Isaiah and Micah, opened their prophecies with the first words of this Song as a prelude to their theme of the Lord's judgements upon His rebellious children. Other prophets quote from or allude to the Song, which was obviously still well known, though probably by that time regarded more as part of Israel's literary and cultural heritage than as the solemn words of their living God. It would be remarkable if the melody had not been preserved as well (see part of the section on "Psalms, and hymns, and spiritual songs" in *The Christadelphian*, 1981, pages 442–445).

Besides being a "sweet psalmist of Israel", author of words and a composer of music, David was "a man after God's own heart". His works, therefore, were full of the spirit of God in both senses of that phrase. As he sang and made melody in his heart to the Lord in the cool of the day or in the night watches, his meditation was of the Lord's mercy to His people in the wilderness when He led them as a shepherd does his flock. And when he became a fugitive from Saul, what more natural than that he should plead for God to be merciful to himself also, setting his prayer to the ancient melody *Al-Taschith*, "Destroy Not"?

If we look briefly at the Psalms which bear this subscription (56–58), we shall see this confirmed and another Divine principle enunciated. The tune at the head of Psalm 56 in the Authorised Version is "The Dove of the Distant Terebinths". We shall see that it is appropriate to Psalm 55 in which David longingly proclaims "Oh that I had wings like a dove!", so that he could fly far away and be at rest. It seems evident then that "Destroy Not" was the tune for Psalms 56–58. In them David cries to God for judgement upon the wicked and mercy for himself and all the righteous. The three Psalms should be carefully read in the light of this; here we briefly outline their contents:

"Be merciful unto me, O God …
For thou hast delivered my soul from death …
For thy mercy is great unto the heavens …
Be thou exalted, O God, above the heavens …
Verily, there is a reward for the righteous:
Verily he is a God that judgeth the earth."

A remnant shall be saved

David was delivered not only for his own sake but for the sake of the Lord's covenant. He was the Lord's anointed, and therefore "under the shadow of his wings" as Israel had been in the wilderness. For he had already been anointed before he had been forced to flee before Saul, although the full import of Samuel's action that day in Bethlehem could not have burst upon him until, sitting on the throne of the Lord in Zion, he had exclaimed:

"Who am I, O Lord GOD (*Adonai Yahweh*)? and what is my house, that thou hast brought me hitherto? And this was yet a small thing in thy sight, O Lord GOD; but thou hast spoken also of thy servant's house for a great while to come …"   (2 Samuel 7:18,19)

David was therefore like Moses and the few faithful with him in the wilderness—the remnant, with whom God would work to preserve His covenant in the midst of a perverse and crooked generation. There *was* a reward for the righteous and in wrath the Lord would remember mercy. The strains of "Destroy Not" would combine with David's words to express his deep longing that the Lord should become his salvation.

Psalm 74 brings the point out further:

"O God, why hast thou cast us off for ever?"

The vivid picture given by the Psalmist of the destruction of the very sanctuary of the Lord itself is set, again appropriately, to the tune "Destroy Not", because it is a prayer to God that He should—

"Remember thy congregation, which thou hast purchased of old; the rod of thine inheritance, which thou hast redeemed."

Again the remnant are brought before God in words reminiscent of the pleading of Moses that the Lord should remember His covenant love and not destroy the righteous with the wicked:

"O deliver not the soul of thy turtledove unto the
  multitude of the wicked:
Forget not the congregation of thy poor for ever.
Have respect unto the covenant:
For the dark places of the earth are full of the
  habitations of cruelty.
O let not the oppressed return ashamed:
Let the poor and needy praise thy name."

(verses 19–21)

A song of the vineyard

Some commentators have seen in the words of Isaiah 65:8, "Destroy it not; for a blessing is in it", a fragment of "an ancient vintage song". However, it would certainly have been no secular song, part of the folklore of an ancient people, but a sacred song to the Lord, gathering up all the symbolism of the vine brought out of Egypt to be planted in the vineyard of the Lord (Psalm 80; Isaiah 5:1–7), which failed to bring forth fruit unto Him. Just as the Psalmist envisages that God will answer his prayer and "Turn us again, O LORD God of hosts … and we shall be saved", so Isaiah throughout his prophecy combines the theme of judgement upon a rebellious people with that of the remnant that shall return, the humble and the contrite to whom the Lord will have respect. Isaiah 65 is full of these themes, and we cannot miss the harmonies from the theme of Deuteronomy as we read the words (verse 8 onwards):

"As the new wine is found in the cluster, and one saith, *Destroy it not*; for a blessing is in it: so will I do for my servants' sakes, that I may not destroy them all. And I will bring forth a seed out of Jacob, and out of Judah an inheritor of my mountains ..."

(1) "Yet they are thy people"
(9:29)

Paul explicitly draws lessons from the incident of the golden calf (1 Corinthians 10:1–12) which, in the context of all the foregoing, bring out the relevance of Deuteronomy for disciples. The example of the Israelites reminds us that for us all to have been baptized into Christ and to partake of spiritual food and drink is not of itself a guarantee of our righteousness. The fathers "all" did similar things, "but with many (with most, RV) of them God was not well pleased". As we know, this expression goes deeper than simply that God was displeased and angry with the people, true though that was. *He could not work His purpose out in them*; since they resisted His will, He could not do in them His *good pleasure*.

Goodwill towards men

The reader will be rewarded if he follows this theme throughout Scripture, from its origin in "the good will of him that dwelt in the bush" (Deuteronomy 33:16), the purpose with Jerusalem in Psalm 51:18, the execution of God's will through His angels in Psalm 103:21, and the Lord's delight in His servant (Isaiah 42:1), to the New Testament working out of this wonderful Old Testament concept. This begins with "good will toward men" in Luke 2:14, extends through the passages recording the Voice from heaven at the Lord's baptism and on the Mount of Transfiguration (e.g. Luke 3:22, Matthew 17:5), to the passage we are considering. It is also to be found in Ephesians 1:5,9; Philippians 2:13; 2 Thessalonians 1:11 and 2 Peter 1:17.

Our chapter in Deuteronomy has brought out most clearly that "the people sat down to eat and drink, and rose up to play" under the very shadow of Sinai, where the smoke was still rising. They murmured, complained or rebelled while within sight of the glow of the consuming fire. Such is human nature that Paul warns the disciples against the same basic sins as those which had beset Israel. We should not:

(a) lust after evil things as they also lusted;

116

(b) be idolaters, as were ssome of them;

(c) commit fornication as some of them committed;

(d) tempt Christ as some of them also tempted;

(e) neither murmur as some of them also murmured.

The force of these warnings is brought home to us when we remember that the Apostle is giving them in the context of a relationship to the Breaking of Bread! We are also reminded that in the very presence of the Lord Jesus, with all the attendant solemnity of the approaching hour when he would in reality give his body and shed his blood, the hand of him that betrayed him was with him on the table, and "there was also a strife among them, which of them should be accounted the greatest" (Luke 22:24)!

The Apostle referred to the making of the golden calf as one of the things that "happened unto them for ensamples", written for our admonition, to drive home two lessons. First, "Let him that thinketh he standeth take heed lest he fall"; and second: "God is faithful, who will not suffer you to be tempted above that ye are able". The wilderness experiences now as then are the discipline imposed by a Father "to see what is in thine heart, whether thou wilt keep his commandments or no".

We have an intercessor more powerful than Moses could ever have been. Moses did not offer himself as a sacrifice for Israel's sin, but Christ gave himself for our redemption. Indeed, by that figure of metonymy described earlier, our sin has been taken away by him, "for he was *made sin* for us, who knew no sin, that we might be made the righteousness of God in him" (2 Corinthians 5:12). In Jesus, the Saviour, the Lord has become our salvation—a deliverance as signal as the coming out of Egypt. He ought to be our strength and song, and His mighty power and outstretched arm be celebrated with a song in our hearts as triumphant as that which was sung "in that day".

The assurance goes even deeper: "Faithful is he that calleth you, who also will do it" is the apostolic form of "He hath brought us out, that he might bring us in". On the lips of the Lord Jesus it was "Fear not little flock; for it is your Father's *good pleasure* to give you the kingdom". Far from being left to ourselves once we have been set upon the way, "it is God that worketh in you both to will and to do of *his good pleasure*". Like Paul we can be "confident of this very thing, that he which hath begun a good work in you will perform it until the day of Jesus Christ" (Philippians 1:6).

(m) "Two tables of stone like the first"
(10:1–11)

In the preceding chapter Moses has driven home his exhortation with a summary of Israel's outstanding acts of rebellion at Taberah, Massah, Kibroth-hattaavah, Kadesh-barnea and above all in the making of the golden calf. All these incidents revealed the perversity of human nature even in the people of the covenant, and left them without room for spiritual pride. The record also brings out the grace of the God of the covenant who in His infinite wisdom could remain true to Himself by judging the rebellious and faithful to His promises to the fathers by forgiving and restoring the repentant.

The Covenant restored

Chapters 10 and 11 are linked together by the "Therefore" of 11:1 and form the climax to the hortatory part of Moses' second speech, before he sets out the details of the constitution of the Land into which the people are to enter. The opening words of this section are:

> "At that time the LORD said unto me, Hew thee two tables of stone like unto the first, and come up unto me into the mount, and make an ark of wood. And I will write on the tables *the words that were in the first tables* which thou brakest, and thou shalt put them in the ark."

The precise statement of the time indicates that the restoration of the covenant on the part of the Lord was the direct result of Moses' intercession. The rest of the section takes up the theme of intercession and mediation and the abiding covenant, a fact which will guide us through what some have regarded as one of the most difficult passages of Deuteronomy as far as its chronology is concerned.

For we have to ask whether there were *two arks*, the ark of the covenant proper and the one referred to with such emphasis here. Was this latter a special container to receive the tables of the testimony prior to the construction of the tabernacle furniture? When did Moses put the law into the ark: immediately after his descent or much later when the tabernacle was erected, as Exodus 40 describes? Why is the death of Aaron introduced into the record at this point, although it occurred some 39 years later than the event being considered? And why was the separation of the tribe of Levi the subject of special reference at this time?

Far from presenting all the difficulties encountered by the commentators (one Jewish commentator was constrained to incorporate a legend about Aaron into the account by way of explanation!), there is a remarkable spiritual lesson to be learned.

Bread of life

The chronological question is resolved when we bear in mind that Scriptural records often bring together events which have a spiritual relation to each other though they were separated in time. An example from Exodus 16 bears directly on our immediate point. After the provision of manna for the first time, Moses told Aaron to fill a pot with it and "lay it up before the LORD, to be kept for your generations" (Exodus 16:33). The literal bread became both a memorial of what the Lord had done and a reminder throughout all generations that His care for His people is everlasting. At that time there was no ark of the testimony and the tables of the testimony had not yet been given from Sinai. Yet we read, "As the LORD commanded Moses, *so Aaron laid it up before the Testimony* to be kept" (verse 34). From Exodus 25:16 we learn that the commandments for the making of the tabernacle and the ark in particular were given before the handing over of the stone tablets: "Thou shalt put into the ark the testimony which I *shall* give thee". So what Moses had said to Aaron about the manna and what the Lord had said to Moses about the testimony were commandments to be carried out in due time when all the conditions could be fulfilled. The same principle is at work in the passage we are considering.

The parallel account in Exodus 34:1 makes no mention of any commandment to make a special ark, nor is there any record of a placing of the tables in the ark made at that time. The command to make an ark which we find here in Deuteronomy 10:1, therefore, did not refer to another ark. It was a declaration that the tables hewn by Moses would be as truly the Testimony as those which the Lord Himself had made; the significance of this we shall discuss below. The instructions about the ark had been already given on the occasion of the earlier visit to the top of the mount and the statement that Moses made it does not mean that it was the work of his own hands but that it was made at his command: he had it made. This manner of speaking is common enough in most languages: "We are building a house in London" only rarely means that the speakers are labouring with their own hands at the bricks and mortar.

The testimony was actually placed in the ark of the covenant at the time of the erection of the tabernacle, according to Exodus 40:20. Years later, to drive home his point that the covenant was still in force, in spite of the rebellion of their forefathers, Moses emphasises that the new tables on which the covenant had been rewritten were later put into the ark which he made just as the originals would have been (Deuteronomy 10:5). (There is no Hebrew tense corresponding to the English "he had made", so we are justified in omitting the "had").

An everlasting covenant

The important point to grasp is that it was the Lord Himself who restored the covenant. It is abundantly plain from this record and that of Exodus 24 that it was He who wrote the words on the new tables and that they were exactly the same as those He had written before. The covenant was an everlasting one, for it was to be laid up before Him as a memorial to the children of Israel for all generations.

In all this there is strong comfort and powerful exhortation for the disciple. In spite of Israel's lack of faith in the Lord,

"... yet he abideth faithful: he cannot deny himself."
(2 Timothy 2:13)

There is another point of supreme importance here. In the restoration of the covenant the words were indeed exactly the same; but this time they had been written *on tables prepared by man*, in this case the mediator of the covenant. Moreover, there was to be a place prepared in which the Testimony could be preserved for future generations. In the diligent preparation of the tables by Moses prior to his encounter with the Lord on Horeb we see in fact the preparation of his own heart. In the placing of them in an ark of wood there was the promise that what was by nature corruptible could be made to endure. And in the proclamation of the Name and of the glory that was in it, he was taught the meaning of mercy and judgement:

"Mercy and truth are met together;
Righteousness and peace have kissed each other."
(Psalm 85:10)

The whole incident foreshadowed the time when:

"Behold, the days come, saith the LORD, that I will make a new covenant with the house of Israel, and with the house of Judah: not according to the covenant that I made with their fathers in the day that I took them by the hand to bring them out of the land of Egypt; *which my covenant they brake*, although I was an husband unto them, saith the LORD. But this shall be the covenant that I will make with the house of Israel; After those days, saith the LORD,

I will put my law in their inward parts, *and write it in their hearts* ... for I will forgive their iniquity, and I will remember their sin no more." (Jeremiah 31:31–34)

In the hands of the mediator

We are brought at once to Hebrews and 2 Corinthians. The Apostle to the Hebrews quotes in full the Jeremiah passage at the end of the eighth chapter. This opens with the words: "Now of the things which we have spoken this is the sum." By this he does not mean simply *the summary*, but rather *the very essence* of the argument—we have a High Priest and mediator, superior to the angels by reason of his more excellent name and superior to the Levitical priesthood because he has—

"a more excellent ministry, by how much also he is the mediator of a better covenant, which was established upon better promises."

Writing to the Corinthians Paul is in effect giving an apostolic commentary upon the incidents which form the background to the Mosaic record we are considering. He too emphasises that the "tables" which receive the Divine law must be those prepared by man, so that the ecclesia becomes:

"... the epistle of Christ ministered by us, written not with ink, but with the Spirit of the living God; not in tables of stone, but in *fleshy tables of the heart*."

(2 Corinthians 3:3)

The power of intercession

In Deuteronomy we are taught the power of intercession by a faithful servant of the Lord. How great must be the power that lies in the intercession of "the Holy One of God", the Son of God Himself. For if Moses, mediator of the Old Covenant, was able to obtain forgiveness for the people and turn away the immediate destruction of the entire nation, much more is the mediator of the New Covenant in his own blood, shed for many for the remission of sins,

"able also to save them to the uttermost that come unto God by him, seeing he ever liveth to make intercession for them." (Hebrews 7:25)

The reason for the apparent interpolation of the death of Aaron and the choosing of the Levites at this point in Moses' speech (Deuteronomy 10:6–9) is thus apparent. As they listened to the record of Moses' several acts of intercession on behalf of their fathers, the question would quite naturally have arisen in the minds of the people as to who would take his place upon their entry into the Land. Aaron, the first

121

High Priest, had been dead six months; Moses was to die before they entered the Land. Would there be no more intercession then on behalf of a people compassed with infirmity?

The answer lay in the reminder that although Aaron was dead the priesthood had not died with him: "Eleazar his son ministered in the priest's office in his stead". Moreover—and this was to be brought out clearly in the ceremonial handing over by Moses of his spiritual charge to priests and Levites (31:9,24–27)—in the Land the priests and Levites would continue to exercise a mediatorial function, having been accepted of the Lord in ransom for the firstborn of the people (Numbers 3). It would be appropriate for the children of Israel to remember this, and because the Levites would have no other inheritance than the Lord Himself (Deuteronomy 10:8,9), they were to be offered all the natural support and sustenance they needed while they occupied themselves with the service of the tabernacle and the priests with the work of mediation and intercession.

Above all, however, was the lesson, no doubt appreciated by Moses alone at that time, that their salvation was a matter of God's grace and not of any man's achievement. Elijah later had to be taught that the ministry of the prophets did not *depend* upon his work, even though he should cry "I, even I only, am left; and they seek my life, to take it away". The work did not cease with his removal from the scene, however, and the very manner of his departure was the symbol of that continuity, as the mantle fell upon Elisha. In like fashion the people did not see the death either of Aaron, or of Moses whom the Lord Himself buried. So the ministry of reconciliation survived those through whom it was first introduced and Moses, Aaron and Elijah were all types of him who ever liveth to make intercession for us.

(n) "What doth the LORD thy God require of thee?" (10:12—11:32)

Closing the record of his intercession with the words "And the LORD hearkened unto me at that time also, and the LORD would not destroy thee" (verse 10), Moses added: "And the LORD said unto me, Arise, take thy journey before the people, that they may go in and possess the land, which I sware unto their fathers to give unto them". The two verses are closely linked. Secure in the knowledge that the Lord was also with them the new generation could now prepare to cross over the Jordan and enter into the long-promised inheritance. Moses calls once more upon Israel to "hear the conclusion of the whole matter". In words to be uttered once more by the prophet Micah, at a time of apostasy in Israel, he gives the essence of the Ten Words of the covenant written on the stones: "And now, Israel, what doth the LORD thy God require of thee" but to fear Him, walk in His ways, love and serve Him and keep His commandments? Many of the details of this section we have already considered, so we shall concentrate upon the special emphasis placed on some of them which is appropriate to a final exhortation. In sum, Moses is saying that since it was through God's grace that they were able to stand that day upon the plains of Moab, their responsibility to fulfil their part of the covenant was all the more pressing.

The great commandment

The basic ideas forming this exhortation are a further exposition of the "Great Commandment" of chapter 6: the Lord is One, and there is none like Him in all the earth; therefore He is to be worshipped in single-mindedness (10:12). He is Possessor of heaven and earth and all that is in them: yet He delighted in the fathers of Israel "and chose their seed after them, *even you above all people*, as it is this day" (verse 15). There follows the first reference in Scripture to circumcision of *the heart*. Circumcision was instituted as "my covenant, which *ye* shall keep", a token of the covenant betwixt me and you" (Genesis 17:9–11. It is important to notice the plurals "ye" and "you" here, although God is talking to Abraham. The covenant and its token were for him personally but also for "thy seed after thee in their generations"). The genuine keeping of the covenant lay not in the outward observance, imperative though that was (Genesis 17:14), but in the devotion of the people to the Lord. We have seen this illustrated also in the incident of the remaking of the stone tables. Once more we perceive the deeply spiritual quality of the Book of Deuteronomy, and indeed of the whole Law of God, from which the Lord Jesus himself and his apostles constantly drew lessons for the disciple which are valid today.

The meaning of the Name in practical terms is expounded once more in the concluding verses of chapter 10. The supremacy of Israel's God lies not only in His might and "the terror of the LORD" in the doing of the great and terrible things "which thine eyes have seen", but in His love for the fatherless, the widow and the stranger. His people would be like Him and so "know his name" if they remembered their sojourn in Egypt and were kind to the stranger in their turn. The whole passage (Deuteronomy 10:14–21) is pure poetry and has a hymn-like quality about it appropriate to the injunction "He is thy praise, and he is thy God" (verse 21). It reminds us of the way in which the Psalmist treats of a similar theme in Psalm 8: "O LORD our Lord (*Adon*, our Lord and Master), how excellent is thy name in all the earth ... What is man, that thou art mindful of him?"

The promises to the patriarchs had already had a partial fulfilment in the increase of their seed. Jacob had recognised the goodness of the Lord in this regard when he said:

> "I am not worthy of the least of all the mercies, and of all the truth, which thou has shewed unto thy servant; for with my staff I passed over this Jordan; and now I am become two bands." (Genesis 32:10)

Now his descendants were about to pass once more over "this Jordan", and Moses could say:

> "Thy fathers went down into Egypt with threescore and ten persons; and now the Lord thy God hath made thee as the stars of heaven for multitude." (Deuteronomy 10:22)

"Your eyes have seen ..."

As in the Letter to the Hebrews, the pattern of Deuteronomy is built around the "Therefores", such as the one with which chapter 11 opens. The charge was all the more urgent because it was immediate: it was not to the generation to come, but to those who had seen the greatness of the Lord and known His chastisements. The mighty judgements had fallen upon Egypt and upon Israel alike when they had proved stiffnecked and rebellious.

There is a relevance in the one incident Moses refers to explicitly out of all that "he did unto you in the wilderness" (verse 5). The rebellion of Dathan and Abiram concerned the question of leadership. Though Korah the Levite is not referred to here, he challenged the right of Moses to intercede and of Aaron to exercise the priesthood, at the same time as the sons of Reuben were challenging their right to lead. All but the very young amongst Moses' hearers must have witnessed God's dramatic demonstration of who it was that He had chosen to be nigh unto Him.

The dramatic destruction of Korah, Dathan and Abiram, recalled by Moses out of all the incidents in the wilderness to reinforce his warnings and exhortation, had demonstrated the power of the Lord, the God of the covenant, as "Lord of Lords", the Disposer Supreme in all His creation (Numbers

16). For He had "made a new thing", or "created a creation" as the Hebrew has it, when the earth opened its mouth and the rebels went down alive into the pit.

The incident was so outstanding that when Peter alluded to it, in the context of the false prophets and teachers who deny "the Lord that bought them" and cause many to "follow their pernicious ways" (2 Peter 2:1–4), he passed by the usual words *Hades* or *Gehenna* in favour of a word unique in the New Testament: God "cast them down to *Tartarus*", that cavern underneath the earth which the Greeks believed was the specific area below ground reserved for the judgement of the wicked. It is even possible that the Greek legend derived from the historical Biblical event.

The "therefore" which follows the allusion to this incident, in Deuteronomy 11:8,9, has an even greater urgency than the preceding ones, if that were possible. Israel would only prolong their days in the Land which the Lord was giving them in fulfilment of His covenant with the fathers by their own observance of all the commandments.

The LORD and His land

The verses which follow present a remarkable picture of the Land of Promise. Some modern visitors find it difficult to recognise amongst the barren hillsides of Judea or the rocky caverns of the desert the "land that floweth with milk and honey". It must be remembered, however, that the desolation of the land was one of the curses laid upon the people for their disobedience, and that it was caused by the physical depredations of a succession of invaders. Even now where water can be made to flow, fruit and flowers spring out of the sandy ground, and during an exceptionally rainy period even hills around Jerusalem are tinged with green.

Egypt had been dependent upon artificial irrigation (verse 10). The ground had to be marked out with channels dug with the foot through which the water would flow. In the Land, however, the Israelites would not be dependent upon human techniques. The hills and valleys were natural irrigation channels which would enable the fertile soil to "drink water of the rain of heaven". Such favour was shown to it because it was "land which the LORD thy God careth for (Heb. *seeketh after*): the eyes of the LORD thy God are always upon it, from the beginning of the year even unto the end of the year" (verse 12).

Rejoicing in His works

It is an extraordinarily beautiful concept, that the Lord takes such delight in the things which He has made, and even more so that His loving care in sustaining His creation is equally for the benefit of man, the crowning glory of the work of His fingers. We are taught much in the Scriptures about man's responsibility for the dominion over the earth which God has given him and it is made very clear that the groaning and travailing in pain of creation (Romans 8) is inseparable from man's abuse of his privileges. The prosperity and desolation of the Land itself were reflections of Israel's obedience and disobedience. While their love of the Lord was full, with heart and soul, the joyful land would yield its increase. Its fruitfulness was not ultimately dependent upon man's labour, since if Israel obeyed the law of the sabbath year, then the uncultivated land would of itself produce more than enough (Leviticus 25:1–7).

For the disciple abundant lessons can be drawn from this exhortation, which are set out in principle in the Sermon on the Mount. There the Lord Jesus sets before us the beauty of the grass of the field which surpasses the glory of man's raiment because God clothes it, and the abundant provision made for the fowls of the air who neither sow nor reap; and concludes: "But seek ye first the kingdom of God, and his righteousness; and all these things shall be added unto you" (Matthew 6:25–33).

Christ said: "Ye cannot serve God and mammon". Those commentators are probably right who see the word *mammon* as a word from the same root as *amen*, "truth", but meaning man's *false* concept of truth, opposed to the Divine standard. God was "the God of truth" or "the God of *Amen*" (see Isaiah 65:16, RV margin) and in Christ "all the promises of God ... are yea, and in him *Amen*, unto the glory of God by us" (2 Corinthians 1:20). The worship and service of anything other than God, especially one's own wealth or talent, is the service of mammon; search for security by one's own efforts is covetousness, "which is idolatry" (Colossians 3:5). The counterpart of *mammon* in Israel were the idols, those "no-gods", or things of nought by which the people's heart could so easily be deceived, to make them turn aside. It would be a vicious circle. Their neglect of their God would cause heaven to be shut up. They would turn with all the more fervour to the fertility gods of the former inhabitants of the land, falling deeper into moral degradation and excess, and would ultimately perish from off the good land which the Lord gave them.

(o) Summary of the exposition of the commandments (11:18–25)

The farewell speech of Moses is, in a sense, completed in the concluding sections of this chapter. Indeed, the whole book has been set before us in condensed form, since chapters 12–25 are the detailed setting out of the principles already covered, in terms of the constitution of the Lord's kingdom and worship in the Land, while the remaining chapters are foreshadowed in 11:26–32.

Verses 18–25 are mainly repetition of material found earlier, although this repetition is not exact. The underlying message of the preceding chapters is gathered up and emphasised in a skilful peroration. The lessons of the past— the Exodus, the wilderness and its temptations, the historic blunder of Kadesh, the provocations at Massah and Meribah—have been set forth to strengthen the warnings and encouragement for the future. It will not be necessary for us to cover the ground again, since the parallel references set out below will direct the reader to a fuller commentary should he seek one.

Verse 18 see 6:6,8
Verse 19 see 6:7; 4:9–10
Verse 20 see 6:9
Verse 21 see 6:21; 4:40
Verse 22 see 6:17–20
Verse 23 see 4:38; 9:1,2
Verse 24 see 1:7,8
Verse 25 see 2:24,25; 7:23,24

If only Israel had hearkened to the voice of the Lord speaking through Moses then "there shall no man be able to stand before (them)" (verse 25).

(p) "A blessing and a curse" (11:26–32)

The words with which this section opens form a kind of a refrain to the detailed setting forth of the blessings and the curses described in chapters 28–30. There was an immediate application in the sense that Moses was quite literally setting the alternatives before them on that day. It was the day of decision, for they were to go forward on the basis of the choice they then made. There was also a future application (verses 29,30), for the statutes and judgements set forth in the intervening chapters would become the law of the Land, ratified by the people in a series of Amens after they had been written "very plainly" upon plastered stones on Mount Ebal. The blessings and the curses would be the sanctions whereby that law was enforced.

A more detailed comment on these Divine Sanctions can be reserved until we come to the relevant chapter. We can note here the precision of Moses' geographical location of the mountains of blessing and cursing. Looking westward from Jordan by Jericho it is possible, according to some travellers, to see "where the sun goeth down" between Ebal and Gerizim, lighting upon Shechem, where the Lord had said unto Abraham, "Unto thy seed will I give this land: and there builded he an altar unto the LORD, who appeared unto him" (Genesis 12:7). There would lie the bones of Joseph, carried from Egypt to his resting place in the Land; and there, by the oak tree which concealed the teraphim purged from the house of Jacob, the patriarch's descendants would put away the strange gods which were among them and incline their heart unto the Lord God of Israel (Genesis 35:2; Joshua 24:23).

We conclude this section and introduce the specific legislation of the next with a comment from *The New International Commentary*:

"The nature of the commandments emerges in a striking manner in verse 28: 'If you do not listen to the commandments ... and you turn aside from the way ...' Again it becomes clear that the commandments were not simply a body of legislation which was to be obeyed for its own sake. The commandments reflected a way of life, the good way of life which God determined for His people; therefore, to disobey (or *not listen to*) the commandments was to *turn aside from the way* that alone could lead to happiness and prosperity in relationship with God, and to take a false trail that could lead only to separation from God and disaster. Thus, in the exposition of the details of the law that follows, Moses' rôle was not that of a great legalist or jurist, but was that of a man deeply concerned that the people who were under his charge should enter into the fullness of life that was potential in the covenant relationship with God."

128

7

LAWS OF THE LAND AS THE SEAT OF THE LORD'S WORSHIP (12:1–16:17)

(a) "The place which the LORD your God shall choose" (12:1–32)

THE RELATIONSHIP between the *Torah*, the Divine teaching and "the statutes and judgments" which give it practical expression has already been discussed (Chapter 5). The Law sets forth the principle, the statutes define how the principle is to be carried out in a given set of circumstances. The complete destruction of idols, the places where they were worshipped and every cult object associated with them was the first practical step to be taken on the entry into the Land. The First and Second Commandments required wholehearted devotion to the Lord who had redeemed Israel. The *principle* underlying the commandments would be negated if, while not themselves making graven images to worship, they were still surrounded by those already made.

The approach to this question was to be entirely realistic. The weaknesses of human nature are fully recognised, for not only were the graven images to be destroyed with their temples, but even the nations which had practised idolatrous worship were to be destroyed. The command is repeated and re-emphasised in various forms in this part of the book, notably in 16:21,22, where the planting of a grove of trees near the altar of the Lord was expressly forbidden. Such groves were associated with idol-worship, although all the background of this cannot be discussed here. From the earliest times there was a certain sense of superstitious dread attached to such plantations as they were considered in the pagan mind to possess a kind of awesome divinity of their own. This was something vastly different from the reverential fear of the Lord, the Holy One of Israel.

We can gather some impression of the abhorrence in which the degrading and quite literally soul-destroying influences were held from 17:2–7. Anyone, man or woman "within thy gates", who *transgressed the Lord's covenant* by serving other gods, even if they were not the obscene idols of Canaan but "the sun, or moon, or any of the host of heaven", was to be stoned to death. "So shalt thou put away the evil from among you." From Paul in Romans 1 we learn the reason for such a command: by worshipping and serving the creature more than the Creator they would "turn the truth of God into a lie". The subsequent verses of this powerful chapter show that complete moral and ultimately physical destruction inevitably follows.

Verses 29–32 of our chapter in Deuteronomy offer a further solemn warning. Even when the symbols of idolatry and its adherents had been completely destroyed, the danger was not past:

"When the LORD thy God shall cut off the nations before thee, whither thou goest to possess them, and thou succeedest them, and dwellest in their land; *take heed to thyself that thou be not snared* by following them, after that they be destroyed from before thee; and that thou enquire not after their gods, saying, How did these nations serve their gods? even so will I do likewise. Thou shalt not do so unto the LORD thy God: for every abomination to the LORD, which he hateth, have they done unto their gods; for even their sons and their daughters they have burnt in the fire to their gods."

The word "snared" is important. The word or its equivalent occurs many times in connection with the idols of Canaan especially in Joshua and Judges (see also Exodus 23:33; 34:12). The possibility that after the destruction of the very nations who worshipped the idols there could be such a reaction that the Lord's people should themselves go after their idols seems remote—until we recognise the justice of the Scriptural assessment of human nature.

In the context of the present Deuteronomy passage it will be profitable for us to consider briefly the origin of sin and strive to understand the reason for the apostolic warnings against its "deceitfulness".

"As the serpent beguiled Eve ..."

Twice Paul refers to the first transgression as a "beguiling" or a deception (2 Corinthians 11 and 1 Timothy 2). The first of these passages makes it quite clear that the basis of the deception is the representation of something as being "other" than what it really is. Disciples, he maintains, could be misled by "another gospel", which turns out to be "not another (gospel)" at all (Galatians 1:6–9). They could receive "another Jesus, whom we have not preached", and be led astray by "false apostles, deceitful workers, transforming themselves into the apostles of Christ". In other words, wholly plausible reasons could be set forth for the pursuit of the *counterpart of the true* which retained certain elements either in name or profession or vocabulary of the truth which it counterfeits. It is easy to distinguish a £10 note from the dollar bill or the rand and all have their value. It is more difficult to recognise the counterfeit, which in any currency has none at all.

"And no marvel ..."

What then does Paul mean by adding, "And no marvel; for Satan himself is transformed into an angel of light"? No doubt there is a spiritual comparison between light and darkness, apostles and false apostles, messengers of the "good news" and those who lead into the way of death. But is there a closer connection with the words of Genesis 3 than we have realised?

For the *nachash*, or serpent of Eden, was apparently attractive in itself: it gleamed like bronze (copper or brass in the AV), the word for which is closely related to, sometimes identical with, the word *nachash*. The words for "enchantment" and "beguiling", and even "to learn by experience" (in a good sense, although it is by the hard way: see Genesis 30:27), are all derivatives of the same root idea. Without going into questions about the serpent's faculty of speech or whether it went upon its belly before, or as a result of the curse, it seems evident that the serpent did not become something to flee from until after the events described in Genesis 3. Surely then a creature such as this "which the LORD God had made" had something to offer? The "subtlety" (*arum*) of the serpent found a response in the man and his wife who were themselves *arum*, "naked", though not yet in a shameful or embarrassing sense.

"Yea, hath God said ...?"

We have in this account then, the facts out of which grew the symbolism of gold for the word of God and man's faith in it, bronze for flesh in its instincts and reasonings, and nakedness for the sin that needs to be covered. For sin is yielding to the attractiveness of the pleasurable and the determination to pursue it without reference to the purpose for which God has made all that is "good for food, pleasant to the eyes, and much to be desired to make one wise". The principle is neatly illustrated in a passage from Ezra: "... two vessels of fine copper ("shining *nachash*"), precious ("desirable") as gold" (8:27: see margin and a good concordance).

The attractiveness of the serpent's appearance as a *nachash*, bright and shining, its subtlety (*arum*) finding a response in the nakedness (*arum*), albeit innocent, of the man and his wife, the plausibility of its words so nearly indistinguishable from the words of God Himself, the curse it brought upon the ground, the man and woman and itself—all combine to make the serpent the very symbol of sin, deceitful, beguiling, yet with a sting that brought death. When the Apostle writes of "the deceitfulness of sin" it is to warn against the possibility of becoming "hardened" by it (Hebrews 3:13).

No wonder, then, that the Second Commandment should find its logical exposition in the destruction of all idolatrous symbols in the Land. For even if that were done, man's insatiable thirst for knowledge other than the knowledge of God would ensnare Israel as it had beguiled Eve. The forbidden tree in the garden, "much to be desired to make one wise", would be replaced by the remnants of a former culture, "fashioned by art and man's device", which would prompt an updated version, as it were, of the serpent's question: "How did these nations serve their gods?"; to be followed inevitably by *"Even so will I do likewise"* (Deuteronomy 12:29,30).

The testimony of Israel's history

The solemn truth behind the warning is amply illustrated by the history of Israel in the Land, both immediately after the death of Joshua and in the times of the Judges and the Kings. If there could have been a danger that they would be ensnared even *"after* that they be destroyed from before thee"*, in how much greater peril must Israel have stood when the destruction was not after all completed. The stratagem of the Gibeonites, itself an act of beguiling or ensnaring, ensured their own preservation and had far-reaching consequences for Israel. The leaders, including Joshua, "asked not counsel at the mouth of the LORD". Like the affair at Kadesh, the incident marked a crisis in Israel's affairs since it signified their failure to complete the occupation of the Land (see Judges 2:20–23).

One classic illustration of the peril envisaged by Deuteronomy 12:30 is the case of Ahaz. He had travelled abroad to meet the king of Assyria in Damascus. He "saw an altar that was at Damascus: and king Ahaz sent to Urijah the priest the fashion of the altar, and the pattern of it, according to all the workmanship thereof. And Urijah the priest built an altar according to all that king Ahaz had sent from Damascus". Thus, as God had warned Moses, the worship of the Lord was displaced by a system more attractive to the king.

Lessons for the disciple

The disciple should take his lessons from all this. The sinful nature of the alternative worship, even in its grossest forms, was clearly not immediately obvious to minds insensitive to Divine requirements. Indeed, it seemed more suited to the needs of the worshipper—"relevant" is the modern term for this—concerned as it was with the fulfilment of natural functions, the satisfaction of fleshly appetites, and the fertility of the land.

There was, moreover, an intellectual, even aesthetic appeal, about some forms of idolatry. It was easy enough for Israel to rationalise the worshipping of *Baal-berith*, the Lord of the Covenant; it was attractive to worship through the medium of a culture linked with groves and streams, sun, moon and stars. Job himself, that servant of the Lord, "a perfect and an upright man, one that feareth God, and escheweth evil", makes a most revealing statement in chapter 31, which shows the nature of the restraint he had to impose upon himself:

"If I beheld the sun when it shined, or the moon walking in brightness; and my heart hath been secretly enticed, or my mouth hath kissed my hand: this also were an iniquity to be punished by the judge: for I should have denied the God that is above." (Job 31:26–28)

If it be objected that the twenty-first century disciple is not likely to be deceived by the grosser forms of idolatry prevalent in the time of Moses, then Romans 1 should be read again in conjunction with any daily newspaper, and the disciple should ask himself how many of the social, aesthetic or even economic values of modern society he has unconsciously absorbed. The rest of the chapter of Job is also helpful, since it links many other aspects of "the pride of life" with the secret idolatry he describes.

The Deuteronomy record is, therefore, entirely realistic, since it recognises the beguiling nature of "other-worship" and the way in which the seemingly innocent deviation becomes the abomination. The serpent of bronze in the wilderness had been Divinely appointed that the sin-stricken people should *look* to it with the eye of faith, recognise the nature of their transgression and be delivered. True to the instinct of human nature, however, they eventually ascribed divinity to the creature and burnt incense to it until the time when Hezekiah broke it in pieces, revealing the shining *nachash* for what it really was: *nehushtan*, a thing of brass (2 Kings 18:4). In this at least the commandment through Moses was carried out.

"Thou shalt not do so unto the LORD thy God: for every abomination to the LORD, which he hateth, have they done unto their gods; for even their sons and their daughters they have burnt in the fire to their gods. What thing soever I command you, observe to do it: thou shalt not add thereto, nor diminish from it." (Deuteronomy 12:31,32)

"Ye shall not do so unto the LORD your God" (12:4)

There was a positive side to the commandment to resist idolatry—a fact which should also offer guidance to the disciple. Life in the Truth is not simply an avoidance of that which is inconsistent with its practice: it is an active involvement in a life which leaves neither time nor inclination for purely worldly pursuits.

Pagan worship was closely associated with certain *places*—the high mountain or hill, or the luxuriant tree. Here were set up the altars and the poles, the *asherim* (a tree or wooden pole symbolising a fertility goddess) and the images of the gods. The systematic destruction of these places was a rejection of the false gods and the banishing of their name from the place, as well as a degrading of the locality. But since the Land was to become the seat of the Lord's worship, He would appoint the place where it was to be practised. The singular "place" in verse 5 is in significant contrast to the Canaanite "places", *every* high hill, under *every* green tree.

Subsequent history shows that the emphasis is to be laid upon the phrase "(the place) *which the LORD thy God shall choose*", since the actual location changed from time to time until God said of Zion: "This is my rest for ever: *here* will I dwell; for I have desired it". The Divine choice precluded the multiplication of sites and therefore the temptation to invest each of them with a special sanctity of its own. For to do this would almost inevitably result in the number of the objects of worship being multiplied as well.*

---

*See the interesting point made by Brother R Purkis that even the memorial stones set up at the passage of the Jordan might have been worshipped as idols later: *The Christadelphian*, December 1982, page 447.

It is important to note that, in the history of God's covenant up to the time when the Temple was built in Jerusalem, "the place" had always been where God was. In the Hebrew of Genesis 28:11 Jacob came to "*the* place" (not "a certain place" as in the AV text) where God confirmed with him the covenant with Abraham and Isaac. It was the place where Abraham had first built an altar and called upon the name of the Lord and the place to which he returned from Egypt, "unto the place where his tent had been at the beginning" (Genesis 12:8; 13:4). After the Temple itself became "idolised", that is, treated as an object of worship in itself and eventually destroyed, the mercy-seat would be found "wherever, Lord, Thy people meet …" This truth Stephen eloquently proclaimed in his speech when he traced the record of God's people at their worship from the time when "the God of glory appeared unto our father Abraham, when he was in Mesopotamia" up to the point when the Lord in glory appeared unto Stephen himself (Acts 7).

The commandment to bring all offerings to a place to be chosen by the Lord was also a promise to the people waiting to enter the Land. "There *shall* be a place", a place for the rejoicing before the Lord which a loyal obedience on their part and a generous blessing on the Lord's would bring (Deuteronomy 12:7,12). They were thus encouraged to look beyond the conquest which was the necessary prelude to inheritance, for they would be unable to fulfil the commandment while campaigning. They were also to put behind them the memory of the wilderness where they had done "every man whatsoever is right in his own eyes" (verse 8). For with the inheritance would come rest. They had every incentive, therefore, to "take heed to thyself that thou offer not thy burnt offerings in every place that thou seest" (verse 13). For even legitimate offerings could not be made in illegitimate places.

"Whatsoever thy soul lusteth after"
There was a recognition made both of human needs and the future development of the nation. To eat of the blessing which the Lord their God had given them in the increase of their cattle could prove impracticable if the place chosen by the Lord was too far away, as it would certainly become "when the LORD thy God shall enlarge thy border" (verses 15,20,21). Moreover there were many animals such as the gazelle and the roebuck which could lawfully be eaten as clean beasts but could not be offered in sacrifice. Sacrificial animals of the herd and the flock could also be eaten in "secular" use. So the

regulation to eat at the sanctuary covered only those things which properly belonged to the Lord in sacrifice, the tithes of all increase, or that which was to be eaten as part of an offering as such.

But surely we cannot fail to draw a lesson from the discipline imposed upon the eating for food and not for sacrifice. "Secular" it might be, but it was sanctified by an act of obedience which recognised the Lord as the Giver of "life and breath and all things". The blood of the sacrifices was poured out before the Lord and *so was the blood of all flesh wherever it was eaten.* So even the family meal was "before the Lord" and the act of restraint afforded the opportunity to bless Him for His goodness while showing forth the principle of sacrifice: "for the life thereof is in the blood".

So today God's people everywhere partake of their food not as they that fly upon the spoil, but after sanctifying it by giving thanks.

The themes of the Land as the seat of the worship of the Lord and of "the place" which He was to choose figure prominently in this section of the Book of Deuteronomy (chapters 12–16) and there are further references to it in later chapters. Since we are not offering a detailed study of the book itself but rather of its principles for the present-day believer's guidance, we can briefly consider these references here.

In chapter 14 there is a reminder about what may and may not be eaten, with a repetition of the command to bring all that belonged unto God and eat it "before the LORD thy God, in the place which he shall choose to place his name there" (verse 23). There is a concession to practicality made here, however, for it would be difficult to drive animals a long way or transport firstfruits over mountainous terrain. The people were then permitted to turn their offering into money and buy their sacrificial meat at "the place". This permission if anything emphasised the importance of offering only before the Lord.

"Year by year before the LORD"

The commandment is repeated in connection with the redemption of the firstborn and the year of release, both commemorations of the deliverance from Egypt (15:19–20), and of course in connection with the three great feasts, when "Three times in a year shall all thy males appear before the LORD thy God in the place which he shall choose" (16:16). So important was the positive command to avoid all association with the former idolatry of the Land that the place of God's choice is referred to no less than six times in this chapter. Significantly it closes with this solemn warning:

"Thou shalt not plant thee a grove of any trees near unto the altar of the LORD thy God, which thou shalt make thee. Neither shalt thou set thee up any image; which the LORD thy God hateth." (Deuteronomy 16:21–22)

The remaining references (chapters 17, 18, 26 and 31) deal with justice, service in the sanctuary, the firstfruits, and the reading of the Law.

(b) "If there arise among you a prophet" (13:1–18)

We might have thought the commandments of the preceding chapter to be far-reaching enough. There was, however, yet another eventuality to be guarded against, one more subtle and therefore more dangerous. We may link with a consideration of this chapter part of chapter 18 which deals with the ministry of the prophets in a different context, but sets forth principles relevant to our immediate discussion. And if there be any who believe that the warnings against idolatry of the previous section are too strong for our contemporary situation then they must surely admit that both the Lord himself and his apostles uttered warnings to the first century ecclesias based upon the very theme of chapter 13.

The ministry of the prophets

The ministry of the prophets was in effect established at Sinai (see page 69), at the request of the people themselves. Unable to endure "the voice of the living God speaking out of the midst of the fire", they pleaded that Moses should act as a mediator and tell them all that God had said to him. Thenceforth they heard the voice of God no more, but Moses spoke all His words unto them. His prophesying was a "speaking forth on God's behalf", as the word implies. In the nature of things the words of Him who knows the end from the beginning involved "foretelling" as well as "forthtelling", and the Book of Deuteronomy contains abundant examples of both.

In chapter 18 is described the prophetic succession from Moses up to the coming of "that prophet", the Word of God made flesh who spoke only the words which his Father had given him to speak. The words of verses 15–22 make it clear that it is this succession which is in question here. The

137

prophet was to arise "from among their brethren", as the record shows was always the case. Angels might speak to individuals but the people heard only the voice of the prophets. The phrase "from among their brethren" had therefore a dual application and found its complete fulfilment in him who was "born of a woman, born under the law".

The prophet would speak only by commandment. There were times when there was no "open vision" and the Lord remained silent. Any who claimed to speak in the name of the Lord went in danger of his life if his claim was proved to be presumptuous. The message was to be clear and unambiguous. Whether revealed in "open vision" or by dream or oracle, the people were to be left in no doubt what the Lord had said. To seek for a mystic experience through divination, enchantment, charms or wizardry was an idolatrous practice, "an abomination unto the LORD: and because of these abominations the LORD thy God doth drive (the nations) out from before thee" (18:9–14).

The false prophet

So powerful would be the pull of idolatry, however, and so ready the people to receive the unusual with delight, that clear evidence had to be given that the word spoken by the prophets was indeed of God. In chapter 18 the emphasis is laid upon the quality of "foretelling" as a guarantee of authenticity:

"When a prophet speaketh in the name of the LORD, if the thing follow not, nor come to pass, that is the thing which the LORD hath not spoken, but the prophet hath spoken it presumptuously: thou shalt not be afraid of him."

There is an outstanding example of true and false prophecy in this category in the case of Hananiah (Jeremiah 28). He prophesied "smooth things", the swift return to Jerusalem of the king and the temple furniture which Nebuchadnezzar had taken to Babylon. This, he categorically proclaimed, was the word of the Lord. Jeremiah, on the other hand, while personally anxious for such a happy outcome (verse 6), charged Hananiah with dangerous falsehood, making the people to trust in a lie. The presumptuous prophet would die within the year as the penalty for his misleading words (verses 16,17; see Deuteronomy 18:20). The fulfilment of Jeremiah's prophecy should have given the people a signal demonstration that the Lord had indeed spoken through him.

The people could be exposed to an even more subtle danger, however—a prophet who seemed to have the power to do signs and wonders, even speaking words that came to pass. Was a miracle the only sign of authenticity? What was the final proof that the Lord had spoken? These questions are answered in chapter 13.

A sign or a wonder

With such an important matter as the word of the Lord, it was right that anyone claiming to speak in His name should give evidence of his authority in "a sign or a wonder." This would involve a proof that he possessed knowledge or power which he could not display of himself, such as a prediction or similar evidence of prophetic insight, or a "miracle" in the stricter sense of control over the laws of nature. All these signs were displayed by a prophet like Elisha, who "saw" the invisible chariots of fire which camped around him and his servant, made iron float, and foretold the lifting of the siege of Samaria by the Syrians.

In the case of some so-called predictions, or "signs and wonders", there could be the possibility of coincidence or illusion. The Delphic oracle in Greece, for example, maintained its reputation for infallibility for centuries by the simple device of the riddling response, which the enquirer interpreted according to his own whim. When the Persian king, Xerxes the Great, consulted it on the eve of his invasion of Greece in 480 BC, the "inspired gibberish" of the drugged prophetess was translated by the attendant priests (for a fee) as: "The day you set foot in Europe a mighty empire will fall." The king, already determined on his course, accepted the omen as predicting his own victory over the Athenian maritime empire. He was sadly disillusioned when he returned home with his mighty forces shattered.

The finger of God

In Egypt some of the very signs which the Lord had given Moses to perform before Pharaoh as evidence of his mission to deliver Israel from their bondage to the king, were reproduced so exactly by the magicians with their enchantments that the king refused to recognise the Lord's authority. The nature of the illusions—rods becoming serpents, the calling forth of frogs from the Nile and turning water into blood—is beyond our power to explain. Yet the Scripture soberly records that they were performed. The actual creation of life, even of the simplest form, however, was beyond the scope of illusion. When the dust of the land became lice throughout all the land of Egypt, the magicians were the first to confess, *"This is the finger of God"*.

We have to accept that there are more things in heaven and earth than we can expect to yield to our limited faculties of reasoning. The Lord Jesus made it clear that "great signs and wonders" of a certain type can be displayed by false prophets, who can wield a dangerous power to deceive (Matthew 7:22; 24:24). Since they would, *if it were possible*, deceive the very elect, we must ask, How then do the elect avoid deception? What defence have they against the false prophet? The answer is clearly set out in Deuteronomy 13. The content of his message was to be tested against the known, authoritative word of the Lord.

The people of Israel were forbidden outright to listen to a prophet, whatever device he used to attempt to validate his words, if his message was:

"Let us go after other gods, which thou hast not known, and let us serve them." (verse 2)

We can assume that "which thou hast not known" is the Lord's parenthesis, not part of the prophet's words, blatant though the rest of them are. No prophet of God could speak words which so flatly contradicted the First Commandment and the command to love the Lord with all the heart, soul and strength. The seriousness of the prophet's crime, for which death was the only possible penalty, is brought out in the contrast of verse 5:

"He hath spoken to *turn you away* from the LORD your God, which *brought you out* of the land of Egypt, and *redeemed you* out of the house of bondage, to *thrust thee out of the way* which the LORD thy God commanded thee to *walk in.*"

A curse upon the disobedient

The false prophet taught *faithlessness* towards the *faithful* God, and *ingratitude* towards the Lord of the covenant who had delivered them from slavery. If he were to achieve his aim then the curse of God proclaimed in 11:28 would fall summarily upon the whole people who had been deceived. So the severe penalty upon the prophet was decreed that they might "put away the evil" from their midst.

The rest of chapter 13 develops the theme of apostasy in different cases. Instead of the public declaration of the false prophet and the equally open response of the people, temptation could arise within the immediate family or the circle of close friends (verses 6–11). Here would be no sign or wonder, but a more secret enticement rendered all the more subtle because of family ties or the intimacy of the marriage relationship. There would be an added psychological pressure in such a temptation. We can deduce from Genesis 3 that it was because Eve offered the forbidden fruit to her husband that Adam consented to follow her in disobedience.

As in verse 2 there is the Lord's parenthesis—"which thou hast not known, thou, nor thy fathers". Had this been part of the deceiver's words the force of them would have been diminished for all except the hardened rebel. God is emphasising that the proffered blandishments are entirely contrary to the faith of the fathers and the faith of the Israelites themselves hitherto.

Once again the magnitude of the peril is matched by the severity of the penalty. To carry it out would be a dreadful experience for all concerned. It is spelt out in fuller form than the punishment of the false prophet, as though to leave no loophole for evasion, especially on the part of the person who would naturally shrink from causing the death of one close to him. Not only was he forbidden to conceal the matter, however, but "thine hand shall be first upon him to put him to death"! It is difficult to over-emphasise the horror with which the attempt to *thrust* others *away* from the Lord was to be regarded.

The apostate city
In verses 12–18 a similar situation is envisaged, but on a larger scale, in the apostate city. It is pointed out that the cities in the land would be part of the Lord's gift to His people. All the more tragic, then, that one of those cities should turn their backs upon Him at the instigation of "men of Belial".

Here we have no private apostasy but what amounts to an urban revolution, since such a falling away was a violation of the constitution of the Lord's land, as well as an act of faithlessness and ingratitude. The character of the nation— its *ethos*—as well as its very existence was threatened by such behaviour and it was to be treated with the same summary destruction as that commanded for the cities of the Canaanites whom God was driving out before them. There is a close parallel between the instruction to destroy Jericho and the fate pronounced upon the rebellious Israelite city. The purpose was the same:

"There shall cleave nought of the cursed thing to thine hand: that the LORD may turn from the fierceness of his anger, and shew thee mercy, and have compassion upon thee, and multiply thee, as he hath sworn unto thy fathers;

141

when thou shalt hearken to the voice of the LORD thy God
..." (13:17)

A brief comparison of these verses with 2:33–36 reveals the surprising fact that the apostate Israelite city was to be treated with greater severity than the cities of Sihon the Amorite, where the cattle and the spoil were not given over to destruction. The dangers of deception for the twenty-first century disciple are no less subtle nor the consequences less severe. It was of those who would be living in the days of his coming that Jesus spoke when he warned against the false prophets who would deceive, if it were possible, the very elect. It is the capacity to resist the deception and continue grounded and settled in the faith once delivered to the saints which distinguishes the elect: it is not possible for those who take their stand firmly upon the word of the Lord to be deceived in such a way.

"The God within"

The word is their "sign and wonder" in an age when others seek their guidance either through the subjective experience, like the Greeks who followed the dictates of human reason and worshipped "the god within", or with an increasing interest in the occult and other evil practices. Isaiah in effect provides a commentary upon Deuteronomy and gives guidance for our times in a chapter which offers comfort to them that fear the Lord and threatens judgement upon those who turn aside to idols:

"Sanctify the LORD of hosts himself; and let him be your fear, and let him be your dread. And he shall be for a sanctuary; but for a stone of stumbling and for a rock of offence to both the houses of Israel ... Bind up the testimony, seal the law among my disciples. And I will wait upon the LORD, that hideth his face from Jacob, and I will look for him. Behold, I and the children whom the LORD hath given me are *for signs and wonders* in Israel from the LORD of hosts, which dwelleth in mount Zion. And when they shall say unto you, Seek unto them that have familiar spirits, and unto wizards that peep and that mutter: should not a people seek unto their God? on behalf of the living should they seek unto the dead? (RV). To the law and to the testimony: if they speak not according to this word, it is because there is no light in them."

(Isaiah 8:13–20)

To this we may add the words of Peter in his Second Epistle. In the first chapter the apostle exhorts to "diligence to make your calling and election sure". To this end Peter does not neglect to repeat what the disciples already well knew and also to commit it to writing, so that they could hold fast to the faith after his death. In following his teaching they would be delivered from the "cunningly devised fables" that were prevalent even alongside the apostolic witness of the first century.

Eyewitnesses

Peter, however, with James and John, had heard the Voice from heaven, as it had been heard so long ago at Sinai. To them it proclaimed the authority of "the prophet like unto Moses", God's only begotten Son: *"Hear him"*. They had been eyewitnesses of his majesty, both in the healing powers he had displayed as proof of his Messiahship and on the Mount of Transfiguration. (The word for "mighty power" attributed in Luke 9:43 to the healing of the child at the foot of the Mount, is the same as that for "majesty" in 2 Peter 1:16.) By this experience the three apostles had had "the word of prophecy made more sure" (verse 19, RV), for its authors were not speaking of themselves but by the Holy Spirit sent from heaven in the same manner as the Voice had come. (The "came" of verse 18 is the same verb as "were moved" in verse 21).

Then comes the warning:

"But there were false prophets also among the people, *even as there shall be false teachers among you*, who privily shall bring in damnable heresies, *even denying the Lord that bought them*, and bring upon themselves swift destruction. And many shall follow their pernicious ways; by reason of whom the way of truth shall be evil spoken of." (2 Peter 2:1,2)

The perils of losing the faith in the last days may not seem at first sight to be so great as those set before the people in the Land. Between the civilisation of the early twenty-first century and the idolatrous culture of Canaan there would seem to be a great gulf fixed. We recall readers once more (with no apology for our repetitions, since they follow the pattern of the Book of Deuteronomy itself) to Romans 1, and point out that belief and conduct are linked together. When a man changes his beliefs he changes his behaviour, and any age in which the truth of God is changed into a lie will be given over to idolatrous practices in one form or another. The Brotherhood would change its character as completely as did Israel if it were to lose its hold upon the faith which is our hope.

143

It is right, therefore, that we should follow the commandment to teach the word of the Lord and His way diligently unto our children, to insist upon it as the basis of acceptability for membership and to proclaim the apostolic teaching that acceptable marriages should be "only in the Lord". Where they are not "in the Lord", and at least one member of the family remains uncommitted to the standards of the Truth, there follows the grave risk that other values and standards will be accepted within the household.

(c) "Thou art a holy people to the LORD thy God" (14:1–29)

In Deuteronomy 1:31 the Lord's care and compassion for His people in leading them through the wilderness is likened to the love of a man for his son. Israel's response to the Lord's tenderness should therefore have been that of obedient children to their father. As children of the Lord their God the people were to be holy as He is holy. Chapter 14 sets out some of the practical aspects of that holiness. We shall not discuss these instructions in detail in these pages, since we are concerned with the underlying principles which it is the duty of the disciples of Christ to show forth in their own daily lives.

Most of the regulations were set out in Leviticus, "the book of holiness", but are repeated since they are to become part of the constitution of the Lord's own land. They teach us that while holiness is a matter of separation in heart and mind from the surrounding world while we continue to live in it, there are outward standards of personal dignity and cleanliness to be kept, proprieties to be observed and acts of compassion to be performed.

Deliberately to disfigure the body fashioned by God was forbidden, even though it were done under the influence of grief. The reason given (14:2) is that such restraint was proper in a people chosen by the Lord for His own, who should therefore be distinctive in their habits among "all the nations that are upon the earth". We are not necessarily to assume that in our day the disciple is prohibited from following any of the mourning customs of our own time, especially where they are dictated by decency and decorum. The simplicity of the Truth and the very nature of our hope, of course, forbids ostentation or empty ceremony and certainly disfigurement.

For the Israelites the prohibition was in fact linked with the First and Second Commandments. Disfigurement and the pouring of one's blood upon the ground were connected with certain fertility rites and a cult of the dead, and so were idolatrous practices. Isaiah referred to the practice of the living consulting the dead in the verses quoted above from chapter 8. In 1 Kings 18 Elijah called mockingly to the prophets of Baal, the fertility god, to make him hear them: "And they cried aloud, and *cut themselves after their manner* with knives and lancets, till the blood gushed out upon them."

Laws of eating

The rest of this chapter deals with

Clean and unclean animals (verses 3–8)

Clean and unclean fish (verses 9,10)

Clean and unclean birds (verses 11–20)

Dead creatures (verse 21)

Cooking a kid (verse 21)

Tithes: where they could be eaten (verses 22–27)

The tithe of the third year (verses 28,29).

There were undoubtedly good dietary and sanitary reasons for many of the prohibitions. The overriding principle, however, was what the Lord commanded. He alone declared what was clean and what unclean in this connection as Peter, in his vision described in Acts 10:14,15, was forcibly reminded.

We may add a word or two on the principle of the laws concerning foods outlined above.

Undoubtedly a holy people will pay attention to the health of the body which God has given them. Likewise the disciple will abstain from defiling habits which either render his body unclean or dull his senses so that his spiritual and moral judgements are impaired. We may classify amongst such habits those which pollute the mind as well as impair the physical health, bearing in mind the Lord's own reminder that evil thoughts retained in the heart are the equivalent of the evil deeds they contemplate.

Meats clean and unclean

We may be sure, therefore, that the prohibitions of Deuteronomy 14 were health-giving and sanitary in themselves, but the overriding principle was what the Lord commanded.

In *The Law of Moses*, chapter XXIX, Brother Robert Roberts searched for the underlying symbolism of the regulations concerning clean and unclean meats which are set out at greater length in Leviticus 11, and he drew some interesting lessons for our instruction. His main thesis was that since the dead body, the carrion eaters, the serpentine and that which arouses instinctive abhorrence were to be avoided and the ruminants and the sure-footed could be eaten, they all represented types of men who were either abhorrent or pleasing to God, and whose fellowship therefore should be avoided or sought after by the man of God. Eating is, of course, a process of assimilation, and finds its highest figurative expression in the words of the Lord Jesus in John 6. What he gave for the life of the world was himself—the bread of life—and the men who allowed the thoughts and deeds of the Lord to become part of themselves would live for ever.

It is our personal conviction that the line taken in *The Law of Moses* is worthy of our attention, especially in the light of Peter's vision. It was designed to convince him, by means of God's cleansing of animals for food, that he should not consider Gentiles like Cornelius and his household unclean either. For Cornelius was "a devout man, and one that feared God with all his house, which gave much alms to the people, and prayed to God alway". The principle is Scripturally sound, therefore, that those given to meditation on the things of God will walk more closely in His ways, and that "he that walketh wisely walketh surely".

On the other hand, we must not be deceived: "Evil communications corrupt good manners", or, "Do not be misled: 'Bad company corrupts good character'" (1 Corinthians 15:33, JBP). It is all of a piece with the prohibition against idol worship and fellowship with those who take part in it. For the Lord's own summary of the commandment under consideration was:

"Thou shalt not eat any *abominable thing*."

(Deuteronomy 14:3)

The word "abominable" is the same as that used for the idols and idolatrous practices which were "an abomination unto the LORD". The prohibitions, therefore, go beyond the simple question of dietary laws as such, and refer to the association of the proscribed foods with foreign religions. We have a link with this idea in Romans 14 and 1 Corinthians 8, where the brethren were faced with serious problems connected with the eating of meat.

"With conscience of the idol"

Meat offered for sale in the market at Corinth had often been used for sacrificial purposes and then sold to the dealers, either by the priests, who received a large share of the sacrifices for themselves, or by the worshipper out of the surplus of his own portion. It was not necessarily "unclean" in the sense that it came from one of the prohibited animals: it could be venison or some other permissible meat. The disciple, however, was faced with the question of conscience, since it had been offered unto a pagan idol. The meat itself was "clean" for, said Paul,

"I know, and am persuaded by the Lord Jesus, that there is nothing unclean of itself." (Romans 14:14)

As he said to Timothy:

"Every creature of God is good, and nothing to be refused, if it be received with thanksgiving: *for it is sanctified by the word of God and prayer.*"

(1 Timothy 4:4,5)

Conscience and offence

By comparing verses 14–22 of 1 Corinthians 10 with verses 23–31, it is evident that for the Apostle Paul the issue was one of "spirituality" versus "legality". The question of whether a man was defiled or not was settled in his own heart and conscience. Not all meat sold in the market at Corinth had been offered to idols and a brother was not under obligation to enquire more closely. If by eating it he gave offence, however—which in its Scriptural context means led his weaker brother into sin (see 1 Corinthians 8)—then he should refrain.

From verse 30 we understand that Paul does not have in mind those who claim to be of "strong principle" and manifest it by harshly criticising their brethren and sisters for doing what they have no inclination or opportunity to do themselves. As he himself says:

"For if I by grace (or, with thanksgiving) be a partaker, why am I evil spoken of for that for which I give thanks?"

(1 Corinthians 10:30)

Critics of this type are not likely to be led astray by their brother's behaviour, unless it be further into the sin of judging unrighteously. It is not the "strong" but the weak brother whose conscience we have to consider, and harsh critics would rarely admit to having a weak conscience.

147

Remarkably, the reasons given for exercising one's freedom of conscience to eat with thanksgiving *and* for practising self-discipline for the sake of one's brother are exactly the same: "The earth is the Lord's, and the fulness thereof."
(verse 26)
The Lord created all things to be received with thanksgiving; it is the same Lord who redeemed our brother through the precious blood of His Son. How then can we contemplate doing anything to destroy him "for whom Christ died" (Romans 14:15; 1 Corinthians 8:11)? To eat what God has graciously provided and to abstain from eating for the sake of another's salvation are both alike acts of worship and thankfulness.

There was another aspect of the Apostle's code for disciples in this matter, which arises directly from what we are considering in Deuteronomy. The Jews have always been strictly conscientious in following their dietary code. The case of Peter is an illustration and we may cite also the experience of the prophet Ezekiel. He felt genuine horror at the command to prepare defiled bread to eat as a parable of the straitness of the famine that would come upon the people of Jerusalem in the impending siege. It is noteworthy that the Lord had compassion on His servant and modified His instructions to spare His prophet some of his distress (Ezekiel 4:14,15).

At the same table

Paul's advice to the Romans and Corinthians was in the spirit of that given by the apostles at the council in Jerusalem when the delicate question of "table fellowship" with the Gentiles arose. It is clear that Paul had the same problem in his mind when discussing the whole question of relationships and causes of offence in the ecclesias. The Letter to the Romans is a deep theological discussion of the relationship between the Law and salvation—"to the Jew first, and also to the Greek". It led to the practical advice on personal and social responsibilities in chapters 12–15. The chapter in Corinthians which we have considered concludes with:

"Give none offence, *neither to the Jews, nor to the Gentiles*, nor to the church of God." (1 Corinthians 10:32)

As a good Jew Paul himself kept the Law since it was the very basis of the Jewish national life in which he had been brought up. Indeed, the issue was not on whether the Law was valid as a code of behaviour for Israel but on whether a man's righteousness (and therefore his salvation) depended upon his keeping it. Towards the end of his life Paul could still thank God as Him "whom I serve *from my forefathers with a pure conscience*" (2 Timothy 1:3). Jewish disciples, however, were not to seek to impose upon their Gentile brethren the burden of keeping the Law. The wise apostles in Jerusalem nevertheless laid upon them "these *necessary* things; that ye abstain from meats offered to idols, and from blood, and from things strangled, and from fornication" (Acts 15:28,29). From then on, with a clear conscience, Jews could sit at the same table with Gentiles in fellowship. How wise a provision, then, that the communion of the body and blood of Christ should be by the simple partaking of bread and wine together, and not of some more elaborate but potentially more controversial feast.

A modern counterpart

The same careful, spiritual sensitivity ought to be exercised in all matters of corporate life today, but perhaps the experience of brethren and sisters who have served overseas with the Bible Missions serves to highlight the need for it. They have sometimes found it both expedient and helpful to take account of the cultural and social background of their work. The Truth is never to be compromised or concessions made to superstition; nevertheless the spirit of fellowship can be fostered and the work of preaching unhindered if certain things are taken account of. For example, if an African brother invites a European brother to his home for a meal he may sometimes offer him the supreme courtesy of preparing and serving it, and then with his family retiring from the room to leave his brother to dine alone. To protest could cause at best embarrassment, at worst a sense of hurt. But when the African is invited home in his turn, he will gladly accept his brother's courtesy to him and sit with him at his table — as of course they will do for the Breaking of Bread.

It is worth noting here, perhaps, that in some societies the use of the left hand in the partaking of food is strictly avoided. Although in European society "we have no such custom", for others it is not a matter of superstition but a custom based upon hygiene, and it gives less offence to avoid the practice in such company for fear of creating misunderstanding.

Before leaving the section on clean and unclean foods in Deuteronomy two other points call for comment. In 14:21 we see repeated the prohibition against seething a kid in its mother's milk (see also Exodus 23:19; 34:26). This law is interpreted as forbidding the eating of meat and dairy products at the same meal, and is rigidly observed in orthodox homes, and in kosher restaurants and kibbutzim in Israel, where there are usually two distinct sections with entirely separate menus.

We still retain vivid (and happy) memories of a young Jewish student who occupied an adjacent pitch in a camp in Rome in 1963. He was "travelling light" as he hiked across Europe with all his camping equipment on his back. He nevertheless carried two complete sets of cooking utensils, since meat and milk dishes had to be prepared and handled separately. He also bore witness to his faith each morning as in all weathers he stood outside his sleeping tent, in which he could only lie down, to say his daily prayers.

A difficult passage

Various explanations of this law have been offered by the commentators, none of them entirely satisfactory. It has been suggested, without real foundation, that there was a pagan custom connected either with sacrifice or a fertility right which involved seething a kid in its mother's milk, and so the practice was rightly classified under the "abominable things" which the Lord hated.

Leaving aside the Rabbinical extrapolation which extends the prohibition to any combining of meat and dairy products, the strong inference from each of the three records is still that the kid was being prepared for food. Moreover, the practice is mentioned on each occasion in connection with the eating of the tithe of the increase of the flock (verse 21: there are no verse divisions in the original text). We think, therefore, that the most probable explanation is that the commandment is of the same type as the prohibition against slaughtering a cow and her calf or a ewe and her lamb on the same day (Leviticus 22:28), or the taking of a bird together with her young or her eggs in the nest (Deuteronomy 22:6). It is a law, therefore, against excess and also against callousness. If God takes thought for sparrows He teaches His people a respect for His creation, and "the merciful man doeth good to his own soul; but he that is cruel troubleth his own flesh" (Proverbs 11:17). To take the young with the mother implied also a greedy partaking of the richness of God's gifts, rather like the eating of the fat of the animal which should have been offered to God.

Learning to fear the Lord

The other point in this chapter concerns the eating of the tithes. Again it is a matter of the self-discipline in a holy people who rendered again unto the Lord for all His benefits. The Lord had given the increase, which was therefore especially His. It is important to realise, however, that the offering of the tithes envisaged here in verse 23, was in effect a sacrificial meal in which the priests and Levites took part, and the purpose of the commandment to eat it "in the place which the LORD thy God shall choose to place his name there" was "that thou mayest learn to fear the LORD thy God always".

That the offerings of the Lord were intended to be a delight to His people is evident from the generous provision of verses 24–26:

"And if the way be too long for thee, so that thou art not able to carry it ... then thou shalt turn it into money ... and thou shalt bestow that money *for whatsoever thy soul lusteth after*, for oxen, or for wine, or for strong drink, or *for whatsoever thy soul desireth* ... and thou shalt rejoice, thou, and thine household."

From verses 28,29, we learn that every three years the tithes were to be stored in one's own locality, to form a local "benevolent fund" for the needy or the Levite within their gates. It appears from Deuteronomy 26:12–15, however, that the people still went up to worship the Lord at the sanctuary, but on this occasion, since they brought no tithes, they were to confess before the Lord that:

"I have brought away the hallowed things out of my house, and also have given them unto *the Levite, and unto the stranger*, to *the fatherless, and to the widow*, according to all thy commandments which thou hast commanded me: I have not transgressed thy commandments, neither have I forgotten them: I have not eaten thereof in my mourning, neither have I taken away ought thereof for any unclean use, nor given ought thereof for the dead ... Look down from thy holy habitation, from heaven, and bless thy people Israel, and the land which thou hast given us."

Could anything be clearer or more expressive for disciples of the Lord Jesus? Let us look and see how many answers there are here to questions of social behaviour. On what principle do we eat, or abstain from eating? To what extent can we *enjoy ourselves*? What place should the "benevolent fund" occupy in our personal or ecclesial giving? What about

151

those outside the household of faith—"the stranger"? What overriding principle enables us to assess our behaviour in any given circumstance?

The standard of perfection

The answers may be summed up in one phrase, as they were for Israel: "Thou art an holy people unto the LORD thy God". Or as the Lord Jesus puts it: "Be ye therefore perfect, as your Father in heaven is perfect". And holiness and perfection in this context is a joyful dedication of oneself to the Father in work and recreation; in the enjoyment of all that we can genuinely offer thanks for, and so sanctify by the word of God and prayer; in realising "that in so labouring ye ought to support the weak, and to remember the words of the Lord Jesus, how he said, It is more blessed to give than to receive" (Acts 20:35).

(d) "Thou shalt remember that thou wast a bondman" (chapter 15)

The reference at the end of the 14th chapter to the fatherless and the widow and the three-yearly collection on their behalf naturally introduces the theme of the 15th: "At the end of every seven years thou shalt make a release". After two three-year periods the cycle was completed by the carrying out of this commandment relating to the seventh year.

The spirit of the law

Did this law mean that debts were cancelled altogether, or that they were not to be collected in the seventh year, but like the land were to "lie fallow" as it were? The argument for the second interpretation is that since there was no labour that year the poor man would have nothing with which to pay.

It is strongly implied in the text that the debts referred to are those of the poor man who had been forced to borrow of his brother, rather than those of the businessman borrowing capital. We adopt the first interpretation, therefore, as being more consistent with the promise that in the sixth year the land would yield so abundantly that there need be no fear of dearth or want in the seventh, or even in the eighth before the harvest. The poor man would have had the same increase as the rich man and their relative status would have been maintained even in the seventh year.

The people were warned against making the imminence of the release an excuse for not lending at all. We need not be detained by the apparent contradiction between verses 4 and 11. The Lord Jesus himself declared in effect that "the poor shall never cease out of the land" (see John 12:8). Their burden, however, will be made light if it is shared by their richer brethren. The AV margin yields an excellent understanding: "That which is thine with thy brother thine hand shall release *to the end that there be no poor among you*". The principle, which was to be one of the laws of the Land by which the Lord was worshipped, found its expression in the behaviour of the early church, when once more the Lord founded a holy nation, a peculiar people, "that ye should shew forth the praises of him who hath called you out of darkness into his marvellous light" (1 Peter 2:9). At that time:

> "All that believed were together, and had all things common; and sold their possessions and goods, and parted them to all men, *as every man had need* ... neither said any of them that ought of the things which he possessed was his own; but they had all things common."
>
> (Acts 2:44,45; 4:32)

Preaching and pastoral care

The same spirit lay behind all the apostolic preaching, as is evidenced by the conversation between Paul and James, Cephas and John, as recorded in Galatians 2. The brotherly agreement to divide the responsibility for preaching to Jew and Gentile among them was sealed with "the right hands of fellowship" and the exhortation: "Only they would that we should remember the poor; the same which I also was forward to do" (verses 9,10).

When the brethren at Jerusalem fell on hard times then "the great collection" was organised on their behalf, and Paul comments: "for if the Gentiles have been made partakers of their spiritual things, their duty is also to minister to them in carnal things" (Romans 15:27); and in the two whole chapters in 2 Corinthians which he devotes to this theme he describes it as "the fellowship of ministering to the saints". He reinforces his exhortation with a significant quotation from Exodus 16:18:

> "... that now at this time your abundance may be a supply for their want, that their abundance also may be a supply for your want: that there may be equality: as it is written, He that had gathered much had nothing over; and he that had gathered little had no lack."
>
> (2 Corinthians 8:14,15)

Thus are we all taught that in our diligent attention to the whole counsel of God we must so labour "to support the weak, and to remember the words of the Lord Jesus, how he said, It is more blessed to give than to receive" (Acts 20:35).

A similar principle operated in the case of the law of the release of bondmen (Deuteronomy 15:12–18). We are not dealing here with slavery in the usual sense of that word in the Ancient World, in which the individual was the *property* of a master. The Israelites were not forbidden to follow the practice in the case of Gentiles, particularly those taken in war. The Hebrew man or woman was bound in service to a master in discharge of a personal or family debt. It seems evident that it is not the sabbatical cycle which is in question here, but a period of six years from the date of entry into service.

The years of an hireling

From Isaiah 16:14 we learn that the usual period of service for a *hired* servant was three years. Hence the bondservant had been "worth a double hired servant" (Deuteronomy 15:8), and his dismissal was not to be grudging but generous. Nor was the servant to resume his freedom in a state of destitution, but well supplied by the liberality of a generous master.

Therein lay a deep spiritual significance: the people of the Lord would remember their own bondage in the land of Egypt and the generous provision made for their deliverance by the open hand of their God. The disciple too sees in his brethren and sisters those "for whom Christ died", and seeks at all times to deal with them gently in consequence. The Apostle sums it all up for us in the words:

"Remember them that are in bonds, *as bound with them*; and them which suffer adversity as *being yourselves also in the body*." (Hebrews 13:3)

There were servants, however, who had no wish to leave their master, and who said, "I will not go away from thee; because he loveth thee and thine house, because he is well with thee". After the ceremony of the piercing of the ear such a one became an *ebed olahm*, a "servant for ever" (Deuteronomy 15:17), a term incidentally of some dignity and importance in the master's household. Some have seen a reference to this in Psalm 40:6: "Mine ears hast thou opened (margin, digged)". The context is indeed the perpetual devotion of the Lord's servant to his Master's will, but the more satisfactory interpretation, and also the simplest, is to follow the AV text in the Psalm, which means that the servant's ears are open to the master's call.

We are on sure ground in our spiritual interpretation, however, for all disciples are bondservants of the Master, as John, James, Jude, Peter and Paul are proud to declare themselves in the salutations in some of their letters. Such disciples love their Master and his house, knowing that they are well with him: and to dwell in the house of the Lord for ever is all their salvation and all their desire.

The law of the firstling

The law of the firstling already alluded to in 12:6 and 14:23 is also linked with the deliverance from bondage, as we learn from Exodus 13:1ff:

> "And the LORD spake unto Moses, saying, Sanctify unto me all the firsborn, whatsoever openeth the womb among the children of Israel, both of man and of beast: it is mine … Remember this day, in which ye came out of Egypt …"

The children and certain animals were redeemed with a purchase price, the animals that could be used for food were eaten *"before the LORD thy God year by year in the place which the LORD shall choose"*. It is to be noted that the sanctification of the firstlings did not deprive the children of Israel of their use or enjoyment of them. The law demanded an act of consecration, whereby it was recognised that what they were enjoying was the Lord's and that their family life with its daily labour and its wealth was all dedicated to Him, not simply because He had given it in the first place, but because it was only through the great salvation He had wrought in Egypt that they were able to enter into the Land and their great possessions.

For us, however, there is more to it even than that. The *exodus* which the Lord Jesus accomplished at Jerusalem (Luke 9:31) delivered us from the bondage of corruption, a deliverance to be consummated in "the redemption of our body" (Romans 8:23). The best of our service and the stewardship of our goods is to be set apart for the Lord's work.

Yet like Israel of old we are permitted to enjoy the good gifts which are given us, all of which we can receive with thanksgiving and sanctify by the word of God and prayer (1 Timothy 4:4,5). We can even eat and drink in fellowship in the Lord's presence, with the prospect of the full realisation in the Kingdom of God. For God Himself illustrated the law of the firstling, if we may so speak with reverence, in that He first gave His firstborn, His beloved Son. Through him we live, being redeemed not by silver and gold, but by the precious blood of Christ, as of a lamb without blemish and without spot (1 Peter 1:18,19 with Deuteronomy 15:21). We must never underestimate the love of the Father in this gift of His only begotten Son.

(e) "In the place which the LORD thy God shall choose" (16:1–18)

The theme of the Land as the seat of the Lord's worship is brought to a fitting climax with the six references in chapter 16 to "the place which the LORD thy God shall choose".

The main topic of the chapter is the feasts of the Lord—Passover, Pentecost and Tabernacles, all of which were to be celebrated in the place in which the Lord would choose to put His Name. Their main purpose was once again joyous remembrance of their salvation in festivals linked to the rhythm of the year. The recurring seasons were themselves evidence that their God was One who kept covenant. For He had promised after the Flood that—

"While the earth remaineth, seedtime and harvest, and cold and heat, and summer and winter, and day and night shall not cease." (Genesis 8:22)

To this was joined the covenant with Israel themselves, as the prophet was to proclaim several hundred years later:

"If those ordinances depart from before me, saith the LORD, then the seed of Israel shall depart from being a nation before me for ever." (Jeremiah 31:36)

The weekly observance of the sabbath rest was designed to keep before the mind of the Lord's people the fact that the Lord of all creation was their God and that He had brought them nigh unto Him. In the wilderness they had before them the commandment to—

"remember the sabbath day, to keep it holy ... For in six days the LORD made heaven and earth, the sea, and all that in them is, and rested the seventh day: *wherefore* the LORD blessed the sabbath day, and hallowed it." (Exodus 20:8–11)

On the threshold of the Land, when they were about to enter into their inheritance they were to keep the sabbath—

"and remember that thou wast a servant in the land of Egypt, and that the LORD thy God brought thee out thence through a mighty hand and by a stretched out arm: *therefore* the LORD thy God commanded thee to keep the sabbath day." (Deuteronomy 5:12–15)

Rejoicing before the Lord

The hallowing of the sabbath was a remembrance within the family and the local community: in the three great festivals "all Israel", "the whole family which I brought up from the land of Egypt" (Amos 3:1), met together to celebrate what the Lord had done for them and in them. The details of these observances are set out in Numbers 28 and 29 and Leviticus 23, and it will be seen that they could only be carried out in the context of national life in the Land, while "the place" was still in existence. Once again, however, the principles are eternal.

In *The Law of Moses* Brother Robert Roberts offers suggestions for interpreting the symbolism of some of the details. He makes the helpful observation that "the year is a natural period, and the longest natural period in the life of man. His life is but a repetition of years. The year, therefore, would naturally stand as a symbol of his whole life. That 'once a year' certain things should be done was an intimation that the things signified stood related to his whole life, that is, that the will of God required these things in paramount recognition in the lives of those who would be acceptable to Him" (page 198).

It is important for us to remember that the rejoicing was "in the LORD", and He had said, "They shall not appear before the LORD empty (that is, empty-handed)". Out of the bountiful store with which they had been blessed (Deuteronomy 16:15) the people blessed in turn "the Levite, the stranger, the fatherless, and the widow". But there was always the remembrance of the need for forgiveness of sins, especially in the Day of Atonement which preceded the Feast of Tabernacles. They could enjoy the open-air holiday in the autumn sun to the full, in the knowledge that the Lord had accepted the contrition of their hearts presented through the High Priest, who had returned from His presence with the words:

> "The LORD bless thee, and keep thee:
> The LORD make his face shine upon thee,
>   and be gracious unto thee:
> The LORD lift up his countenance upon thee,
>   and give thee peace."

"We keep the memory adored"

We have no such rhythm of the year as a set pattern for our worship, and the weekly observance is a showing forth of the Lord's death and not a keeping of sabbath in the legal sense—we should in any case have "ceased from our own works" in all departments of our lives! Nevertheless from the calendar of events in ancient Israel we can learn much to guide and discipline our own worship.

There is strong evidence that the Feast of Weeks (Pentecost) began on the anniversary of the giving of the Law at Sinai, that is, with the actual founding of the nation. They left Egypt on the fifteenth of Abib and reached Sinai "in the third month" (Exodus 19:1); so at least 45 days elapsed before the third month began. It is not unreasonable to suppose therefore, that "In the third month"could signify somewhere in the first week of that month.

It is good therefore to realise that the basis of our own rejoicing in the Lord should be the salvation wrought for us in Christ's death and resurrection, the founding at Pentecost of "the holy nation, the royal priesthood" of which we are privileged members, and the fellowship of sharing in the blessings which our Father has showered upon us, as He supplies all our need.

8

LAWS OF THE LAND AS THE SEAT OF THE LORD'S KINGDOM (16:18—18:22)

(a) "Thou shalt not wrest judgment" (16:19)

THE REJOICING in the Law which the great feasts of the Lord encouraged emphasised the nature of Israel's unique privilege. If they would but serve the Lord their God with all their hearts then He would open the windows of heaven to rain blessings upon them. In the very rhythm of nature which formed the basis of their life they would see the faithfulness of the Lord of the covenant, confirmed in the ordinances of day and night. The discipline and restraints of the Law would be more than compensated for by the joy of their service: "for his commands are not grievous". So the Land itself was the seat of the worship of the Lord who was honoured in the acts of daily life, even the partaking of food. The focal point of the worship, where all Israel met together in worship as a nation, was "the place which the LORD thy God shall choose".

The kingdom of the Lord

In principle the distinction between Land as the seat of the worship and the Land as the seat the Kingdom did not exist. Israel were to be "a kingdom of priests, and an holy nation" (Exodus 19). The ideal will be realised when they "receive whom God appointed for their Prophet, Priest and King". The setting up of the kingdom in Israel was in fact a rejection of the Lord as King. Nevertheless, from the beginning He exercised His jurisdiction over the people in daily practice through men chosen as His representatives. While the section of Deuteronomy we now consider does not exclude reference to altar and sacrifice, it is mainly concerned with "civil" judgement and justice and the social order.

The local administration of justice was to be in the hands of the "judges and officers" which they should make "in all thy gates which the LORD thy God giveth thee, throughout thy tribes". "The officers" were presumably executives in the administration. There was nevertheless to be a central tribunal "in the place which the LORD thy God shall choose",

159

where difficult civil or criminal cases could be heard "between blood and blood, between plea and plea, and between stroke and stroke" (17:8–13). The word for "stroke" is also "plague", and therefore could refer to questions of ceremonial or other impurity and their cleansing, which had to be referred to the priest "at the door of the tabernacle". For a glimpse of the way in which these arrangements were put into practice later see 2 Chronicles 19:8–11. This arrangement would be an adaptation in their settlements in the Land of the organisation set up in the wilderness, as described in Deuteronomy 1:13–18 (pages 12–14). From Joshua 23:2 we see that the arrangement was well established in the Land by the time of Joshua's death. The principle in each case was evidently that the people "took wise men" and "made them judges", and the appointment was then ratified by the Lord, no doubt through the priests.

The priests and Levites were clearly closely associated with "the judge that shall be in those days", who was probably, or at any rate ideally, a priest or a Levite himself. This principle is reflected in the books of Judges and 1 Samuel. The judges of the Book of Judges were not in fact all Levites. The influence they exercised under the hand of God was over the local tribal area and sometimes its immediate neighbours, but not over all the people. They were outstanding characters among the judges of the type described in 16:18. Eli and Samuel, however, were examples of the judges referred to in 17:9. They served at Shiloh until the ark was taken away, and the latter went on circuit throughout all the tribes. "*All Israel* from Dan even to Beer-sheba knew that Samuel was established to be a prophet of the LORD ... and the word of Samuel came to all Israel" (1 Samuel 3:20–4:1). This arrangement continued until the establishment of the monarchy.

"I said, Ye are gods ..."

It is sometimes said that the title of *elohim*, or gods, was given to the judges as a mark of respect for their office. In practice the word is translated "judges" only in Exodus 21 and 22, where the RV has "God". The underlying principle, however, is that to come before Israel's judges and to come before God should have amounted to the same thing, if they were exercising their function according to the Law. For the Law they administered was God's, the people they judged were God's and they were to exercise judgment as God would do Himself. In short, the judges stood before Israel as the Lord's own representatives.

Their obligations were therefore strict:

"They shall judge the people with just judgment. Thou shalt not wrest judgment; thou shalt not respect persons, neither take a gift: for a gift doth blind the eyes of the wise, and pervert the words of the righteous. That which is altogether just shalt thou follow, that thou mayest live, and inherit the land which the LORD thy God giveth thee."
(Deuteronomy 16:18–20)

In Psalm 82 the judges are described as "gods", amongst whom God Himself stood to judge. That the term goes deeper than simply one of respect is made plain by the Lord Jesus' quotation from this Psalm in support of his own claim to be the Son of God:

"Is it not written in your law, I said, Ye are gods? If he called them gods, *unto whom the word of God came*, and the scripture cannot be broken; say ye of him, whom the Father hath sanctified, and sent into the world, Thou blasphemest; because I said, I am the Son of God?"
(John 10:34–36)

The Psalmist makes it plain that those who stood before Israel as representatives of the Lord had not manifested the attributes of His Name: "for the LORD your God is God of gods ... a mighty, and a terrible, which regardeth not persons, nor taketh reward: He doth execute the judgment of the fatherless and widow" (Deuteronomy 10:17,18). They had judged unjustly, accepted the persons of the wicked, failed to defend the poor and the fatherless or deliver the needy— Psalm 82:2–4 quotes directly from the Law. The Lord therefore pronounced His judgement upon them:

"I have said, Ye are gods;
And all of you are children of the most High.
But ye shall die like men, and fall like
one of the princes." (verses 6,7)

We have already drawn some parallels between the principle of leadership in Israel and in the twenty-first century ecclesia (pages 12–15). There is also a message for the individual disciple who seeks to be perfect as His heavenly Father is perfect. He will be no respecter of persons, and if he judges, which in the sense of passing judgement on others he must not do, but must nevertheless exercise discernment in matters of life and conduct, then he will "judge not according to the appearance, but judge righteous judgment" (John 7:24).

So shall we be the children of our Father which is in heaven (Matthew 5:45).

(b) "So shalt thou put the evil away from among you" (16:21—17:13)

Since the Kingdom was the Lord's it was a *theocracy*: its constitution was its religion, its religion was its constitution. There could therefore be no private religion, and 16:21,22 forbids it explicitly. Altars for local worship there could be, within the limits of the regulations for their construction and use (Exodus 20:24–26), but they were to be *altars to the Lord*. The principles of the Second Commandment were therefore expounded in terms of the law of the Land, and nothing that suggested or encouraged secret rites in a grove of trees or that could entice towards the abominations of the Canaanites could be allowed anywhere near the Lord's altar.

The subject has already been introduced in Deuteronomy 7:5 and 12:3, with a comment on pages 87 and 135. Israel after the spirit should be disciplined by the same principle, and remove from sight and mind all that can entice into sin— "which the LORD thy God hateth". At one Youth Gathering, in an earnest appeal to young people upon the theme "Wherewithal shall a young man cleanse his way?", the excellent point was made by the speaker that it would be profitable to place on the top of every television set, as a guide to the use of the switch, the following verses:

"O when wilt thou come unto me? I will walk within my house with a perfect heart. I will set no wicked thing before mine eyes: I hate the work of them that turn aside; it shall not cleave unto me ... Mine eyes shall be upon the faithful of the land, that they may dwell with me ... He that worketh deceit shall not dwell within my house: he that telleth lies shall not tarry in my sight."

(Psalm 101:2,3,6,7)

The law regulating the purity of things offered in sacrifice is to be found in greater detail in Leviticus 22. It finds its place here since the various topics dealt with in this section of Moses' discourse are all related to the holiness of the individual as a member of God's people, whether he be a petitioner, a judge or a priest. Only the best can be offered in sacrifice or service unto the Lord. Anything less would only widen the breach between the Lord and the offerer which He was graciously seeking to heal in accepting the offering.

"Offer it now unto thy governor"

A further connection of this law with the general theme of this section is suggested by reference to Malachi 1:6–8. If judges were neither to accept bribes nor respect persons, the people were equally forbidden to attempt to influence the course of their judgement by offering them gifts. Those who proffered gifts would know that their cause could never be advanced before a corrupt ruler if the gifts were defective. To offer him the good and reserve the bad for the Lord would be an act of gross disrespect to His Name. The possibility of such dishonour being done is evident from the prophet's words:

"Ye say, Wherein have we polluted thee? In that ye say, The table of the LORD is contemptible. And if ye offer the blind for sacrifice, is it not evil? and if ye offer the lame and the sick, is it not evil? *offer it now unto thy governor*; will he be pleased with thee, or accept thy person? saith the LORD of hosts."

The next section deals with what must surely be the hardest decision the individual first and then the people as a whole had to face. It bears a close relationship to matters which affect us in the ecclesias today and runs counter to the prevailing ecumenical and tolerant spirit of the times.

Where faith and behaviour are matters of opinion or personal preference then a community seeks to contain its unorthodox members. One thing the nation was forbidden to do was to harbour the private individual whose conduct was inconsistent with the foundation principles of the nation. For the worship of other gods, even if they were the things which God Himself had created, was a transgression of the First Commandment, and therefore *a breach of the covenant*: it was nothing less than "an abomination in the sight of the LORD". It must be remembered that such practices had *moral consequences*. The idolater was not simply misguided in his thinking: he had turned the truth of God into a lie and was given over to all kinds of depravity.

"At the mouth of two or three witnesses"

The law of the Land regulated the procedure to be followed. The knowledge of wickedness brought responsibility upon the witness, which went beyond the act of informing to participation in the carrying out of the sentence. The occasion could not be one of private vengeance, since at least two or three witnesses were necessary to establish the charge before the judges. If the charge were false then the informers would be guilty of murder in the death of their countryman.

The paramount crime of the Israelite community is dealt with in greater detail in the treatment of the apostate city or of the closest relative (Deuteronomy 13:6–8). The natural human reaction to a tragedy of this kind is recognised, but it has to be overridden by a higher loyalty to the Lord Himself!

"Neither shall thine eye pity him, neither shalt thou spare, neither shalt thou conceal him: but thou shalt surely kill him; thine hand shall be first upon him to put him to death."

The law of the witnesses has its New Testament application in Matthew 18:16, 2 Corinthians 13:1 and 1 Timothy 5:19. In each case the point is driven home that we are dealing not with abstractions but with people. If God is to purge the world ultimately of evil, then it will be evil men who are rooted out in the judgement. He deals with offenders not offences. As Paul says, quoting from Deuteronomy 17:7 in dealing with the case of fornication in Corinth: "Therefore put away from among yourselves *that wicked person*" (1 Corinthians 5:13). The Hebrew word for "put away" is very strong: it is "to consume", and is found in the place name of Taberah, where fire destroyed those who lusted after flesh.

What lessons and warnings are here! For there is not only the responsibility to honour the Lord in preventing or eradicating corrupting moral influences from among us, but the even heavier responsibility of avoiding private or personal malice, or accusation which cannot be substantiated, having no foundation, but which may nevertheless effectively destroy our brother's reputation. "With what judgment ye judge, ye shall be judged."

The same commandment to "put away the evil" from Israel applied to presumptuous defiance of the judgement of the central tribunal, whose function has already been described briefly above. The New Testament parallel here is the discipline of the ecclesia to be exercised in matters of offence brought before it at the mouth of two or three witnesses:

"If he shall neglect to hear them, tell it unto the church: but if he neglect to hear the church, let him be unto thee as an heathen man and a publican." (Matthew 18:17)

"A man that is an heretick after the first and second admonition reject; knowing that he that is such is subverted, and sinneth, *being condemned of himself*." (Titus 3:10,11)

(c) "I will set a king over me like the nations" (17:14–20)

One thing above all emerges clearly from the foregoing law and the penalty of presumption—the supremacy of the written Law in Israel. The emphasis is laid upon the fact that the final court of appeal is "the place which the LORD thy God shall choose" and that the judgement is to be based upon "the sentence which they of that place which the LORD thy God shall choose shall shew thee ... inform thee ... teach thee ... tell thee".

This anticipates the command in chapter 31, given by Moses before his death, that the copy of the Law which he had just completed writing should be placed in the side of the Ark of the Covenant as a witness against the children of Israel. The Levites were constituted its custodians, and the principles of the covenant were enshrined in the words of the song which Moses "put into the mouths" of the people, also for a witness.

The only authority by which the priests and Levites could judge the people was therefore by God's Law. The same was to be true of the king they would set over them later. The true prophetic nature of the Book of Deuteronomy in both senses of that word is evidenced by this law of the Kingdom.

Moses was not only *forth*telling the words of God, but in dealing with eternal principles was of necessity *fore*telling the course the nation would follow and the blessings and the curses which would be the consequences of their behaviour. Chapter 28 is the outstanding example of this.

It was inevitable therefore that eventually the people would demand a king, as God had foreseen. It was implicit in the blessings of Jacob's sons in which the royal tribe was designated as Judah. That the true significance of these blessings, which with hindsight we can recognise as so comprehensive, should be only gradually unfolded is a mark of Divine revelation. It is also a further proof that Deuteronomy was not written late in the times of the Kings, when the record could hardly have passed over in silence so much that was then known.

It is remarkable that the people should have demanded a king in the very terms of Moses' prophecy, almost as though they were citing him in support of a proposition so obviously displeasing to Samuel: "Nay; but we will have a king to reign over us; *that we also may be like all the nations*" (1 Samuel 8:19,20).

The supremacy of the written Law in Israel was emphasised by the commandment concerning the kingdom (17:18–20). It is interesting to note here that this law of the kingdom is unlike the other laws in two important aspects: it is in a sense permissive legislation, inasmuch as it does not demand that a king be appointed, but only sets out principles governing the choice of the king when they were ready to make it. Second, there is no mention of the rôle he will play in the government of the people, only that the people will want to set him over them in order to be like other nations. The true function of the king from God's point of view, however, is abundantly illustrated elsewhere in Scripture: he was to be not a lord over a land but a shepherd to the Lord's flock.

God's purposes stand

Following the principle we have already seen illustrated in Deuteronomy in the election of judges (1:9–17, pages 12–16) and the choice of the spies who were to search out the Land (1:22–24, page 18), what the people or their leaders had determined to do was brought under the Lord's control for the furtherance of His purpose long before revealed. So although the first king had been a man of Benjamin, the kingdom was established under the hand of David, that "the sceptre shall not depart from Judah, nor a lawgiver from between his feet, until Shiloh come" (Genesis 49:10).

It is important to realise then that the appointment of a king in Samuel's day was not in itself a sin, neither does Samuel suggest that it was. How could it be if the prophetic blessing of Judah had specifically linked him with a royal line? The Lord's words to Samuel when he showed himself displeased at the request for a king must be seen in their context. It was not a question of appointing a successor to Samuel after his death, but of setting aside during his lifetime one whom God Himself had chosen to judge His people and to whom the word of the Lord had come. The time and circumstance were therefore wrong, and it is plain that Samuel treated the affair as a personal rejection. However, the Lord said,

"They have not rejected *thee*, but they have rejected *me*, that *I* should not reign over them. According to all the works which they have done since the day I brought them up out of Egypt unto this day ... so do they also unto thee."

(1 Samuel 8:6–9)

The Lord's kingdom

In spite of the unworthiness of many of his descendants, because David had fulfilled so faithfully in himself the requirements of Deuteronomy 17, which clearly emphasised that, whoever sat upon the throne of David, *the kingdom was the Lord's*, the kingdom was established in his house.

For David was "from among thy brethren". It is remarkable to see how this principle was uppermost in the minds of "all the tribes of Israel" when, after the death of Saul, they came to David and said, "Behold, we are thy bone and thy flesh" (2 Samuel 5:1). There was an ironic overtone to the question which the wise men asked at the court of Herod the Great, the Idumean king of the Jews: "Where is he that is *born* King of the Jews? for we have seen his star in the east, and are come to worship him" (Matthew 2:2).

But the principle went even deeper: the law of the king was that he should be he "whom the LORD thy God shall choose" (Deuteronomy 17:15). In David's case that choice had been made and the anointing taken place long before the tribes visited him in Hebron. So it was with the Son of David. In the same "volume of the book" in which it was written that he would come to suffer and to die it was foreordained that he should sit on David's throne, and "reign for God, and dwell with men".

"The manner of the king" as Samuel spelled it out to the assembled people was entirely different from what the Lord had commanded. The Lord's anointed was not to "multiply horses to himself" (Deuteronomy 17:16). No doubt there was a twofold reason for the prohibition. First of all:

"An horse is a vain thing for safety: neither shall he deliver any by his great strength." (Psalm 33:17)

The people, therefore, who had the Lord for their defence and the Holy One of Israel for their King (Psalm 89:19) had no need of a king who put his trust in a multitude of horses. In Isaiah's day the prophet proclaimed:

"Woe unto those that go down to Egypt for help; and stay on horses … but they look not unto the Holy One of Israel, neither seek the LORD … Now the Egyptians are men, and not God; and their horses flesh, and not spirit." (Isaiah 31:1,3)

"I am the LORD"

The king of Syria learned a similar lesson in the days of Ahab, when he lost his chariots and horsemen in battle, and assumed it was because they had fought in the hills, where the Israelite infantry had the advantage. Matching horse for horse and chariot for chariot Benhadad renewed his forces and went forth to meet Israel in the plain, where he supposed that his mounted army would be superior. The Divine comment was:

"Because the Syrians have said, The LORD is God of the hills, but he is not God of the valleys, therefore will I deliver all this great multitude into thine hand, and ye shall know that I am the LORD." (1 Kings 20:28)

Second, the horse, which was used only for fighting and not for agriculture, was a "status symbol", and the amassing of horses was therefore equivalent to the pursuit of great wealth, which was also forbidden (Deuteronomy 17:17). It is fairly clear that horses were not bred in any great numbers in Israel. Egypt was the main market, as can be seen from abundant references to Pharaoh's chariots and horsemen, including Isaiah's above; but note particularly Exodus 15:1:

"I will sing unto the LORD, for he hath
triumphed gloriously:
The horse and his rider hath he
thrown into the sea."

The prohibition against causing the people to return to Egypt to buy horses for the king is an excellent argument against the attempts of the critics to assign Deuteronomy to a late date in the history of the kings of Israel. In the wilderness the children of Israel had frequently declared their desire to return to Egypt with its fleshpots, and had at one time been on the point of electing a leader for that purpose (Numbers 14:4). To claim that the Deuteronomy record belongs to the period after the desolation of the northern kingdom and when the judgment was about to fall upon Judah also is far-fetched to say the least, and amounts to a charge of deliberate forgery of a message from God.

This becomes even clearer when we consider the rest of the commandment concerning the king. It would have been impossible to write it after the days of Solomon without some allusion to the disasters of his reign.

The authenticity of Deuteronomy, however, rests upon other evidence than that contained in these few verses.*

"Thou shalt make no covenant ..."

There is no prohibition for the king against polygamy as such but only against the multiplying of wives. Obedience to this command would set Israel's king completely apart from those of the surrounding nations, for whose kings a large harem was both a mark of prestige and a political expedient. It is not only the moral aspect of the practice which is in question here, although we are well aware that that must be uppermost in the minds of all disciples for whom the teaching of the Master carries the seventh commandment far deeper than any mere "legal" observance.

In the context of this passage, however, it is probable that it is marriage alliances of a political nature which are in view. Remarkably the glory of Solomon's reign in its early stages rested upon the fact that he had sought wisdom from God with his whole heart, and God had added the blessing of the power and the riches which he himself was forbidden to seek after according to the commandment. It was when he began to consolidate his position amongst the nations by marrying many strange wives that disaster came. The sombre prophecy of Deuteronomy 17 was fulfilled to the letter:

> "His wives turned away his heart after other gods: and his heart was not perfect with the LORD his God, as was the heart of David his father." (17:17 with 1 Kings 11:4)

By his marriages Solomon had entered into a "covenant relationship" with other nations, when his covenant should have been exclusively with the Lord his God.

The law was to be in the king's heart, and to that end he had to make his personal copy of it. What constituted "this law" which he was to write out? Was it simply the law concerning himself contained in these verses? Or was it the whole law as contained in the Book of Deuteronomy—the exposition of the Ten Commandments in terms of practical living, as the national constitution in the Lord's Land? The latter, undoubtedly, since the king was to write it in a book "out of that which is before the priests the Levites" (verse 18). In 31:24,25 the book which Moses commits to the keeping of the Levites was all "the words of this law ... until they were finished", to be laid up in the ark of the covenant before the Lord as a witness against them after his death.

---

*See the series on "The Antiquity of Deuteronomy", *The Christadelphian*, September 1951 onwards.

The word hid in the heart

"Thy word have I hid in mine heart, that I might not sin against thee", wrote the Psalmist in that great acrostic poem about the power of the word to illuminate and to cleanse (Psalm 119). And page after page of the Psalms testifies to the conscientious way in which David kept the "law of the kingdom" which required him to read therein all the days of his life:

"O how love I thy law! it is my meditation all the day."

There is no direct record that David or Solomon wrote out their personal copy of the law, although we may safely assume that they did. We do read from time to time of the custom of presenting the newly anointed king with the testimony. The faithful Jehoiada put the testimony into the hands of the young Joash when the crown was placed upon his head (2 Chronicles 23:11); in the reign of Jehoshaphat, who "walked in the first ways of his father David", the Levites went about through all the cities of Judah, "and had the book of the law of the LORD with them" to teach the people (2 Chronicles 17:9).

The custom evidently fell into disuse and when the book of the Law was rediscovered in the Temple it produced a profound effect upon Josiah when it was brought to him to read (34:14–19).

It is clear from the Deuteronomy record that it was a dynasty or line of kings that was in view, for the faithful monarch who turned not aside from the commandment to the right hand or to the left would find that not only were his own days prolonged in his kingdom, but also those of his children "in the midst of Israel". Indeed, the keeping of the Lord's commandment is implicit in the covenant made with David, when the Lord spoke of His "servant's house for a great while to come". The great fulfilment came when he who had read what was written in "the volume of the book" concerning himself did the Father's will so perfectly.

The rôle of the written word

There can surely be no need to emphasise the importance of all this for disciples of the twenty-first century. Those who heard the word proclaimed from the heights of Sinai were still dependent for their continuing instruction upon the Lord's own provision of the tables of the testimony "written with the finger of God". The relationship of these to their daily life, the constitution of the nation in the Land, was set out in the book of the law preserved along with the tables, so

170

that future generations could still learn the authentic word of the Lord, as surely as if they had heard it themselves in the Voice from heaven or had been there when Moses rehearsed all the words of the covenant before he wrote them down and committed them to the keeping of the Levites.

The comment of P C Craigie in *The New International Commentary* on Deuteronomy is helpful here:

"The rôle of the *book* in the life of the king is of importance for understanding the full dimensions of Israel's faith. In the early part of Moses' address, he recalled for his audience the events of past history; on the basis of the experience of God in history (one form of revelation), the Israelites drew strength for the future. But the revelation of the word of God, written down for successive generations, was also a source of strength. Both the acts of God and the words of God were recorded; but while the former gave evidence of the living reality of their God, it was the latter that provided in detail the guidance and wisdom for daily living, in the first place for the king."

It is making a distinction without a difference if in our day we say that the word of the Lord is something more than the Scripture—that the Bible is not the word of God but it contains it. For we are then faced with the problem of defining how we receive the word of God other than through the medium of the written word, which God Himself has chosen as the vehicle for His truth. Were it not so there would be no meaning to the Apostle's words about Scripture in 2 Timothy 3:16:

"All Scripture is *theopneustos* (God-breathed—the nearest Scriptural equivalent to the traditional Christadelphian phrase 'the Spirit-word'), and is profitable for doctrine, for reproof, for correction, for instruction in righteousness: that the man of God may be perfect, throughly furnished unto all good works."

Yet it is *the word intelligently and affectionately received* which contains the cleansing power, and the human heart or the community of believers wherein it is honoured and treasured will know the grace of God as surely as Israel's kings, indeed Israel herself, would have known it, if they had been obedient to the royal law, the lively oracles of God.

The remaining chapters in this section we will pass in brief review before considering in more detail the closing chapters in which the covenant is renewed and the Law is ratified by the people as the constitution of the Land.

171

(d) "This shall be the due of the priest from the people" (18:1–8)

The Lord's kingdom being a theocracy, in which there was no distinction between "church" and "state", some detailed legislation concerning the Levites follows naturally here. The Levites have been referred to several times already in Deuteronomy (in 10:8,9; 12:12,18,19; 14:27,29; 16:11; 17:9,18). This section describes the kind of dues the people were to offer, when they had entered into their inheritance of the Land, to those whose inheritance was the Lord's service.

The priests who ministered at the tabernacle were still to live of the altar, and the significant addition to the law of the firstfruits was the gift of a fleece to the priests. The portions of the sacrifices described, the shoulder, the two cheeks and the maw, represented the best of the meat. It was important to remind the people of all their responsibilities to the rest of the Levites who did not minister at the tabernacle but were scattered throughout Israel, where they performed the duties of teachers and judges (17:8,9). The reminder was made more necessary because the dispersion of the people themselves rendered impracticable the regulation of Leviticus 17 that all animals used for food should be slain at the door of the tabernacle. There were one or two similar commandments suitable for the camp in the wilderness which were superseded by the Deuteronomy code when they entered the Land.

Although Levites had no tribal inheritance assigned to them by lot, there was evidently nothing which prevented their acquiring private property, since the cities allotted them were "for their cattle, and for their goods, and for all their beasts" (Numbers 35:3; cf. Abiathar in 1 Kings 2:26, Jeremiah in 32:7 and Barnabas in Acts 4:36,37). Any who had a deep desire to leave their own district to come and serve at the sanctuary were entitled to the same privileges as the priests who were already there. The proceeds of any sale of his property ("patrimony", Deuteronomy 18:8) he could retain.

David's organisation later regulated this service by assigning the sanctuary duties to all the priests divided into "courses", which fulfilled their ministry by lot. Thus Zacharias, father of John the Baptist, was "of the course of Abia", which brought him from "a city of Juda" to Jerusalem to offer incense in the Temple (1 Chronicles 24:10; Luke 1:5).

Paul applies the whole principle illustrated in this section (18:1–8) to the service of the Gospel, and although our own organisation finds no place for a paid ministry, we should nevertheless ensure that none are debarred from service by reason of expense alone. For, says Paul:

"Do ye not know that they which minister about sacred things eat of the things of the temple, and they which wait upon the altar have their portion with the altar?"

(1 Corinthians 9:13, RV)

Living of the Gospel

It is not the place here to discuss all the questions raised by the concept of "living of the gospel" as the Lord ordained it (1 Corinthians 9:14), since in general the community has come to terms with it. True, the question of "expenses" (which in spite of the occasional jocular references to the labourer being worthy of it are not the speaker's *hire!*) often seems to cause some embarrassment. There can be few ecclesias left nowadays, however, who do not expect to meet out-of-pocket expenses when they have invited someone to minister to them. Few now believe that it costs you nothing if you come by car instead of by train, but many would be surprised if the true cost of the journey was claimed; for every motorist knows that the fuel bill is only part of it.

The service rendered cannot be measured in terms of finance in any case, since time spent in preparation and the actual process of delivering an address—which should be an imparting of *oneself* to the ecclesia (1 Thessalonians 2:8), are all part of the service "as unto the Lord". And many will no doubt remember, at least in their prayers, the situation of those brethren and sisters who have suspended, if only for a limited period, the pursuit of their own careers in order to do preaching and pastoral work overseas, often while still labouring for their daily bread.

In view of the wide range of financial capability in the Brotherhood some feel they need no reimbursement and so decline expenses when they are offered; others cannot manage without, but are reluctant to ask if they are not. It might be a good principle that the ecclesia should always ask and the speaker always accept at least some contribution. Those who can afford to do without them can always return their expenses by way of the collection bag, or make them an anonymous contribution to some other cause. In this way no invidious distinction is made between him and the brother who cannot afford to travel at his own charges, and the ecclesia is thus made aware of the true regular running costs of their yearly programme.

There is another aspect to such ecclesial service which has nothing to do with finance but nevertheless represents a genuine contribution of the ecclesia to the speakers who serve it. All ecclesias, and especially the sisters, should know of the immense contribution they are making to a speaker's service to their ecclesia and the gratitude he feels when he is received into a home, or even just met with an open door at the meeting room after a long journey.

"Thy peace upon our homeward way"

The speaker is too much of a realist not to know that it is sometimes necessary, especially if he has gone over his allotted time, for members of the ecclesia who live at a distance to depart before the close of a meeting, to avoid missing a bus or a train. Being human, however, he may occasionally reflect that *he* will not be home after the lecture until nearly ten—or eleven—o'clock. The occasions when the final prayer includes a request for a blessing on all those who travel home are relatively few, but even a privately-expressed wish can be a comfort to a rather tired and flat-feeling speaker going out alone into the darkness. Some ecclesias, incidentally, request a certain limit to addresses in a courteous note well in advance, explaining the reasons for the restriction and asking for the speaker's cooperation. Some tell him by means of a curt printed notice which he sees as he stands up to speak. Some just tell him afterwards!

One more reflection arises from a consideration of the Levites' service to the Lord and their due from the people. They were entitled to receive it by reason of the fact that they had been called to a service which the people could not do for themselves and which by its very nature prevented them from labouring at anything else at the same time. To turn the situation round, there are brethren and sisters amongst us who earn their living through the profit of their own business or the skill of their own hands, in the "supply" or "service" industries.

This provides them with "substance" with which they serve the Master and their brethren. We should not on that account expect them to attend to our personal needs—service the car, decorate the room, sell us goods, or anything of that sort—for nothing, as though they have a duty to support their brethren.

Without exception such Christadelphians gladly help their fellows who are *in need,* minister of their substance in the Truth's service, and often out of brotherly feeling treat us all generously. We should be grateful that, being brethren or sisters, they will work for us "as unto the Lord", and that we can be assured of quality and reliability in their work, without demanding that they actually subsidise us out of their "patrimony" as well.

(e) "The LORD thy God hath not suffered thee so to do" (18:9–14)

Our next section deals further with the exposition of the Second Commandment, which we have discussed earlier in some detail. The worship of demons and idols led the surrounding nations into abominable practices, amongst which were spiritualism and necromancy. The vestiges of such worship in Canaan, even after the Lord their God had driven out the nations because of those abominations, could prove a snare for Israel.

There is a deep significance in the context of this prohibition against foreign practices in religion: the preceding passage deals with the legitimate worship of the people through the mediation of the priests; the succeeding passage concerns the true prophet from whom they could seek the authentic word of the Lord. The evil practices were forbidden precisely because they had formed the ground of God's judgements upon the previous inhabitants of the Land.

The Apostle Paul had read deeply and carefully in the book of Deuteronomy. In the section in 1 Corinthians in which he emphasises that to drink the cup and break the bread were acts of "communion of the blood of Christ … of the body of Christ", he draws an analogy from the service of the priests:

"Behold Israel after the flesh: are not they which eat of the sacrifices partakers of the altar?"

Paul clearly has both our chapter and the Second Commandment in mind throughout the whole of 1 Corinthians 10, for he calls upon the Corinthians to avoid pressing their freedom in Christ to the point of "provoking the Lord to jealousy" (verse 22; Exodus 20:5) by following the example of Israel in the matter of idols. For sacrificing to an idol, or indeed any pursuit of alien religious practices at all, was an act of fellowship with that which was not God, which could only be a breaking of the covenant of fellowship with their God. The whole Corinthian passage is worth reading in this light:

"But I say, that the things which the Gentiles sacrifice, they sacrifice to devils, and not to God: *and I would not that ye should have fellowship with devils*. Ye cannot drink

175

the cup of the Lord, and the cup of devils: ye cannot be partaker of the Lord's table, and of the table of devils."

(verses 20,21)

The principle is the same whether we engage in necromancy or devil worship or not. The communion of the body and blood of Christ is something more deeply spiritual than the mere act of partaking of the emblems: it is full association with the Lord in heartfelt love and obedience. To come before him while regarding iniquity in our hearts or striving to serve both him and mammon, is as much a provocation to jealousy as the more explicit worship of an idol.

(f) "A prophet unto thee, of thy brethren" (18:15–22)

We will let the words of the prophet Isaiah, also based upon Deuteronomy, provide both the link between the sections and a fitting conclusion to this chapter of our book. We pass from the cult of demons and the sacrifice of children, as a special propitiatory rite when seeking a revelation, to the source of true knowledge of God, the Law and prophet. We have considered the founding of the ministry of the prophets and the test of the true prophet in some detail and so need not repeat ourselves here.

The written word under the guardian care of the Levites was a sufficient guide for the people in their life and worship, provided "the priest's lips kept knowledge" and the teaching ministry was not neglected. The seven-yearly reading through of the Law in the hearing of the whole people (to be inaugurated in chapter 31:9–13) would keep the Law before them and their "children, which have not known anything". At times of crisis, however, usually brought on by the neglect of both priest and people to obey the word of the Lord, God Himself would raise up a man to recall them to their obedience or proclaim His judgement on the unrepentant. It was vitally important that at such times the people could distinguish the false prophet from the true, in the manner laid down in chapters 13 and 18. Like the king, the prophet was to be "of thy brethren", and being also like Moses, with whom the Lord would speak "mouth to mouth, even apparently, and not in dark speeches" (Numbers 12:8), such a prophet would be distinguished from those to whom the title could be applied in a lesser sense—"the sons of the prophets" of Elijah's day, for example. Samuel is an obvious example but there were others who had the same testimony: "He is

176

faithful in all my house." They all foreshadowed the coming of the Word made flesh, who was "like" yet "greater than" Moses and all the others. For God, who at sundry times and in divers manners spake in time past unto the fathers through the prophets, would speak in His Son, their Prophet, Priest and King.

So, as Isaiah the prophet said to the people who were going back upon the Lord's commands in Deuteronomy 18:

> "And when they shall say unto you, Seek unto them that have familiar spirits, and unto the wizards, that chirp and that mutter: should not a people seek unto their God? on behalf of the living should they seek unto the dead (*necromancy*)? To the law and to the testimony! if they speak not according to this word, surely there is no morning for them." (Isaiah 8:19,20, RV)

(g) "Thou shalt prepare thee a way" (chapter 19)

The second part of the Decalogue contains the Commandments which regulated Israel's behaviour (and the disciple's) towards man. It forms what the Lord Jesus described as "the second commandment", the first being in fact the summary of Commandments one to five:

> "Hear, O Israel: the LORD our God is one LORD: and thou shalt love the LORD thy God with all thine heart, and with all thy soul and with all thy might."

This is not to say that love of the Lord and love of one's neighbour are separate features of the covenant; in fact the reverse. In these days when the trend is to emphasise the second of the great commandments, or to assume that even sincere humanitarianism of itself is love of the Lord without reference to what He has revealed concerning Himself, it is worth restating the principle: "Love to God always brings the love of men in its train; while love to men has not the same power to bring about love to God, and in those ignorant of God's ways sometimes occasions a special embitterment against Him" (author unknown).

Commandments 5–10, therefore, set out a code of behaviour by which the Lord is honoured in social relationships. They are expounded in Deuteronomy chapter 19 onwards, beginning with the theme of "Thou shalt not kill".

The sovereignty of God as Creator: as the giver of "life, and breath, and all things", in whom "we live, and move, and have our being" is declared by this Commandment: for man who cannot give life must not take it away. The chapter opens with the words "When the LORD thy God hath cut off the nations". We are not therefore dealing with warfare, which Israel were at times commanded by God to undertake, but with murder, manslaughter or accidental homicide. The stringency of the law is seen in every aspect of the Divine code which became part of Israel's daily life, which also emphasised God's justice.

The avenger of blood

"Whoso sheddeth man's blood, by man shall his blood be shed: for in the image of God made he man." So God said to Noah (Genesis 9:5,6; see also 4:14), and the principle of "the avenger of blood" received Divine sanction. The man who killed his fellow by accident was delivered only by the law covering the cities of refuge. The man's life was regarded as forfeit, but there was a way of escape for the innocent in heart, provided he kept to the rules laid down. They were inconvenient, since he had to leave home and dwell within the city's precincts until the death of the high priest. For the man guilty of premeditated murder the city of refuge offered no escape from justice.

An interesting alternative translation of verse 3 is: "You shall fix the distance of the roads", which in conjunction with the command to divide the land into three when deciding the location of the cities, and the addition of another three on the east of Jordan, indicates the great care which was taken to make the refuge as convenient to reach as possible. It was important to maintain the roads in good condition, and to make the direction plain. Perhaps there is an allusion to this in Isaiah 35:

"And an highway shall be there, and a way, and it shall be called The way of holiness; the unclean shall not pass over it; but it shall be for those: the wayfaring men, though fools, shall not err therein." (verse 8)

There is much beautiful symbolism in this for the disciple. He, realising that he is worthy of death, makes the Lord his refuge and strength. While he remains with Him he is safe, for his High Priest never dies, and so he goes no more out. On the practical level, however, it is worthy of note that although the man's life was spared because he was innocent, there could be no pretending that the accident had not happened. The pattern of life was irrevocably altered by what had occurred. It is the same with the forgiveness of sins. The *consequences* of our actions may remain with us, as in the case of David, even though the burden of guilt the Father graciously removes.

Even if one were found slain in the open field with no means of discovering the killer, expiation of the crime had still to be made, so abhorrent was such a deed in the eyes of the Lord (chapter 21). The elders of the nearest city were held responsible, and had to purify themselves by slaying a heifer and declaring before the priests "Our hands have not shed this blood, neither have our eyes seen it … And the blood shall be forgiven *them*".

The remainder of chapter 19 deals with landmarks and false witness.

Removing the landmark

Nothing is more eloquent of the nature of Israel's inheritance of the Land than this short command:

"Thou shalt not remove thy neighbour's landmark, which they of old time have set in thine inheritance, which thou shalt inherit in the land that the LORD thy God giveth thee to possess it." (verse 14)

In the first place it spoke of inheritance for a great while to come, since the boundaries had not yet been set. Then it made clear that the Land was the Lord's, although He had given it unto them. In effect the boundary marks had been set by the Lord also, since the division of the Land and the allocation of it to the tribes by lot was all at His command. Just as the individual bore a certain geographical relationship to the tabernacle in the wilderness according to his family and tribe (Numbers 2), so it was in his permanent settlement. The form of stealing implied by moving the landmark was therefore an act against the Lord.

The seriousness of the offence made it the subject of a special curse when the sanctions of the Law were proclaimed in the Land itself:

"Cursed be he that removeth his neighbour's landmark. And all the people shall say, Amen." (Deuteronomy 27:17)

9

RULES OF WARFARE, SOCIETY, PROPERTY AND PERSONAL BEHAVIOUR IN THE LORD'S LAND (CHAPTERS 20–27)

(a) "When thou goest out to battle against thine enemies" (chapter 20)

THE RULES for the conduct of warfare by the people of Israel were firmly based upon the principles of the covenant and the occupation of the Land. They were in no way an infringement of the Sixth Commandment, "Thou shalt not kill". This referred to the act of murder, the taking away for personal reasons of profit or revenge of a life which God had given. Warfare in Israel, however, was to be at God's command, subject to His laws and for the occupation and later the defence of the Land of Promise. It was therefore entirely part of God's own purpose, the means by which His Land would be rid of idolatry that it might become the seat of His worship.

A true defence

Accordingly it was not the captain but the priest who addressed the troops: "The LORD thy God is with thee, which brought thee up out of the land of Egypt" (verse 1). So the *best* army would be not the *most numerous* (compare Gideon and his 300 men; Judges 7:2), but the one in which faith in God was as effective as shield and buckler, even in the face of the enemy cavalry, a military arm in which Israel was always outnumbered: "Some trust in chariots, and some in horses: but we will remember the name of the LORD our God" (Psalm 20:7).

The prelude to any battle, then, was to be the proclamation by the priest of the name of the Lord and the reminder of His saving power. It was implicit in this act that the campaign was one sanctioned by God. There were many occasions in their subsequent history when Israel were routed because they had acted on their own initiative or in their own puny strength.

The limited scope of their warfare made a permanent standing army unnecessary, although in David's day at least there were prolonged periods when an organised force was maintained. In earlier times the army was mustered for the

180

occasion, as we can gather from the records of the Judges and Saul. The proclamation in verses 5–8 must therefore have been made at the beginning of every campaign, the "officers" presumably being the leaders of the tribes responsible for the muster of their own people. The exemptions from military service detailed here further illustrate the purpose and scope of the Divine warfare, initially the settlement and development of the Lord's Land.

Exemption from military service

The principles of exemption were both practical and compassionate. The building of a house to dwell in, the planting of a vineyard, the marrying of a wife, all these were the very foundations of life in the Land, and there was no purpose at all in warfare if these activities had to cease. Priority was given, therefore, to these important aspects of normal life. The blessing of God both upon the army and those who stayed at home was essential, for the idealistic approach to "national service" envisaged in this chapter would be impossible without it. Indeed, it could not be followed in the total warfare of today, which God may indeed turn towards the fulfilment of His purpose, but has its origin in naked aggression or desperate defence of a sovereignty in which He has no place.

The fourth category of exemption was equally practical as well as compassionate, but only in a state whose strength lay not in its army but in God. The fearful were to depart— 22,000 of Gideon's 32,000 men left on this ground! (Judges 7:3)—since they had not the necessary faith for the Lord to accomplish His purpose in them. Moreover, panic and fear can spread like wildfire through the ranks of an army: high morale and trust in the Lord are the surest means of attack as well as of defence. The classic illustration of this is seen in the account of "the army that sang" in 2 Chronicles 20, during the invasion by the Moabites. In the days of Jehoshaphat who, in fear at the "great multitude" of the enemy, cried unto God, the Spirit of the Lord came upon a Levite who stood up before the congregation and said:

"Thus saith the LORD unto you, Be not afraid nor dismayed by reason of this great multitude; for the battle is not yours, but God's ... Ye shall not need to fight in this battle: set yourselves, *stand ye still and see the salvation of the LORD* with you (cf. Exodus 14:13) ... Believe in the LORD your God, so shall ye be established; believe his prophets, so shall ye prosper ... he appointed singers unto the LORD, and that should praise the beauty of holiness, as they went out before the army, and to say, Praise the LORD, for his mercy endureth for ever... Then they returned, every man of Judah and Jerusalem, and Jehoshaphat in the forefront of them, to go again to Jerusalem with joy; for the LORD had made them to rejoice over their enemies."

(2 Chronicles 20:14–30)

"Be strong and of a good courage"

Two other considerations may be noted briefly in this section. First, it is *defensive* warfare against possible invaders that is chiefly in view in this chapter, since the reference is to "cities which are very far off from thee, which are not of the cities of these nations" (verse 15). For these there was to be made an offer of peace, though not of alliance. If there was no submission or consent to becoming a tributary, then the Lord's people were commanded to smite the city and take the spoil for themselves. A war of aggrandisement played no part, therefore, in the political life of the nation which the Lord Himself would establish within the boundaries covenanted to the fathers. For the Canaanite, however, there was to be no quarter, "that they teach you not to do after their abominations".

Secondly, there was to be no wanton devastation of the countryside such as has become only too familiar in modern warfare. Even in the felling of trees for military purposes, in the siege for example, the Israelites had carefully to avoid the destruction of fruit trees, "for the tree of the field is man's life".

Balancing essential duties

The disciple concerned with the Lord's warfare can draw his own lessons from the foregoing. It will help him to strike the delicate balance between duty in the home and family with the service of the preacher and campaigner, the principle being clearly set forth in the conditions of military service in Israel, where the citizen was the soldier, and might be called upon to leave his domestic comfort to defend both hearth and home.

The enduring of hardness as a good soldier of Jesus Christ certainly involves not being entangled with the affairs of this life. The maintenance of a godly home and the bringing up of a family in the nurture and admonition of the Lord are not "affairs of this life" in the sense the Apostle had in mind (2 Timothy 2), since they are part of the Lord's service. And just as in Israel, the building of the spiritual house, cultivation of the good ground and going forth in the Lord's name are all obligations laid upon us.

If we would "war a good warfare", we too must remember that the Lord is our helper, a thought which should make us strong and very courageous. The strength which comes through such faith has another important aspect: it strengthens our brethren also. The prohibition against service for the faithless or faint-hearted teaches us the parallel lesson: "Let him go and return to his house, lest his brethren's heart faint as well as his heart" (verse 8).

(b) "That the land be not defiled ..."

Amongst other rules in this section which have a relevance for the modern disciple, we may cite those concerning personal hygiene and the cleanliness of the camp, "for the LORD thy God walketh in the midst of thy camp" (23:12–14). It was the military camp in question here, but the principle, surely, is that the realisation of the Lord's presence amongst the people should encourage us to do the best we can in removing "unseemliness" or disorder from our surroundings, at home or in the meeting place. As Brother Islip Collyer once said, "Sometimes we worship God in conditions we would not tolerate in our own homes".

Respect for the person and property of others, even when punishment was to be meted out to an offender, and a sense of responsibility for the lives or safety of others is set against the background of the Ten Commandments, as were divorce, marriage and extra-marital relations. All was designed to bring home to the people the holiness of the Lord and consequently the standards of behaviour which alone were appropriate to those who were in covenant with Him.

There is an interesting and revealing comment in 22:1–4 which refers to something which has its counterpart in spiritual Israel, with its concept of "*the Brotherhood Near and Far*", in the home ecclesia or in the Bible Mission field. Israel like ourselves bore a family relationship to one another which had a spiritual rather than a social basis, which embraces all those "that *in every place* call upon the name of Jesus Christ our Lord, both theirs and ours" (1 Corinthians 1:2). So we, like them, have a responsibility for one another's welfare even "*if thy brother be not nigh unto thee, or if thou know him not*". We in effect bring his goods "unto thine own house, and it shall be with thee until thy brother seek after it, and thou shalt restore it to him again".

"A Syrian ready to perish ..."

The recognition of all this by the individual member of the people was to be gathered up in the ceremony of the presentation of the firstfruits of the Land after its occupation and settlement, when confession was to be made of all the Lord's goodness in bringing the people out of Egypt to a land that flowed with milk and honey, and the offerer rejoiced in every good thing that the Lord his God had given. Upon the contrite and obedient the Lord would look down from His holy habitation, from heaven, and bless His people Israel, and the land which he had given them, as He sware unto their fathers (verse 15). The prayer was in fact for God's *continued* blessing, the tithe of the firstfruits being the sign that the people were already experiencing His favour.

The conclusion of the whole matter

Moses concluded his speech to the people in words which were in effect an exposition in summary of the whole covenant relationship of the Lord with His holy nation:

"This day the LORD thy God hath commanded thee ... Thou hast avouched the LORD this day to be thy God, and to walk in his ways ... And the LORD hath avouched thee this day to be his peculiar people, as he hath promised thee, and that thou shouldest keep all his commandments; and to make thee high above all nations ... and that thou mayest be an holy people unto the LORD thy God, as he hath spoken."

The speech is framed, as it were, between the statement of the covenant in terms of the Decalogue and the enactment of the covenant in the succeeding chapters. It is also a beautiful thought, as Ellicott remarks in his *Commentary,* that the speech is prophetic of its own fulfilment.

10

THE ENACTMENT OF THE LAW
(CHAPTER 27)

WE now come to what has been described as the Enactment, that is, the ceremony by which the Ten Commandments in exposition were actually to be brought into force as the law of the Land when the people had crossed over Jordan. It is important to note that the command to do this was given to the people by Moses *with the elders*, the first time that they were associated with him in his leadership.

This is a clear indication that although the Enactment was to be carried out according to the Divine authority vested in Moses, the elders would bear the responsibility as agents since Moses was not to pass over Jordan. Joshua, who later fulfilled this charge as leader was at this time one of the elders, but had not yet had the full responsibility of that office laid upon him (see chapter 31). The people were therefore left in no doubt that the elders would be executing the Lord's command when the time came for them to put it into practice.

The word "keep" (verse 1) is in Hebrew "to keep", and is either an infinitive used as a general command, or an expression which is in sequence with the preceding chapter: "To keep the commandments I have described, you must write them". Either understanding makes excellent sense, and the chapter describes a natural sequel to the events at Horeb. There the Lord Himself wrote the Law on tables of stone, "with the finger of God". The first tablets had been hewn by Himself, the replacements by Moses at His command. The Ten Words were now to be engraved by the hand of man upon stones prepared to receive them, but still in their unhewn condition, as God had left them.

These stones were to be set up in the heart of the Land, to represent both the title deeds of the inheritance which God had given and the constitution by which it was to be governed. From the record in Joshua 8 we understand that no time was lost in establishing these pillars, almost immediately after the capture of Ai, and long before the whole land was settled.

Not only was the importance of the *written* word re-emphasised but another ceremony, the building of an altar for burnt offerings and peace offerings, imparted a special sanctity to the occasion. The choice of location for the two ceremonies and for the blessings and cursings was also highly significant, for Mount Ebal and Mount Gerizim overlooked the valley of Shechem. It was there that Abraham built an altar unto the Lord who had appeared unto him and said, "Unto thy seed will I give this land".

Why should Ebal, the mount of the curses, be chosen for the setting up of the pillars of the Law? And why should there be a record of the curses and not of the blessings pronounced upon Gerizim? One or two possibilities exist, the least likely being that the record of the blessing was lost. Some think that we must seek for them in the counterparts of the curses. There is no evidence at all for the incomplete record theory. It is, on the other hand, not improbable that blessings and cursings were pronounced alternately across the valley, and the loud Amen echoed in response to each.

"A witness for Me against Israel"

The Divine account records only the cursings, and for a good reason, or so it seems to us: on the threshold of inheritance of the blessings it was the consequences of disobedience, every aspect of which described here was distinctively Canaanitish, which needed spelling out clearly. In accepting this aspect of the law as the sanctions of the covenant, the people were witnessing against themselves, as they were to do later in the learning of the Song. See 31:19–22, noting especially the "therefore" of verse 19, which links the Song with the people's disobedience foretold in the preceding verses.

Many fascinating questions suggest themselves; to the answers we can allude only briefly here. What significance can be found in the disposition of the tribes on the mountains, or in their particular rôle in the ceremony? It should first be noted that they are the *ancestral* tribes, those who were the actual twelve sons of Jacob. Levi is therefore included and Joseph counts as one tribe, whereas in the usual numbering of Israel he is represented by his sons, Ephraim and Manasseh. In the patriarchal blessing a "double portion" centred on Shechem was granted to Joseph (Genesis 48:21,22). The ceremony of taking possession—the performing of "the truth to Jacob and the mercy to Abraham" which the Lord had sworn unto their fathers from the days of old—was therefore appropriately in the hands of the representatives of Jacob's sons.

"The generations of Jacob"

Moreover, the pronouncing of the blessings upon the people was committed to the more honourable of Jacob's sons, Simeon, Levi, Judah, Issachar, Joseph and Benjamin, all with one exception sons of Jacob's wives Leah and Rachel. The exception is Zebulun, Leah's youngest son, whose tribe is joined with the four sons of the handmaids, Bilhah and Zilpah. Again, appropriately enough in the context of a ceremony marking inheritance, Reuben the firstborn of Jacob is on the mount of the curses, in partial fulfilment of his father's prophecy that he should not excel. He had forfeited his birthright and put himself on the side of Bilhah's sons by lying with her (Genesis 35:22; 49:3,4; 1 Chronicles 5:1).

Is there any pattern to the list of sins which came under the formal cursing? We have suggested one above—they were all Canaanite abominations. It is a worthwhile exercise to consider them, the Dodecalogue (the "Twelve Commandments") as they have been called, in the light of the Decalogue itself. It will be seen that in sum they represent the exact opposite of the conduct of the man in whose heart is the Law of the Lord and who will love his neighbour as himself.

Much could be written about other details of this chapter which describes the Enactment so forcefully, stage by stage until the final curse sets the seal upon it all: "Cursed be he that confirmeth not all the words of this law *to do them*. And all the people shall say, Amen".

11

THE SANCTIONS OF THE LAW OF THE LAND (CHAPTER 28)

THE *ENACTMENT* of the Law, to make it the Constitution of the Land as the seat of the Lord's kingdom and worship (chapter 27) was followed by the list of *sanctions* of chapter 28. Although it lies beyond the scope of our immediate purpose to go through this chapter in detail we shall consider a few of its characteristic features.

Almost every specific portion of law in Scripture ends in similar fashion: the blessings of obedience are set out first, followed by a list of denunciations against those who disobey. This chapter, which is highly prophetic in character, contains denunciations which have been classed as "the most tremendous in all Scripture". The code of law in Exodus 21–23 ends with a declaration of rewards and punishments (verses 20–33); and the laws of holiness, both ceremonial and moral, in Leviticus are closed by chapter 26, a close parallel in content with this chapter in Deuteronomy. There are other parallels in Matthew 7:21–27 and Apocalypse 22:10–19.

Overtaken by blessings and curses

So the blessings come first (verses 1–14). They would "overtake" the people whom the Lord would set "on high", an echo of the title of the God whose people they were—"the most high God", whose priest, Melchizedek, had blessed their father Abraham. The curses (verse 15—end) would far outweigh the blessings, however, and would invade every aspect of their daily life, from the kneading-trough to the store. The prophecy of the removing into all the kingdoms of the earth was a vivid forecast of the Dispersion or *Diaspora*, the actual word used in the Greek version (LXX) of this chapter. And in the midst of all their trouble they would have "none to rescue them" (verse 31). The words here mean "no saviour", and portray the hopelessness of their situation.

In the closing section, on the conquest of Israel by a strange nation, we have those poignant words so completely fulfilled in the siege of Jerusalem, which ushered in the sufferings which would be "of long continuance"—nearly 2,000 years in fact. There were none more poignant and prophetic, however, than those which portray the plight of the people in the more recent days of the Holocaust:

"In the morning thou shalt say, Would God it were even! and at even thou shalt say, Would God it were morning! for the fear of thine heart wherewith thou shalt fear ..."

The end of the Sinaitic covenant

Ironically, the curses of this book, which mark the end of the exposition of the Sinaitic covenant, include a return to the Egypt from which the people had been delivered, and to a bondage more severe than that from which they had been set free. Happily the chapter is immediately followed by the description of another covenant, equally prophetic and longer lasting, which looked forward to the fulfilment of the wider covenant with Abraham than that of which the entry into the Land was the token.

12

THE SECOND COVENANT IN THE LAND OF MOAB (CHAPTERS 29,30)

IN chapters 29 and 30 there is recorded a fascinating prophecy, the making of the *second covenant*. The record is quite explicit that, on the threshold of the Land, the people were assembled to hear the words of—

"the covenant, which the LORD commanded Moses to make with the children of Israel in the Land of Moab, *beside* the covenant which he made in Horeb." (verse 1)

The curse, then, was not after all the end of God's dealings with His people, for the second covenant sees beyond that of the Law of Moses. At first sight this covenant seems to go over ground already covered. The mighty acts of the Lord and "the blindness of Israel" are set out (verses 2–8), and the exhortation to "keep therefore the words of this covenant, and do them" is repeated once more. Once more also the curses for disobedience are stated in summary form, with both an individual and a national implication. Those who turn aside to idols ("dungy gods", verse 17, AV margin; Baal-zebub was "lord of the dung flies", an unpleasant fertility symbol) would be "a root that beareth gall (*rosh*, a poisonous herb) and wormwood" (verse 18). This prophecy found fulfilment in the Northern Kingdom as Amos declared in 5:7 and 6:12; and could have its counterpart even amongst the children of the New Covenant, if any became, like Esau, "profane persons", that is, "outside the sanctuary" according to the root meaning of the word "profane". Esau was "a root of bitterness" in the family of Abraham (Hebrews 12:15,16).

But though "the anger of the LORD and his jealousy shall smoke against that man" (Deuteronomy 29:20), and the nation be driven out from a land that, like Sodom and Gomorrah, became "brimstone, and salt, and burning" (verse 23; see also Isaiah 1:9; Romans 9:29), the Lord would turn the captivity of the faithful remnant who turned again to Him (Deuteronomy 30:1–3). Though their Dispersion be "unto the outmost parts of heaven", He would still gather together in one the children of God that are scattered abroad.

The forward-looking covenant

As though to emphasise the forward-looking character of this covenant into which the people passed that day, to be *established* as the people of the Lord according to the oath sworn unto the fathers (29:13), Moses added:

"Neither with you only (all the men of Israel, their wives, little ones, *and the stranger* that was in their camp) do I make this covenant and this oath; but with him that standeth here with us this day before the LORD our God, *and also with him that is not here with us this day.*"

(verses 14,15)

It is much to be regretted that in all the discussions that have centred around the application of Acts 2:39, the link with these verses in Deuteronomy has been for the most part ignored. The New Covenant in Christ's blood, by which he was to gather together in one all the children of God that were scattered abroad (John 11:52), saw the beginning of its fulfilment in that day when the faithful of Israel were constituted the "chosen generation, a royal priesthood, an holy nation, a peculiar people" (Acts 2; 1 Peter 2:9), and heirs of the Abrahamic covenant. At Pentecost, as at Sinai, the covenant was made with all the people. Future generations later enjoyed the privileges and bore the responsibilities of being the people of God, as though the covenant had been made directly with them personally—as in effect it had. The Acts tells us that the preaching spread abroad even to them that were afar off: for such was the nature of the promise, as Peter said:

"The promise is unto you, and to your children, and to all that are afar off, even as many as the Lord our God shall call."

The language is surely based upon the words of Deuteronomy. That the call of the Gentiles, implicit in the covenant with Abraham, was foreshadowed in these remarkable chapters of Deuteronomy is further confirmed in the terms of this second covenant in the land of Moab. The Lord declared (30:6):

"And the LORD thy God will circumcise *thine heart, and the heart of thy seed,* to love the LORD thy God with all thine heart, and with all thy soul, that thou mayest live."

This surely anticipates the words of Jeremiah concerning the new covenant which was to be—

"Not according to the covenant that I made with their fathers ... which my covenant they brake ... After those

191

days, saith the LORD, I will put my law in their inward parts, *and write it in their hearts*; and will be their God and they shall be my people." (Jeremiah 31:33)

The law of righteousness

These words are taken up in Hebrews 8 and applied directly to the covenant of the forgiveness of sins, the covenant of which the risen Lord seated at God's right hand, is the mediator and minister. The fact that the word was "very nigh unto thee, in thy mouth, and *in thy heart*, that thou mayest do it" (Deuteronomy 30:14) meant that the law of this second covenant was to be the Law of the Righteousness which is by faith, and Paul says in Romans 10:6–8, choosing his words carefully from these chapters:

"Say not in thine heart, Who shall ascend into heaven? (that is, to bring Christ down from above:) or, Who shall descend into the deep? (that is, to bring up Christ again from the dead) ... The word is nigh thee, even in thy mouth, and in thy heart: that is, the word of faith, which we preach."

We note this interesting use of the word "beyond" in Deuteronomy 30:13, with the sense of "on the other side of", in this case of the surface of the sea, and therefore below it. Compare the experience of Jonah, that prophetic type of the Lord in his burial and resurrection. He spent three days and three nights the other side of the surface of the deep. See also Ephesians 4:9,10. So for disciples these chapters have a clear message of hope and consolation. The Lord's covenant does not rest upon man's capacity to achieve, but upon the faithfulness and mercy of God. Our part is to believe and to obey: and with life and good, death and evil so manifestly set forth before us (verse 15), who would not elect to choose good that we may live?

13

MOSES HANDS OVER HIS CHARGE
(CHAPTER 31)

W ITH his exhortation faithfully delivered and the Lord's command still heavy on his heart—"Thou shalt not go over this Jordan"—Moses prepared to lay down his burden of responsibility. Once more we are made aware that such men, great as they were, exercised their leadership under God, so that the Divine purpose was not affected by the weakness or mortality of men. "The LORD thy God, he will go over before thee ... and Joshua, he shall go over before thee, *as the LORD hath said*" (31:3). Joshua was therefore the successor whom the Lord had chosen, although he was to learn later that he was not in fact "the captain of the LORD's host", when he saw standing before Jericho (Joshua 5:13–15) the angel with the drawn sword who had come neither as enemy nor as ally, but as "prince" (margin).

"I will be with thee"

So Joshua had faith in the Lord, who said, "As I was with Moses, so I will be with thee: I will not fail thee, nor forsake thee" (Joshua 1:5, taking up Moses' words in Deuteronomy 31:6); and the people could have faith in Joshua, to whom Moses had entrusted his commission in the *sight of Israel* (verse 7; see also Numbers 27:15–23).

Moses then delivered "this law" (verse 9) to the priests, the Levites, whose lips were to "keep knowledge" in Israel, with the charge that they should read it "before all Israel in their hearing" every seven years at the feast of tabernacles. "*This law*" is almost certainly the Deuteronomy rather than simply the Ten Commandments, which were to be inscribed on plastered stones. Evidently a multiplication of copies was not envisaged, since the words were intended to be "in thine heart". Thus an added importance is to be attached to the words of the Song referred to later in the chapter.

In verses 14,15 is recorded the formal ratification of what had been done, when Moses and Joshua went to present themselves in the tabernacle of the congregation, where the Lord appeared in a pillar of cloud, which stood at the door of the tabernacle.

Final acts

The ceremony over, Moses gave the book to the Levites, to be put inside the ark with the tables of the testimony, "for a witness against" the children of Israel. Moses' final acts were to teach them the Song which the Lord had commanded and to pronounce his patriarchal blessing upon the tribes before his death. Thus his leadership began and ended with a song.

14

A SONG TO REMEMBER (31:19–32:43)

NOTHING can impress upon the disciple the importance of music and song in worship more than a consideration of this "Song of Moses". The joy and the solemnity of the act of praising the Lord can be gauged from words such as those of Psalm 50:23: "Whoso *offereth* praise glorifieth me." In the Temple the sacrifice of praise was a priestly duty and both singers and players were said to *prophesy* before the Lord.

The Lord's song

The sacred song had a practical as well as a spiritual and cultural importance. The songs were not folk songs but "the Lord's song", the "songs of Zion", whose form was an aid to memory as well as a medium for expressing praise and devotion, particularly essential for a people who, possessing no personal written copies of their law, were yet commanded to have it in their heart. True, if the commandments in Deuteronomy 6:7–9 were carried out, then the Lord's goodness in salvation and their own obligations would be the theme of daily conversation as well as being impressed upon the forehead and the doorpost. This Song of Moses, however, was to be a witness *for* the Lord *against* His people!

The need for such a Song arose from the foreknowledge of God, as expressed in 31:16–21. He knew "their imagination, which they go about, even now, before I have brought them into the land which I sware".

Thus in the Song the Lord's benefits were spelled out—the deliverance from Egypt, the provision of food in the wilderness, the entry into a fruitful land, the promotion of Israel to be the head of the nations, riding "on the high places of the earth" (32:13). The people's disobedience to the Lord's commandments is also described in some detail and also their turning to idols away from the service of the living God. The penalties to be incurred, both actual and prophetic, were set out, as well as the ultimate mercy of the Lord (verse 43). All this the people had to learn by heart as the Song was "put in their mouths" (31:19).

195

It would be fascinating to discover the method of teaching a multitude such a song as this. Perhaps the Levites were first instructed by Moses and the people learned it by rote from them. Some readers old enough to remember being taught songs by the tonic sol-fa, will retain hazy recollections of the teacher translating the musical intervals from the wall-chart, or modulator, into a series of hand-signs. By this means a halting melody was coaxed from a class of varying ability. The cantillation marks in the Hebrew text of Psalms and Prophets could conceivably be so translated, and Moses could have used some such method to teach the Lord's Song. At any rate, it must have been a thrilling experience to hear the great congregation lift their voices in loud acclamation as they had done once before at the Red Sea—like "the fulness of the sea, when it breaks upon the shore" (Hymn 297).

But the singing of the Song was to be no mere emotional experience, making the spirit soar for a while, and then to be forgotten. Nor was it a piece of "community singing" because they felt like it. It was an act of worship—and remembrance. Each time it was sung, throughout successive generations, the people were not merely to utter words but express devotion. To draw nigh with the lips when the heart was far from God was, and for the disciple still is, entirely unacceptable—a thought which should discipline our choice of words, our musical idiom and certainly the manner of our singing even today. For the Song endured as a witness for the Lord who had revealed His goodness *against* the people who had despised it.

The song recalled

Over 700 years later, at a time of impending judgement because the nation had lapsed into the condition foreshadowed in the Song, and only the presence of the faithful remnant ensured that the land would not finally be treated like Sodom and Gomorrha (Deuteronomy 32:32; Isaiah 1:9), the prophet Isaiah opened his account of "the vision which he saw concerning Judah and Jerusalem" with the opening words of the Song:

"Hear, O heavens, and give ear, O earth: for the LORD hath spoken ..."

How this must have struck to the hearts of the contrite, as it should have smitten the rebellious with dread! Micah had adopted a similar approach in the opening words of his prophecy, directed this time against both Samaria and Jerusalem:

"Hear, all ye people; hearken, O earth, and all that therein is."   (1:2; see also Psalm 50:4)

The Song merits a detailed study beyond the scope of this book but attention to the one or two salient points to be noted in the concluding chapter will greatly enhance the reading of this poetic summary of the whole Book of Deuteronomy.

The whole "doctrine" of the Lord, summed up in His *Torah*, or teaching, is like the beneficent and refreshing rain (32:2; see also Isaiah 55:10). The word Rock (verse 4) is introduced as a title of God, and the contrast between building and trusting on the Lord and turning instead to idols is a characteristic theme of the Song (see verses 18,31,37). It gathers up the themes of the Rock that flowed with water, and the smitten Rock, and looks forward to "the rock that followed them" (1 Corinthians 10:4), the Christ, the true Son of the Living God, upon whom the true church, the chosen generation, was to be built. For the children of that generation had corrupted themselves, to become, in effect, the "no-sons" of the "no-gods", as the Hebrew word for idols often signifies.

Yet the Song should have caused them to "remember the days of old" (verse 7), when their fathers trusted in Him who set the bounds of the nations with respect to His purpose with the people of "his inheritance" (verse 9).

"The shadow of His wings"

The beautiful theme of "the shadow of his wings", taken up in Ruth 2:12, Psalms 17,36,57,61,63, and then by the Lord Jesus in Matthew 23:37, is introduced in verse 11, where the rare word (*rachaph*) for "fluttereth over" picks up the sense of the creative spirit of God "hovering" (*rachaph*) over the darkness of the waters to bring life and light (Genesis 1:2).

The people, however, turned from their God, who had revealed Himself to their fathers as *Ail Shaddai*, Creator, Sustainer, and Bestower of blessings both natural and spiritual, to "worship and serve created things more than the creator" (see Romans 1:18ff.). By attributing to the creature a kind of divinity, they became vain in their imaginations and were destroyed by those very same material things. Created things became for them "devils" (verse 17) or "destroyers" (*shed*), as the word here means. To these idols, in some cases a "hairy goat", the people even sacrificed their sons and daughters (Psalm 106:37) and *worshipped that which should have been offered in sacrifice to the Creator*. Compare "devils" in Leviticus 17:7 with the "goat" offered on the Day of

Atonement: the word is *sair*, "hairy one" in each case. No wonder that, as Paul puts it, they "were destroyed of the destroyer" (1 Corinthians 10:10)!

In confirmation of the point made in considering the new covenant, we have the Apostle's authority for seeing in the Song also a promise of the call of the Gentiles. According to Romans 10:19, Israel knew of this future development for (quoting from Deuteronomy 32:21):

"First Moses saith, I will provoke you to jealousy by them that are no people, and by a foolish nation I will anger you."

Also in Romans 15:10 (from Deuteronomy 32:43), in the context of the work of the Lord Jesus Christ in confirming the promises made to the fathers, and that the Gentiles also might hope in God's mercy, Paul says:

"And again he saith, Rejoice, ye Gentiles, with his people."

The mystery of the Gospel

The fulness of all this constituted at that time some of those "secret things" which belonged unto the Lord their God—the mystery that was yet to be revealed (29:29 with Ephesians 1:9; 3:3–6; Romans 16:25). There was sufficient that belonged unto the people of that day and to their children, however, to enable them to understand the will and purpose of their God, even if there were only a remnant who would look and long for the time when the Lord would finally "avenge the blood of his servants, and will render vengeance to his adversaries, and will be merciful unto his land, and to his people" (Deuteronomy 32:43).

15

FAREWELL BLESSINGS
(CHAPTER 33)

THE LORD announced the time of Moses' death the "selfsame day" upon which he had "made an end of speaking all these words to all Israel" (32:45,48). The words of the Deuteronomy (the title of the book in Hebrew is *The Words*), like the words of the Song were timeless, and it is as true for disciples today as it was then that "it is not a vain thing for you; *because it is your life*". Although Moses was instructed to climb Mount Nebo to die because he had struck the rock and failed to sanctify the Lord before all the people, he nevertheless died as "Moses the man of God", and therefore still had the right to pronounce patriarchal blessings (33:1). The blessing was almost certainly pronounced on the "selfsame day" as well.

The blessings are cast into poetic form like the Song, and may have been recited on formal occasions or celebrations in Israel's calendar. The actual writing need not be that of Moses, however, as we can deduce from verses 4 and 5. The record, like that of Moses' death, was probably Joshua's. Comparison may be sought with the blessing of Jacob upon his sons (Genesis 49), but the Mosaic blessing does not follow the same pattern and is more specifically related to the occupation of the Land.

The **Introduction** (verses 2–5) takes us back to the foundation of the nation at *Sinai*, the only time in the book when this appellation is used for Horeb. The intention is probably to link Moses and his patriarchal authority directly with the giving of the Law (verse 4) and his establishment as "King in Jeshurun" and the "theophany" of the Lord, who comes with the sunrise over Seir. The military character of some of the blessings points to the immediate future, the conquest of the Land, but as with the Song there is a more distant prospect. Indeed, Habakkuk uses the opening of the Blessings in a similar fashion to Micah and Isaiah in their use of the Song.

The prophet's prayer in chapter 3 recalls this second verse to foretell the filling of heaven and earth with the glory of the

199

Lord (see Habakkuk 2:14). This time the "fiery law", by which the people were to be judged, would also judge the invaders of the Land, until the fruitfulness thereof was restored — a consummation for which the disciple, like Habakkuk, will quietly wait (3:17–19).

We note that even in the context of "the fiery law", the Lord's acts were all done because "he loved the people, especially the saints" in His land, who received His words. We are reminded that among all the characteristic phrases of the Deuteronomy, which speak of the relationship between the Lord and His people, such expressions as "the LORD *thy* God" figure about 300 times.

The Blessing of Reuben (Deuteronomy 33:6) was a necessary prayer for an unstable tribe, descended from an unstable ancestor. In the wilderness they had suffered the most terrible destruction ever inflicted on a tribe, when Dathan and Abiram "and all they that appertained to them went down live into the pit". Though little is heard of the tribe of Reuben again (but see 1 Chronicles 5:18 ff), they did not perish from the nation.

The Blessing of Judah (verse 7), though much shorter than that given by Jacob in Genesis 49, is still a kingly blessing, which reflects the prominent, even dangerous position held by the tribe. They formed the vanguard of the nation on the move and of the army in the battle-line. So the prayer is for the continual presence of the Lord to be with them to help and protect.

The Blessing of Levi (verses 8–11) is one of the more extensive and is in marked contrast to that pronounced by Jacob. The terms of the blessing recall the historical events by which the tribe advanced to their position of honour before God — events which concerned first Moses and Aaron, as personal representatives of the tribe, and then those in which the Levites were involved collectively. They were put to the proof at Massah and Meribah, and again at Rephidim and Kadesh (Exodus 17:1–7; Numbers 20:1–13). Then there was the tribe's action (verse 9), when after the incident of the golden calf they were set apart for the Lord's service (Exodus 32:26–29). So they were to be responsible for the Urim and Thummim, by which the divine will was to be made known (verse 8); they were the teachers in Israel, whose lips were to keep knowledge; and they were the mediators in the worship of God (verse 10).

The Blessing of Benjamin (verse 12) was that the Lord, of whom he was beloved, would keep him in safety. The Lord was "a man of war" (Exodus 15:3), and through His protection the tribe survived the great dangers which brought it near to extinction (Judges 21).

The Blessing of Joseph (verses 13–17), like that given by Jacob, sets forth the prominence the tribe was to achieve, even rivalling Judah, and ultimately leading to the great schism between Judah and Israel (Isaiah 11:13). The passage takes account of the fact that the tribe was already beginning to split into two parts, which are often treated as two distinct tribes, especially in terms of inheritance. The fertility of Joseph's inheritance in the Land is foreshadowed in terms of the fruitfulness of heaven and earth, and all the deep rivers in their courses. Thus was confirmed the prophecy of Jacob that Joseph's main portion was centred in *Ephraim* (fruitfulness), although he was not the firstborn.

But we must not miss the force of the spiritual aspect of this blessing, coming as it did from "him who dwelt in the bush". His "good will", or good pleasure, it was to bring His people into a fruitful land, but also to crown them with all spiritual blessings in Christ, the man "that was separated from his brethren".

Both Zebulun and Issachar (verses 18,19) dwelt in the camp of Judah in the wilderness, and were to be blessed in their "going out and coming in". Zebulun did in fact later dwell by the sea (verse 19), although Issachar did not. The two tribes, however, are often grouped together as here (see Genesis 49:13–15 and Judges 5:14,15), probably because of their descent from Leah as the fifth and sixth sons of Jacob.

The Blessing of Gad (verses 20,21) is in fact both an exhortation and a reminder of responsibilities. Along with Reuben and the half tribe of Manasseh they had been granted "by the law giver" territory across the Jordan—"the broad lands" (= "enlargeth"), and had "the first part for himself". They had covenanted to march with the whole army, and would play a lion's part in the victories, "with the heads of the people". As Leah had said, prophetically, at the time of Gad's birth (Genesis 30:11): "A troop cometh!"

The Blessing of Dan (verse 22), although the tribe was one of the four under whose banner two others encamped, receives but brief mention. The "lion's whelp" (cf. Judah in Genesis 49:9) was originally allocated land close to Judah, but eventually migrated to the far north, whence he could "leap from Bashan".

DEUTERONOMY FOR DISCIPLES

The Blessing of Naphtali (verse 23) appears to have no connection with Jacob's blessing. It is of a far more general nature, concerned with their inheritance in the Land. Evidently "the west and the south" were not absolute terms with respect to their geographical position in the Land, but were appropriate to their position near Dan's northern territory (see Joshua 19:47).

The Blessing of Asher (verses 24,25), the "happy tribe" (cf. Genesis 30:13), is largely an exposition of their name in terms of the fertility of the land they would inherit. Like Job in the days of his prosperity, they would wash their steps in butter, and the rock would pour them out rivers of oil (Job 29:6). Their territory was said to be rich in olive trees. One version translates "thy shoes" (verse 25) as "thy bolts", that is, the strong defences of their land, which would enable them to live out their days in safety.

No Blessing of Simeon appears in the list, which concerns only eleven tribes. There is nothing unusual in this, since the various listings of the tribes in Genesis, Ezekiel and the Apocalypse all differ. Brethren have laboured to find a meaning for these variations. The most likely explanation of the omission of Simeon from Moses' list is that the tribe had its inheritance within that of Judah, and so shared their blessing and protection (Joshua 19:1).

All the blessings, of course, were to be interpreted in the light of the exhortation of the Book: "When thou art come into the land, then beware lest thou forget ..."

16

FINAL BLESSING AND
THE DEATH OF MOSES (33:26–34:12)

THE FINAL BLESSING (verses 26–29) sets out the blessedness of Israel, if only they would remain obedient. A rich mine for later prophets and psalmists to find their spiritual treasures in, these concluding words of Moses reveal the power of inspiration to produce majestic poetry. The uniqueness of Israel's God—"Jeshurun" is a diminutive of "Israel", the beloved one—lay in His supreme sovereignty over all His handiwork. He rode upon heaven to help His people, "upon a cherub", for example, to deliver David, His servant (Psalm 18). The excellency of His Name in the fulness of its manifestation was above the heavens (Psalm 8). We have alluded elsewhere to the theme of "excellency" in Scripture (in *The Name that is Above Every Name* and *The Spirit of God*, for example)—the "excellent name", "the excellent glory", "the glory that excelleth", "the more excellent way" of the disciple. All these ideas spring out of the books of the Law of Israel's God.

"God is our refuge and our strength", His people still sing today and many a disciple in tribulation takes comfort in the knowledge that

"The eternal God is thy refuge,
And underneath are the everlasting arms."

The Lord of the fountain

And what of "the fountain of Jacob", beside which grew the fruitful vine of Joseph (Genesis 49:22), out of which was to flow salvation (Isaiah 12) and life eternal (John 4), since "the Lord of the fountain of Israel" (Psalm 68:26, with margin) was the Holy One of Israel in the midst of His people? From the Song of chapter 32 we understand that not only do the heavens drop down literal dew, but thence comes also the healthful doctrine, the distilled essence of God's saving truth.

With what heaviness of heart Moses climbed up Mount Nebo to view the Land he was forbidden to enter we can only guess. No feebleness of heart or mind made him welcome the prospect of death, especially when it seemed that the best was yet to be. There, at last, so close at hand, was "the land which I sware unto Abraham, unto Isaac, and unto Jacob".

And yet … "by faith he saw the Land beautified and glorious". No devastation such as was certain to come, according to his own prophecy, marred the grandeur of the scene. He himself had done all he could, and Joshua was full of the Spirit of Wisdom because he had laid his hands upon him. Although the record does not gloss over the events at Meribah and makes it quite clear that it was his own rash act that caused Moses to be debarred from entry, still the Lord was giving His beloved sleep. Moses would have concerned himself not at all for his personal reputation as the greatest of the Old Testament prophets, although with deep humility he would have rejoiced—and marvelled—at the grace of the Lord who said of him that He knew him "face to face".

The true glory

For Moses had seen the true glory of the Lord, a vision of what the disciple can see in Jesus' face, and he believed Him and trusted in Him that one day "the prophet like unto himself", a saviour like unto Joshua, a Rock of Salvation such as had "followed them", would arise. Then indeed would the earth be filled with the glory of the Lord, as the waters cover the sea.

So his last recorded words were:

"Happy art thou, O Israel: who is like unto thee, O people saved by the LORD, the shield of thy help, and who is the sword of thy excellency! And thine enemies shall be found liars unto thee; and thou shalt tread upon their high places."

For fuller treatment of some of the topics alluded to in this book see the author's series on "Cherubim and Seraphim" (*The Christadelphian*, 1972-73) and on "The Whole Family" (*The Christadelphian*, 1978).

SCRIPTURE INDEX
(Excluding references covered by CONTENTS)

DEUTERONOMY FOR DISCIPLES

OTHER WORKS BY THE SAME AUTHOR

The Evangelical Revival

Most Christian sects have been affected by Pentecostalism: the belief that true Christians are only those who have received a Holy Spirit gift. This challenge led to a thorough re-examination of scripture teaching about the Spirit, and the work of God in the lives of believers today.

Interpreting the Book of Revelation

Based on a series of articles in *The Christadelphian*, the book provides an approach to interpretation of the Apocalypse. The symbols employed and the scripture background to the message are examined, leading to the strong exhortational content of the book.

The Name that is Above Every Name

Not only does God reveal Himself as Creator but in many other ways, particualrly shown in His Memorial Name. This book examines the different ways the Lord God has manifested Himself.

Remember the Days of Old

As the foreword states, this book sets out to examine "some distinctive features of scripture teaching as they have been understood from the beginning of our history as a separate community". It aims to "inform and to exhort in days when it has become fashionable in the religious world to discard fundamentals ..."

In recalling "the days of old", the author encourages us to understand and appreciate our heritage, emphasising that what is important is not Christadelphian 'tradition' but the teaching of scripture on which Christadelphian faith is based.

The Spirit of God

In writing comprehensively about the Spirit of God, the author draws on the whole teaching of scripture, both Old and New Testaments, in an endeavour to understand the mind of God on this vital topic. It is a work of devotion and exposition.

Letters to Timothy and Titus

The subtitle is "Sound words for ecclesias under pressure". This section by section commentary is interspersed with a series of "essays" that deal with many of the issues raised in these letters.